TOO MUCH BOOGIE

EROTIC REMIXES OF THE DIRTY BLUES

EDITED BY COLE RILEY

TOO MUCH BOOGIE:
EROTIC REMIXES OF THE DIRTY BLUES

Edited by Cole Riley

ISBN: 9781905091898
Paperback version
© Logical-Lust Publications 2011

Published in the United Kingdom by Logical-Lust Publications, 2011
www.ll-publications.com
57 Blair Avenue
Hurlford
Scotland
KA1 5AZ

Edited by Cole Riley
Additional editing by Zetta Brown
Book layout and typesetting by jimandzetta.com
Cover art and design by Helen E. H. Madden www.pixelarcana.com © 2011

Printed in the UK and the USA

TOO MUCH BOOGIE: *Erotic Remixes of the Dirty Blues* is a work of fiction. The names, characters, and incidents are entirely the work of the author's imagination. Any resemblance to actual persons, living or dead, or events, is entirely coincidental.

TRACKS

INTRODUCTION

"Blues is a feeling. You can write the truth with the blues. In the blues line, it always brings up on somebody you love or somebody who quits you. The blues gets to the nitty gritty with no foolishness in it."

—*Bukka White (1966)*

THERE ARE only a few dream assignments which fall in the lap of a writer. When an editor asked me to pilot a collection of erotic stories based on the blues. I leaped at the glorious moment.

Since the roots of my parents are deep in the red soil of Mississippi Delta and the mad partying in the Crescent City of New Orleans, I knew about the blues in a certain intimate way, because that was the only music heard in my house other than Motown. My father, who was born in the South, knew about the difference of the seasonings in both the country blues and the urban blues. We listened to Robert Johnson, Son House, Bessie Smith, Victoria Spivey, Lightning Hopkins, B.B. King, Leadbelly, Alberta Hunter, and Howling Wolf.

"The blues is like an ingredient to pecan pie or something," another great bluesman, B.B. King once said. "Many people like it, but not too many people can make it. It's about honesty. You can say what you're gonna say with a minimum of words."

In this book, the lyrics of the blues are used as fictional points of departures by some of the finest writers of erotica. Their stories tell about real life in their wise yet raunchy scenes of desire, frustration, anxiety, turmoil and jealousy. Sex always plays an important part in everything in these people, their talk, and their behavior. It has always been a part and parcel of the blues. Sex becomes sheer poetry of wit, humor, sarcasm, irony, sometimes explicit but always complex. The meanings of the words flipped over. The truth inverted and turned on its ear. The blues says that every human being has had the blues or is suffering from it now. Every human being has paid his or her dues on the road of life.

Called "the Devil's music," the stories of the blues goes beyond jump turns, slow drag ditties, reel, jigs, minstrel songs, ragtime, or the buzzard lope. These lyrics connected to these stories celebrate heartache, separation, distrust, betrayal, lust, but they promise a healing love of revival and renewal. It's a celebration of the present, of the now, and it's totally mad at the past and suspicious of the future. But who are kidding? Let us tell the truth. Really, the themes of this raucous collection often wallow in carnal pain, in the weakness of the flesh, and the temptation of sin. Taboo love, forbidden love. Sometimes it's just plain nasty. All of the good stuff.

In *Too Much Boogie*, the spirit of the blues afflicts everybody. Within the emotional pull of the lyrics and its stirring music, there is a common language of the heart and the soul. Although the blues were born and bred in the land of Jim Crow by black people, it has nothing to do with class, color, or category. Even the rich get the blues and do dumb things. The book shows there is a pulse beating within each of us and that pulse is the blues.

These selected stories, contemporary retellings of some of the most familiar blues themes, are inspired from the recorded gems of the Delta blues, Chicago blues, Memphis blues and Texas blues. The themes cover every facet of sexual abandon, betrayal, and obsession: the virile man, the willing woman, and the needs, impulses, cravings and urges of the sensual mating dance. Whether it's Alegra Verde's eager young girl under the commands of an older sugar daddy in "The Things I Used to Do" or Akua Lezli Hope's "Ask the Heart" with a very complex sexual threesome, the blues suggests anyone can have their world turned upside down and all secrets of a private life can be revealed.

Through the blues, you can experience feelings which you never thought possible such as in the tales of Alice Sturdivant's "For Love or Money," Jolene Hui's "The Summer of Bobby," Savannah Stephens Smith's "The Principal of the Thing," and Anne Tourney's "Come for Me, Dark Man." The blues can be hard-stompin', low down, and just devilment like Kalamu Ya Salaam's tale of "What's in the Box," or Art Nixon's sin-enriched "P.K." It can hurt your feelings like the characters in Kevin James Breaux's "Mother's Milk" or Gary Phillips' "Can't Be Satisfied" or Robert Buckley's mind-twisting "Head Games."

D. L. King, known for her hard-edged flesh fables, softens her game with her very sincere "She Had to Go and Lose It at The Astor," following a naughty young woman on a glorious evening of dining and desire at a swank hotel. Often, the blues permits you to be yourself, whispering a gentle argument to not fret. It's when those carefree, rebellious thoughts speak their mind, such as in the dark Zander Vyne's "Tricked," Amanda Fox's brave "Once You Go Black," Victor J. Banis' ornery "Midnight Special," Lisabet Sarai's "Red Eye" and C. Dennis Moore's redemptive "My Strongest Weakness." The blues, at its best, can walk the beam between utter sadness and almost giddy pleasure when properly mixed. That is when it is the most effective, like Hzal's "Heaven is a Blues Café," Remittance Girl's "Hole," Jayme Whitfield's "Rocking Chair Blues," Thomas S. Roche's "Goodbye Blues," and Alicia Night Orchid's "Hurricane Love."

Other voices talk confidence-building boasts and "talk shit," collecting the images and pictures in each experience. This is what the listeners listen for in the music, every juju, every *gris-gris*, every mannish boys or mean gal mistreater. Every juicy detail. The remaining stories have all of this and more: Maxmillian Lagos's "Warming Up," Dean Jean-Pierre's "Sunday Morning," Rebecca Kyle's "The Backup Singer," and Dorla Moorehouse's "Effects of Moonshine." Possibly Dali, Bunuel, or Hitchcock had a surrealist hand of angst in the composer Nick Nicholson's "The Room."

These tales of sex and sensuality mirror the power and sweep of the blues. They say we are people who are constantly under the influence of our urges, needs, impulses and desires. I think these stories will remain with you long after you shut the book.

There is something magical, something sensual waiting for you. So relax and turn the page.

Cole Riley
New York City

THE THINGS I USED TO DO
ALEGRA VERDE

*"No time for marry, no time to settle down
I'm a young woman and ain't done running around."*

Young Woman's Blues – Bessie Smith (1926)

"DADDY don't you do me wrong," I said to the man as I slid into his Cadillac. It was old, but it was clean, just like him.

The tan leather of the seat squeaked as I settled in.

"My momma taught me always to treat a lady right. You ain't got to worry about me, babygirl."

He pulled out into traffic. It was light this time of night, but he did it slow and lazy like his Caddie was a Rolls or a hearse easing out into the center lane.

"What you got for me, baby?" he asked as he slid into a gangster lean, his body low in the seat, and his elbow on the armrest as his warm palm trailed along my knee. I let him, didn't even jump. His finger slipped down to drum lightly against my inner thigh.

"What you want, daddy?"

He smiled. "You ain't a regular around here."

It wasn't a question.

"A little young," he peeked over at me a question in his eye.

"Nineteen."

"A baby," he laughed. "Got a place?"

"Naw." Why he think I let him pick me up at Ruby's. If I had some place to go, I wouldn't be sitting here with him.

"My place then," he said as he turned the corner and headed towards Woodward Avenue.

His place was a one-bedroom apartment on Seward. Not a bad neighborhood, but not the best. In the living room, he had a beige couch with a matching chair, a dark cherry wood cocktail table, and a

TV in a matching wood console. There wasn't much else in the living room. No pictures, not even Jesus. The living room opened into a small kitchenette on one side and the bedroom on the other side. It was neat, but kind of dusty like he didn't spend much time here. Eat, sleep, and off to work. Eat, sleep, and off to play. A pair of blue workmen's pants and a matching shirt hung on a hook on what had to be the door to the bathroom. It was set off in a corner of the bedroom.

I stood on the threshold of the bedroom looking in. He stood behind me, his lips grazing the back of my neck before he headed into the kitchen. A nice bedroom set: chest of drawers, a long, low modern dresser with a mirror that ran its length, and a good-sized bed, bigger than the double bed that momma had in her room.

"Beer?" he asked. I could hear the door to the refrigerator opening.

"Yeah," I said taking a seat on the sofa.

He put the beers down on the table in front of me and went over to the console to leaf through the albums. After a soft click, Ray Charles started singing. The notes were a slow, soft wind that spread throughout the room and rubbed up against any surface they touched.

"You can stay here with me tonight," he said as his lips tugged on the long necked bottle.

"I figured," I said as I took a sip from mine.

He laughed, low, but hearty.

"You a pretty girl." He looked me up and down. "Why ain't you got no place to stay?"

"I'm in between."

He laughed again and reached a hand out to touch my cleavage, tucking a finger in the crease. "I know what I want to get in between."

I didn't say nothing, just looked at him and sipped my beer. He wasn't bad looking. I didn't like the mustache, but he had nice eyes, heavy lidded and dark. I liked his skin too, smooth with a healthy shine. He didn't look that old. The finger was going up and down the crease massaging the damp skin.

"How old are you?" I asked.

"Thirty-five." He leaned down to kiss my lips. I turned my head. He laughed, throaty and deep. Then he took my chin and turned my face back to his. His kiss was long and deep like his tongue as it tussled with mine, rough and warm. He pulled back and nipped my neck and then my shoulder with his teeth. I could feel the wetness starting to pool between my legs. Maybe this would be so bad.

"Why you so old and ain't married?," I asked as his head bobbed in front of me, his long, hot tongue dipping into the crease between my breasts, his thumbs worrying my hardening nipples.

"Ain't got time," he said into my breasts. "Too busy working and having fun."

He unzipped the back of my dress, unhooked my brassiere, and pushed the sleeves down and off my shoulders. My hands cradled the sides of his head, the tight curls of his head, crisp and firm beneath my fingers. The bodice of my dress drooped in the front as he lifted each breast out of its cup and held it in his warm palm. His full lips found the buds and suckled each in turn. His mouth was moist and strong as his tongue lapped and petted the tight buds.

"Sweet," he whispered between nips and sucks.

I laughed and my fingers tightened around his head and the lips of my sex twitched. My thighs tightened. I was nearly breathless when he pulled back to stand up and take his suit coat and tie off. As he unbuttoned his shirt, he tossed the jacket and tie onto the armchair, moved the cocktail table further away from the couch, and knelt down in front of me.

"I want to smell what's baking down there." His words were soft and guttural as his hands went to either side of my dress, easing it up over my thighs. Ray Charles strummed the air, his words like the keys of his piano stroking, urging the nimble fingers along my thighs. My sex clenched creating its fragrant cream.

The long fingers slipped up and over the silky fabric of my panties and skimmed the waistline before tugging the bit of fabric down over the garter belt and along the nylon of my stockings. After flinging the panties atop his jacket, he tucked his head under my dress. I felt his nose first, its blunted tip dipping into my cream, and then that long tongue lapping, licking, and nudging between the tingling lips of my sex. I couldn't help but squirm, my thighs boxing his ears. He nipped a lip, and I yipped, a high squeaky sound. He laughed, the sound like an echo deep in the hollow of my thighs.

The old dude was a surprise. I wasn't used to guys giving head. They were usually too eager to lift my skirt, shove it in, jiggle their thing around and leave their mark. Then they'd lay back and crow like they'd done something and I was supposed to croon, "Oh, daddy that was so good."

His hands were gripping my ass and his tongue was teasing my opening. He held on no matter how hard I squirmed. No matter how my thighs trembled, he continued, relentless. His tongue, and lips, and teeth, and the brush of that mustache creating a surge that started someplace deep, someplace far, that rolled up and spread out causing my teeth to clench and my thighs to tighten. Then he shoved his tongue into me as he spread my cheeks and squeezed the heated skin with his long fingers. I came with a yelp, my cream sloshing out.

He pressed his face to my mound and waited me out.

When the quakes subsided, he got up and found hand towels. He used one to wipe his face and handed me the other. Then he unzipped his pants and pulled out a substantial cock and said, "Do me, baby."

Usually I would have been offended, but I was still tingling, and his cock was a beauty, long, firm, and dark, its head a shiny purple grape. I wanted to put it in my mouth. I wanted to suck on that thick purple grape.

He sat down next to me, his pants down around his hips. I hadn't missed those firm apple-brown butt cheeks.

"I haven't had a lot of experience with this," I admitted.

"Just suck it like a lollypop, baby. I just want to feel your mouth all wet and warm on it." He grasped it with his hand and jingled it at me, the eye peeked up wetly.

I slipped my dress and brassiere the rest of the way off and tossed them both on top of his jacket before kneeling down in front of him.

It was salty and just a little musky like roast beef. I sucked, slowly at first, savoring the feel of the smooth skin, the heat, the rise and fall of the terrain as it butted against my tongue and the roof of my mouth. I liked the way it felt, the way it rubbed against my lips and held my mouth open, the way it insinuated itself into the waiting space seeking its warm wetness. My lips closed lovingly around him and I sucked with relish. My tongue circled the head, tasting and rubbing against its curves, slipping under its hood, and then down the underside. He groaned, his fingers deep in my hair, massaging my scalp. My hand found his balls, damp and hairy. I caressed them. Then, with reluctance, I relinquished the staff and lowered my head to taste his balls. They were saltier, but I liked the weight of them and the texture of the loose skin. I sucked them gently before returning to the hooded grape.

"I need to fuck you," he said from somewhere far above me.

I grunted and continued to suck.

He, with some force, lifted me up. Then he moved the cocktail table further away before pressing me forward onto the couch and kneeling behind me. My behind twitched eagerly and I could feel my cream beginning to coat my thighs. He stroked my bottom cheeks. I could imagine what he saw, the firm golden globes of my ass framed by the white cotton of the garter belt, the elastic strips straining down my thighs as they worked to secure my hose.

Then he was behind me, pressing his thick cock into my seeping opening. I groaned as he slid in, a long slow stroke that rubbed and stroked the walls of my sex as it thrust its way toward the bottom of my womb to make a final, thudding contact. I tensed around him, my muscles flexing, and he gripped my hips tighter, his fingers making red marks in the skin as he held on.

"I'm glad you decided to stop by Ruby's tonight," he groaned as he pulled back getting ready to make another plunge.

"Me too," I breathed. I rocked back against him as he wedged his cock into me again.

He rode me like that for a while, a slow drag as I squeezed at him trying to hold on. I could feel him getting thicker, harder, and more forceful with each thrust until he was riding me fast and hard. His body smacking against mine, the sweat making our skin slick and causing a slapping sound every time he hit bottom. I could feel his sacks like an afterthought as they swiped against my thighs. My nipples were granite beads as they dug into the rough woven fabric of the couch.

"You so fucking hot, baby. I could fuck you all night."

I smiled and backed up, smacking my ass against him as my muscles tightened around him, squeezing. He filled all of me, soothed, and then stroked every corner until it radiated with need again. All I could do was clutch at the hard pillar with the muscles of my sex. I wanted to hold him there, just there and tried to, but the trembling began again, a sort of tingling that ran the length of my body. Then he was jerking behind me, his cock a steel rod as it lunged forward releasing all he had in short, strong spurts. I clutched at him, the muscles of my sex a clamp, trying to hold on, but the trembling tingle consumed me as it ran the length of my body. I must have gripped him again because he cried out before tumbling onto me, his big body making a splat on my back.

After a while, he rose up off of me, but his cock was still tucked in and he moved forward just a bit, testing. "That was good," he said and I could feel him getting hard again. "What did you say your name was?"

"Eula," I said as I backed into him.

"You can stay the night," he said again as his hands went to my hips. "Maybe we'll get some breakfast. Then we'll see."

"And what did you say your name was, daddy?" I said as I squeezed him.

"Ellis," he laughed. It was kind of a choking sound. I could feel him growing inside me. "I like you Eula," he said as he slid in further.

"I like you too, daddy."

FOR LOVE OR MONEY
ALICE STURDIVANT

*"He took out his trusty drill, and he told me to open wide
He said he wouldn't hurt me, but he'd fill my whole inside
Long John, you've got that golden touch.
You thrill me when you drill me, and I need you very
much."*

Long John Blues – Dinah Washington (1948)

MICHAEL awoke with a start, pale arm snapping back from the edge of the feather bed, his fingers sliding across the eyelet coverlet. Grey eyes adjusted to the shadows of the room, midnight blue and orange from the streetlight outside and the hurricane lamp across the room on the dresser. Hurriedly, he turned over, immediately colliding with soft, warm skin.

She was still there, he realized and exhaled. He didn't know he'd been holding his breath.

The soft moan of Alice's usually languid awakening brought a smile to his lips. "Hi," she half-breathed, her voice husky with sleep. The tiny, down-soft spirals of her hair tickled his throat. In the shadows and streetlight, her skin shone in muted tones of sepia. Too many memories of her were in the darkness, the twilight. *I wish I could see her like this in the light someday*, he thought. *Maybe someday.*

She stretched a little, pressing a soft breast into his waiting palm. Thoughts fled. Michael gave her nipple a gentle roll with his fingertips. He could hear the smile in her voice.

"You're going to get in trouble doing that."

His kiss went to her hair. "I know." Michael's voice vibrated through her temple. His sex was lengthening again, pressing against the roundness of her smooth derriere. The hand that snaked around her waist splayed out on the gentle mound of her belly, pressing fingers into her skin, reminding her that it was all too close to her already dampening pussy. Alice's tongue darted out to her lips and a sigh escaped. Slow pressure on her breast and stomach closed her eyes; she could feel the rough whorls of his fingertips and palms.

It was odd, the way just having his body so close could almost make her forget. The excuses, the warnings, the rumors, even the photograph in the society pages. Michael's familiar smile, the scar that always seemed too near his right eye looked more dashing than trouble when featured with a woman and a section of the newspaper that was miles away in more ways than one from Alice's little house on the wrong side of the river with the red door. His gaze stared out at her, as dark as the newsprint, as he grinned beside the sleek blonde whose name was always in bold print. They were, both of them, beautiful. A beautiful couple. A beautiful, *engaged* couple. He'd made his decision.

"She doesn't really want me, Allie," Michael had insisted at her unasked question earlier that evening. The paper had lain on her coffee table, the setting sun slanted gold over the open page. Michael had told her from the beginning, the devil's bargain: marriage to the sleek blonde in exchange for an easy life, one that would let him achieve all his dreams. All *their* dreams. "I'm convenient, and she gets to keep her inheritance. You know how it is with these old money types: they control the purse strings. She knows about us, she doesn't care; we'd just have to be discreet. We can still be together."

"Discreet," Alice answered, acidly.

Michael was quick to rush to her, kiss the implication away. Rich men called it discretion; men from their side of town called it something else, something dirty. "Not like *that*, you know that. *Never* like that." She'd let him lead her to their bed and make her forget how she already felt *like that*.

Liars, all of them. Michael said that the money and the status didn't matter. Alice herself said that his heart was with her, and that she didn't want or need a ring. Both of them, saying that the nights in the little house with the red door were all they needed between them, that only the words they said in bed together were the truth.

Only times like now, when Michael's body was wrapped around hers, and she could feel his quickening breath on her neck, that molasses-smooth voice murmuring into the delicate skin there, she believed every lie they told each other. It wasn't until morning that the truth would come, smelling like cool morning air, making her shiver.

"I love you." His whisper was thickened by sleep, offhand. She believed that too. Would have believed him even if it had been a lie. If only she'd been rich, she wondered. If only she had been born rich enough to claim him as hers.

If only...

She turned in his arms and kissed him, leading with her tongue, surprising him with drugging sweeps of her lips and mouth, her body rolling atop his until she straddled him and his hands were full of her. Michael couldn't help but groan, the sight of her atop him making him almost giddy.

"Alice..."

"You woke me up. This isn't what you were expecting?"

Her triumphant grin and his chuckle turned into satisfied sighs as Alice grasped him, fitted his cock into her, and she slid down on him.

Where she belonged, he thought. "I love you."

She rode him slowly at first, a teasing, sultry wave of her hips, cupping her breasts to his mouth, his hands otherwise occupied with her hips and thighs, holding onto her as if afraid she would stop if he let go. It was as if she couldn't get enough of him: his body, his taste, his talented tongue that was making flickers of pleasure that echoed where she was coiling around his cock.

"More." With him, there was no shame in asking.

"God, Alice..." He nibbled her, using his teeth to graze her nipple. Michael moved faster, the rhythm more of a blues number now, his cock catching her in a spot that made her swallow her breath. She closed her eyes; saw the eyes of the other woman in the photograph. She rode him harder.

"More." Michael sucked at her hard, pulling her down on him, fingers tight enough on her hips to bruise. The staccato slapping of their wet flesh grew louder in the quiet room.

"More." She was asking more than he could give.

"Look at me." Michael's voice was guttural, almost angry. Alice opened her eyes and saw him, his face drawn in a beautiful kind of agony, the lines around his mouth drawn as he pumped into her. "I'm here, baby. Right...here..."

There was only his eyes, his voice, his cock, his scent, his heat. Alice bit her lip to keep from crying out as she came around him. To keep from crying. She felt him stiffen beneath her, groaning as he came, his fingers almost painfully tight on her skin.

"I love you."

He pretended to believe that the sheen he'd seen in her eyes had been from love alone.

"Alice, baby, c'mon. Nothing else matters, but here, now."

THE NEXT AFTERNOON, there was another photograph in the paper. Alice didn't need to read the words of the announcement. The white dress, the woman's triumphant, sky-blue eyes, the beatific smiles of the happy couple, the diamond ring that seemed almost as large as the quarter-page photo. The ring she'd had to have purchased herself: Michael didn't have that kind of money. *Oh but he does,* she reminded herself. *He does now.* His grey eyes reminded her far too much of the way they'd looked at her, through her, the night before.

He'd already chosen. The words might not have been lies, but now they felt like it. Dirty. Wrong. Worst of all: foolish.

Alice folded up the paper neatly, creasing the edges, and looked out at the daylight on the street. *Never in the daytime,* she thought. And he wouldn't be coming tonight, either. Or the next. They'd be on their honeymoon, after all.

He'd made his choice. Love or money. And she had neither.

When the phone rang, she knew who it was.

"Michael."

"Alice, I love you."

She twisted the phone cord in her fingers and frowned.

"Bullshit, Michael. Don't lie to me. You never lied to me before. Don't start now."

There was silence on the other end of the phone, then his voice, wounded. "I'm sorry."

"Don't be." She was fighting tears now, looking up at the ceiling. The day outside was too cheery for this. Sunshine and singing birds and spring flowers. She wished it were nighttime again, when at least the dark made it easier to hide from herself. "All things come to an end, right? We both knew..."

"I don't want to lose you..." His voice was breaking up.

"It's too late for that, Michael."

The line went dead, and Alice felt her heart lurch in her chest. "Michael?"

The knock at the door, insistent, gave him away. "Let me in, Allie.... Please...I have to..."

She was livid. "You have to what!" Half-screaming, she yanked open the door. Her hair was disheveled, half up, half down. Her usually immaculate outfit had been exchanged for a washed-with-something-red, once-white T-shirt emblazoned with a fading university logo. Shapely caramel thighs emerged from the frayed hem. She was barefoot, the crimson polish of her toenails her only nod to her previous role as the woman who'd seduced his senses, made him mad with lust with her intricate costuming once upon a time. Michael noticed the absence of her trademark perfume, smelling instead tea and something else...paper? Newsprint?

She looked at him, fists curled into empty brown threats, makeup-free eyes flat and so very, very sad.

"Go back to *her*." The voice that greeted him was cold—and that frightened him even more than the angry screams she'd opened the door with. She leaned against the doorjamb, trying to block his way in.

"I..." He was pleading.

Those eyes, she thought. *Those eyes slid across every inch of me and I did everything he wanted...he did everything I wanted too...*She was shocked to feel tears on her lips.

"Oh, damn...baby...don't." His arms slid around her, the fine material of his tuxedo jacket crushing against her body. The cell-phone clattered, ignored, to the floor. God, she felt so good...nothing was under that shirt, nothing but her naked skin, her nipples, her pussy...he remembered how she'd tasted on his fingers that first time in his apartment: thick and heady and sweet and musky. He couldn't get enough of her. And now, thanks to his own greed and the life he thought he wanted, and the whole fucking world that wouldn't go away, he would have to get enough of her. He'd have to. Forever. One last time...

He was saying it aloud. "One last time..."

She wanted to kill him. She wanted to kiss him. Looking into his eyes like this, in her doorway, the decision was made. The last time. Alice licked her lips and nodded, brushing her cheek against the rough new growth of beard on his cheek.

He pushed her inside, kicking the door closed, already half-out of the jacket, yanking at the hanging strip of his undone bow tie, tearing at the delicate buttons of his dress-shirt. She stood, dumb in front of him, the light from the kitchen illuminating his chest and his torso...and when he'd shoved down his trousers, his briefs...he stood before her, a golden idol, marvelously erect...in his socks. She smiled at the ludicrousness of it, the juxtaposition of it—a god in socks—but it was soon forgotten when he held out his hand and suddenly she couldn't bear all the space between them.

Her shirt was carelessly thrown across the room, barely making it to the couch and landing on the wood floor instead. Her nipples were hard already for him, plump berries his tongue would always remember. He bent his head to taste them, savoring the texture on his lips. She sighed against him and rubbed against him impatiently.

"Inside me. I need..."

He nodded and kissed her roughly. No words could tell her—anger, pain, love, regret—tongue slipped over lip, tasting, coaxing, then met with hers to mate, moving back and forth over and over. An intimation of things to come. He sucked on her greedily, kneading the soft flesh of her ass. She was almost climbing up his body in eagerness.

"Alice..." was all he could manage before picking her up and pushing her against the wall, lifting her hips, spreading her legs, and entering her smoothly, hard. "Ah, God...Alice..."

"Yesssss..." her breath came out in a hiss and they were bucking together, frantically, almost as if they would be caught. One palm braced against the wall, the other holding her thigh high on his hip, spread wide open while he thrust in and out of her. She held on to his shoulder, his back, moving with him, moaning and writhing.

"Oh, Michael. Oh....oh...*fuck*...."

She came with a loud cry. Surely her neighbors outside the half-shut door could hear her, he thought. The thought sent him over the edge and he slumped against her, hips still pumping, slower now. She was still cumming, her slick walls fluttering around his cock. They remained still for a moment...two....five...? Just breathing, holding, relishing the feel of each other, slick in each other's arms, panting, and the smell of their sex wafting around them to be remembered, held in dreams, regrets.

"Alice." What could he say? He could feel her slipping from him, her warmth, her cocooning comfort easing away.

"Thank you." The flat voice again. She wanted him gone before she could shame herself by begging, pleading for him to stay.

"Alice, please." Plaintive now. He had no such shame.

But she was pushing him away, closing herself to him, drawing her legs together and folding her arms, night-dark eyes gone cold. He'd made his choice; she'd made hers. Michael stood looking at her, wishing he didn't have to leave. He wanted to explain. He wanted to tell her how sorry he was, how he didn't really love that woman, how it had all seemed so simple. How he thought it would have worked out. He wanted to tell her how much she meant to him, that he wanted to give up everything he had for her, that he didn't give a fuck that he was white and she was black, or both of them poor. That it was the marriage that was all a lie, that it was a big mistake. He'd made the wrong choice. He wanted to tell her that he wanted to be inside of her again, with her again, love her.

He looked at her, opened his mouth. Nothing came out.

She smiled ruefully and made her way to her bathroom, stumbling slightly by her couch, ass bobbling slightly with the movement. She was careful not to look back.

"Thank you and goodbye, Michael."

He gathered up the crumpled pieces of the tuxedo and put them on slowly, trying to keep his eyes off the discarded T-shirt on the floor. His keys jangled in his pockets when he put them on, the ring on his finger flashing in the sunlight, reminding him of where he was supposed to be.

The tears didn't come until he shut her locked door behind him. He could hear her latch the door as he stepped into the afternoon, thought he could hear her sob even through the red door that he knew was barred to him for good.

ROCKING CHAIR BLUES
JAYME WHITFIELD

"Kick up my furnace and turn up my heat
Brown my biscuits and chop my meat
That's why I want him around
'Cause I'm the hottest gal in the town."

Hottest Gal in Town — Lil Johnson (1940)

I.

IN AN ATTEMPT to escape the sweltering heat, Abraham ducked into
the first shop he came across. The sign on the door read "Second
Chances," and he rolled his eyes at the cliché name of the used
furniture store. He hesitated in the doorway, giving his eyes a
moment to adjust to the dim light. The room he found himself in
wasn't much cooler than the sidewalk had been, but a small fan in the
back attracted his attention. Weaving his way past occasional tables
and frayed settees, he finally reached the rear of the store. He looked
around furtively, hoping the sales clerk hadn't heard his entrance. He
wanted a few minutes alone with the tepid air the fan was spreading
around.

With a sigh of contentment, he unbuttoned the top of his shirt,
hoping to allow some of the heat to escape. Sweat beaded on his
forehead and pooled in the small of his back. He couldn't remember a
time when he'd been so uncomfortable.

"Makin' yourself at home, I see."

Startled by the woman's voice, Abraham jumped. She laughed, a
rich, throaty laugh that drew his eyes to her. She stood at the base of a
stairwell about four feet from him. The lack of light made her features
hard to discern, but what he could see of her form invited more

inspection. Long legs led to broad hips and a small waist. Her breasts were large, barely contained by the thin green cotton dress she wore.

"Just tryin' to escape the heat," he replied.

"See something you like?"

Abraham was taken aback by the forward question, and then realized she must have been talking about the collection of used furnishings that surrounded him. Realizing that if he didn't at least feign an interest, he'd be ejected from the shop, he pointed to the item closest to him—a wooden rocking chair with cane-webbed back and padded seat. Nodding her approval, the woman moved in his direction, coming to a stop only inches from him. He could feel the heat of her, smell her scent, a curious mixture of lavender, sweat, and Bourbon.

His gaze traveled over her face. She had wide hazel eyes that were fringed by dark lashes, high cheekbones, and full lips. Her skin was almost luminescent, like melted caramel dipped in honey. Thick black curls tumbled down her shoulders and he resisted the urge to touch the silky strands.

She laughed again, and then turned and sat in the chair he'd pointed to. She began to rock, her breasts rising and falling with the motion.

"This is the nicest piece in this backwater town," she grinned up at him, the mischief in her eyes enchanting.

"Is that so?" He crouched down on his haunches, bringing them face-to-face again. She smiled, flashing him a glimpse of even, white teeth.

"Sure it is. I wouldn't lie. She hasn't gotten much use, only by a man or two. I'll make you a deal—you give me $10 and she's yours." Her spiel over, she grinned at him. He laughed and ran his fingers up her bare arm.

"I don't know, looks a lot more worn than you say. I'm not a wealthy man, and $10 is a lot of money for something that I might get one use out of, don't ya' think?"

Raising an eyebrow, she slid her tongue out and licked her bottom lip, as if she were considering his words carefully. Abraham was entranced.

Without warning, she jumped up from the chair. Her sudden movement startled him, causing him to lose his balance and fall onto his ass. She laughed, and then extended a hand to help him up. He caught it, clamping it tight in his own. Once he was back on his feet, he pulled her close to him, his arms circling around her back, her breasts tight against his chest. To his surprise, she didn't fight him. Instead, she pulled his arms down until his hands were on her ass.

"Now listen here, cheapskate. That chair is the best around, ready to accommodate. The weaving is nice and tight, just right for a man your size." She spun around and rubbed her ass against his obvious arousal. "Look at the curves, and those legs—long and sleek. And the color—no, you won't find another one like it, especially at that price."

"Not much use, eh?" he asked, his voice thick. "A man or two, you said. How do I know you're telling the truth? I prefer the things that I pay for to be new. And I'm not cheap, just wary of being takin' for a ride. How do I know the previous owner won't come lookin' for it—or that it has some fault that isn't apparent to the naked eye?"

She pulled away, sitting in the chair, sliding her back down and her knees up. Her dress pooled around her knees, which she casually spread wide, giving him a view he wouldn't soon forget.

"Well, sir—" she began, but he cut her off.

"Abraham."

"Abraham, all I have left to say is that if you're not buyin' it, I'll have to just keep sittin' on it. I'm not in business to be giving things away. My rent has to be paid, same as the rest, and we both know this chair is the best around. So if you're not interested, then I'll just keep sittin' on it—someone else'll be along soon enough." As she finished talking, she slid her thighs shut.

"Ten dollars, right?"

"That's right, Abraham. Ten dollars and it's yours. You can take it home, put it in your room, use it how you like."

"I'll take it."

She laughed again, and then jumped up.

"Let me just take it in the back room and clean it up a bit, then I'll have my boy bring it 'round to your address..."

"I'll come with you and take it now, if you don't mind."

She stopped then, her green eyes flashing.

"I don't think that would be such a good idea, Abraham..."

"But I do, and since I'm the paying customer, you know I'm right."

II.

GEORGIA'S pulse pounded in her ears. She wasn't prepared for this; she'd gone too far this time, and she knew it. A little fun was all she wanted—it was so hot and boring here during the day. She'd teased him like the others...hell, that's what they came here for. She never meant anything by it, just giving them a show to help the sale along. They knew it, too, knew their place, knew that she wasn't some whore waiting for a poke up against the wall of the harbor-master's office.

This one was different, though. She'd known it the moment she set eyes on him. She knew he wasn't from her town, was a stranger to the place. He had the air of a man used to getting what he wanted. She could sense a dangerous edge, a side of him that was unpredictable, almost primal. She'd teased him anyway, testing to see what sort of rise she could get from. Now she hoped his bark was worse than his bite.

He was a handsome man, tall, with well-defined arms and a rock-solid chest. Tightly cropped hair covered his head and highlighted his strong jaw. His warm brown eyes sparkled with intelligence and just the hint of something more, something that made her knees feel weak. He was enjoying watching her as she watched him. Dimples appeared as he flashed her a predatory smile, his thick lips parting to reveal a row of gleaming white teeth.

Georgia shivered but continued her brazen assessment, impressed by his trim waist and long legs. His skin was as dark as midnight, his hands rough from hard work. He also had a package that any woman would be a fool to refuse; she'd felt it when he'd held her close.

Attractive as sin itself, Georgia thought, her gaze locked on the muscles flexing in his powerful arms as he lifted the rocking chair. He turned to face her again, the chair held in his grip as easily as a puff of cotton. She knew he was waiting for her to direct him. She hesitated only a moment before tilting her head in the direction of the faded green door that led to the store's back room. She took the lead, walking up to the door, where she paused, the smooth brass knob in her hand. Glancing back at him, she wondered if she should stop whatever was happening. A part of her wanted to run, to put as much distance between them as possible. Turning the knob, she pushed forward, wondering what there was inside her that could supersede that hesitation.

She stepped into the room, moving out of his way as he came through the door behind her. Still balancing his purchase, he turned around and kicked the door shut. Georgia spun around at the sound, watching silently as he set the chair on the floor in front of her only route of escape. He moved forward like a cat on the prowl, his hand disappearing into his pocket and returning with a wad of dollar bills. They landed on the scarred surface of the work table without a sound.

"Come here."

"I...I don't want to." She eyed him warily, taking a step backwards and away from him. He grinned and moved forward.

"Sure seemed like you wanted to when we were in the other room."

"I think you misunderstood."

"I don't think so."

"No, you did. I was just..."

"Just what?"

"I was just trying to sell that chair."

"Oh, is that what you were selling?"

"Yes, just sellin' the chair. I didn't mean nothin' by it."

"So you were just teasin' me?"

"No...I mean, yes..." Georgia swallowed, and then gave a squeak as he closed the distance between them. The sound was muffled by his kiss, swift and unexpected. His hands slid behind her head, tangling in her hair. She tried to turn her face away, but his fingers locked, preventing her retreat. Breaking the kiss, he pulled her head lower, his teeth grazing her earlobe. Her knees went weak as he whispered in her ear.

"Which is it? Yes or no?"

"No. You see, don't you?"

"No, I don't see. Why don't you explain it to me?" He drew his hands down, caressing her neck and shoulders before sliding lower. His thumbs grazed her exposed collar bone, and then began tracing the outline of her taut nipples with slow, smooth circles. She closed her eyes, common sense warring with natural attraction, trying to assert itself but losing the battle.

"But I can't think straight when you're doin' that."

He laughed.

"You know what I think?"

"What?"

"I think you're tryin' to pretend you don't want this, but we both know the truth."

"The truth?"

"The truth. I can hear your heart poundin', feel your nipples straining against your dress. I can smell your sex from here. I bet if I pull up that skirt of yours, you'll be so hot and wet and ready that I could slide my fingers right in."

Gathering her courage, Georgia broke away from him. She couldn't do this. It would ruin her. She'd be no better than a good-time girl down on the docks. Taking a step back, she brought up her hand to deliver a hard slap across his face. Her teeth clenched as she glared at him.

"How dare you..."

He stopped her with another kiss, his arms circling her waist, and crushing her against his chest. She tried to pull away, struggled against him. He backed her up against a workbench, his hands roaming her body. She resisted, tried to deny the pool of desire building within her.

"You think you got me all balled up, but you're dead wrong. You think I'm just gonna give up and give in. Well, I ain't buyin' what you're sellin'. Sorry to tell you, but it's time for you to go!"

Abraham laughed. He held her face in his hands, his thumbs working a pattern from her cheekbones to her chin.

"Oh yeah. You play the bearcat but you're nothing but a tease. Dishin' it out, givin' the boys a little look-see, maybe even a bit of petting to get 'em all riled up. But when the cards are on the table, well, that's when we know you've been playin' with wooden nickels."

"I am not a tease!"

"Prove it. Baby, that oven of yours is primed and ready to cook it up."

Before she could reply, he grabbed her elbows and spun her around. His hand found the small of her back, pushing her forward and down while his other hand ran up the inside of her thigh. He flipped up her skirt and laughed again when she struggled. Georgia realized that her ass was wiggling back and forth as she tried to loosen his grip, giving him quite the show. Humiliation mixed with desire and Georgia felt her cheeks flame. Closing her eyes, she sucked in a ragged, shallow breath.

Abraham pressed close to her, so close she could feel his heat and hardness against her backside. When he leaned forward, she couldn't help pushing back towards him. Lowering his head, he whispered in her ear.

"You just say the word and I'll scratch that itch for you, baby."

Before she could respond, someone began pounding on the locked door.

III.

"DAMNATION!" Abraham cursed everyone he could think of, starting with whoever was beating on the door and ending with his own mother, for birthing him under an unlucky star. He stepped back, adjusting himself, as Georgia straightened and tried to fix her own disheveled clothing.

"Who is that?" His words were a curt whisper as he tried to tamp down his desire. The pounding was now accompanied by a deep male voice. Her low reply had a touch of panic in it.

"It's my brother, Solomon. He's the one who fixes up all the furniture. I live upstairs with him and his wife Mary. He'll kill us both if he finds us in here!"

Abraham looked around, spotting the glow of sunlight coming through at the back of the room.

"That a window?"

"Yeah, but look at all that stuff in front of it! He'd hear us..." He could see her fear, knew that if he didn't act soon they'd be caught.

"So you just want to go unlock that door and let him in? Come on!"

Tugging her along behind him, he moved as quickly as he could through the congested space. He winced as her dress caught on a broken table leg, sending it crashing into a stack of tin cans. The pounding grew louder, Solomon's angry voice rising to a fever pitch.

"I can hear you in there! I'm gonna bust this door down if you don't unlock it now!"

Abraham didn't worry about being quiet, shoving aside the boards that blocked his escape route and throwing the window open. Despite her protests, he shoved Georgia through first. He hesitated as her skirt worked its way up her thighs, her wiggling legs exposed to him, but got control of himself and followed her out the window. Wincing at the heat, he gave his eyes a moment to adjust. They'd arrived in a back alley, nothing more than a path behind the buildings. Georgia started to shut the window, but he caught her hand.

"Wait!"

"Wait for what? He'll be through that door any second now!"

Abraham moved down the path, obviously searching for something around the doorways and crawl spaces of the buildings. He found what he was looking for behind the butcher shop. Crouching down, he stretched his arms into the small space under the stairs and came out with a large orange tabby cat. The cat was clearly unhappy with its new situation, clawing and spitting as it twisted in his hands, trying to break free.

Trotting back down the alley, Abraham flashed Georgia a grin and tossed the cat into the workroom through the open window. Loud banging and crashing could be heard from inside, and even Georgia had to laugh at his ingenuity. The sound of splintering wood set them into motion again, and they darted down the alley, working their way towards an opening on the main thoroughfare. By the time they reached safety, they were coated with sweat, panting and laughing so loud that it was beginning to attract attention.

He watched her for a moment, enjoying the sound of her laughter and the way the sunlight glinted on her skin.

"Lord, but you're beautiful."

She froze at his words, her dark eyes turning to meet his, her gaze searching his face for something. He wasn't sure what she hoped to find, but knew if he didn't watch his step, she'd bolt for good. Time to change tactics.

"How 'bout a Good Humor bar?"

"What?"

He laughed at her incredulous expression. Taking her hand in his, he began to stroll down the sidewalk. "I asked if you'd like an ice cream. It's hot as Hades out here, and I thought you might want a bit o' somethin' to cool you off." Cooling off was the last thing Abraham wanted her to do, but given the circumstances, it was probably the least scandalous thing he could think to do with her.

"Oh. Ice cream? I guess that would be okay..."

They walked on in silence until she inexplicably began to giggle.

"What's so funny?"

"I just pictured you with that cat, scratchin' and howlin' to beat the band! I thought for sure you were about to lose an eye!"

Abraham couldn't help but laugh.

"I was just praying ol' Solomon the Wise didn't see us!"

They ate their ice cream under an oak, trading stories of their lives. He couldn't stop watching her mouth, fascinated by the delicate way she nibbled on the chocolaty treat. When they finally parted ways, she told him he'd better stay away from the shop, just in case they had been seen. He agreed reluctantly, stealing a final kiss before heading down by the docks.

His mind was full of images of her. He could almost feel her silky skin, taste her sweet lips. He was hard with want and cursing himself for agreeing to stay away. After restlessly wandering the streets until dusk, he finally let his feet carry him home. Flopping on his small cot, he worked his hand under the waist band of his pants, intent on providing himself with some relief from his uncomfortable situation. His frustration rose to new heights as a knock sounded on his door.

Muttering under his breath, he stood, adjusting himself and crossing to the door. Turning the knob, he pulled it open.

"What in Hades do you—" he stopped in mid-sentence, a grin breaking out on his face as he took in the sight before him. Georgia sat leisurely on the rocking chair, gliding back and forth, her skirt hiked up just enough to tempt a man to do bad things.

She smiled at him, her eyes flashing with mischief as she spoke.

"You forgot your chair."

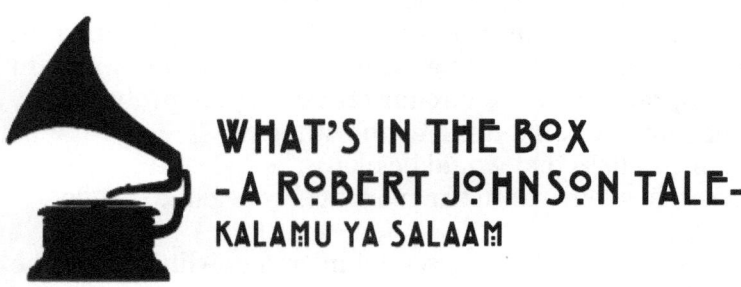

WHAT'S IN THE BOX
- A ROBERT JOHNSON TALE -
KALAMU YA SALAAM

*"Now you can squeeze my lemon 'til the juice run my leg,
You know what I'm talking about."*

Traveling Riverside Blues – Robert Johnson (1936)

IT'S FUNNY how when he walking along sometime Robert get his mind stuck on one thing and no matter what else he try to think on, he come back to the same one thing he stuck on. Robert recognize that it be different things but most of them different things come back to womens and music, maybe that's why most of them songs be about women, and most of the songs the women sing be about men.

Like that Bessie Smith, Lord that woman could sing. All them platters she had. Robert was going to make him some platters, they most likely would not sell like Bessie Smith platters or Leroy Carr's, but they would be his platters none the less. Which bring up the issue of what it would be like to fuck Bessie Smith. Robert done heard musicianeers jawboning over that. Possum Crayton come right out and admit he would be scared to fuck Bessie Smith, said Bessie was too much woman for him.

"See I'm just a average feller when it come to fucking. I ain't got no dick like Long Dick Ned."

"Who dat you talking about?"

"You know Long Dick over to Crystal Springs?"

"Possum, don't nobody know who you talking about. Tommy, you from over Crystal Springs way, you ever hear tell of some Long Dick Ned?"

"Naw, but I can't say as I know everybody."

"I know he going to tell us anyway, but I'm going to ask Possum this question, so as he can pass this lie out the front part of his mouth: why they call him Long Dick?"

"Now you ain't even got to ask that question. The man name advertise his specialty. In fact, his specialty so special, even the white folks refers to him that way. They say he can even fuck a mare and make a mule."

The gentlemen sitting around the stove all roar with laughter. Slapping their thighs, calloused hands against work-worn denim overalls. One or two of them even pausing to feel on themselves, and most of them not-so-secretly wishing they had what it took to be called Long Dick.

"So, Possum, you were saying hows you was just average in the dick department."

"Yeah, I'm like most mens is. I couldn't handle no Bessie Smith. Besides, they tell me she go with women."

"Ain't no such."

"Sho there is. There is women what go with women."

"Ain't such. Can't be."

"Why it can't be?"

"What a woman going to do with a woman? Stick her finger in it?"

"Well, I'm going lay it out like I plows, which is straight down the middle. Ain't going to lie. I done used my hand and I done done it with women, and the hand lose out to nookie every time. Every time."

"Yeah. Yeah. I believe Joe right about that."

Feeling like he had backup from Joe, Possum started getting loud, "Besides all that, y'all knows once a woman done had some of this here good wood I got, her finger wouldn't be nothing but a toothpick compared to this tree I got down here."

"Well, I know many a man be talking," Robert looked dead up in Possum face as he drawled out a quiet rebuke, "you know, talking about they cigar and all, but they don't never much even have a cigarette."

The men laugh at Robert's quiet rebuke. From time to time, they all brag, but ninety-nine out a hundred of them feel somewhat lacking when it come to measuring length and all, at least lacking when measured long side of how long they would like to be.

Just like scared men whistle through a cemetery, the average man lie, brag and laugh when it come to talking about his thing. It's the same thing. Robert just smile because this is something he been figuring on for a long time.

Possum didn't take kindly to young Robert contradict. "Boy, what you know? You so green you still squirting water."

"I knows there is women what likes women, and they be satisfied with each other."

"Ain't such. Might be some what says that just 'cause they don't want to give you none. But just like they ain't no man I desires, I don't believe they got no women what desire a woman."

Which is when Tommy spoke up on the subject. Tommy had been around some, had made platters and all, traveled a ways, probably had more experience than most all of them put together. "Y'all done all heard that song Kokomo sing 'bout if the Lord can't send him no woman, then at least send him a sissy man?"

"That ain't natural."

"But it happen, don't it? Happen all the time up to Parchman, don't it? What's the matter? Y'all was all loud talking a minute ago? What you got to say now?"

"Tommy, you know good and well, when you all locked up and everything, you got to make do. I'm just saying if you had the option, some nookie or some asshole, the average man would go for the nookie every time. Every time."

"Well, Possum, ain't said nothing about every woman likes women, he said he heard Bessie likes women."

"What difference do it make what she do?"

"The difference is it ain't right."

"So, who say what right is?"

Robert peeped where this conversation was headed, "Next thing some one of y'all going to be quoting the Bible and all." Robert looked around at each of the men, they choose not to lock horns with him and instead look off to the side or out the open doorway. Robert continues, raising his voice slightly for emphasis but not loud or shouting. "The fact that the Bible say don't do it must mean that somebody was doing it, even way back then." Robert pause both to let his words sink in and to give space in case somebody want to contradict. Nobody say nothing, so Robert, he continue. "So it would seem to me if it weren't natural, it would of been died out by now, but the fact that it still going on and that it been going on since before the flood back in the Bible and all, that fact alone tell me that not only is it natural, but it's something God is allowing to exist 'cause if He didn't want it to exist, He wouldn't never of made it."

Tommy stare over at young Robert in amazement. The boy not only could play, he could think. How-so-ever, Possum, for his part, remain unconvinced.

"All that sound good, but I knows womens on womens don't work."

Here it was, a big old Saturday evening, they weren't even drunk yet, just sitting around jaw jacking and such, waiting for the crowd to congregate up, and already they were philosophying like they was white men up in one of them big school buildings like to over at

Oxford. Normally, Robert didn't arrive until late so he would not be involved in such conversating, but he was early on that particular evening on account of he had not been home to Callie for two days. Rather than walk four more miles coming and going, he had decided to head straight on over to the juke right off the road. Robert remembered it clear as clear could be, and now here he was walking this Louisiana road and thinking back on that Tommy Johnson discussion.

Tommy had challenged Possum when Possum said how he knowed a woman couldn't satisfy a woman.

"Possum, how you know that? You ain't no woman."

"I ain't got to be no woman to know what a woman got and ain't got. And one thing I know for sure, a woman ain't got no dick."

Which is when Tommy quietly said, "They got women in New Orleans that got dicks."

"Ain't such."

"Yes sir, Possum. I'm telling you what I knows, not what I heard. You said you heard something about Bessie, well, I'm telling you something I know."

"How you know? If a woman had a dick that would make her a man."

"I know 'cause I was friendly up with a woman down there and she showed me."

"Tommy, you saying a woman fucked you with a dick?" Possum say laughing at the same time and making a motion like he humping the air in front of him.

Some of them snickered, but it was a nervous laughter that died down quickly, like trying to light green wood where the flame go out no sooner you pick the stick up out the fire. They was all waiting to hear Tommy's response. Tommy was generally respected and so if he said he seen it, well, it must have been so.

"No, Possum. I'm saying she told me about it and showed it to me."

"Showed it?"

"Yeah, she keep it in a box inside a drawer in this chest of drawers she had. Tell the truth, she had two boxes. One of them was white and one of them was black."

"What color she was? I know she weren't no white woman. Wouldn't no white woman show you her dick."

"Well, it's hard to say what color she was 'cause she was mixed up colored and white. You know they got what they call that Creole thing down there. They be colored but they look like they white."

The men whistle and get all big-eyed quiet like the first time they watch a stallion mount a mare. They all hanging on every word Tommy Johnson got to say.

In fact, the fact that Tommy Johnson was going to be there was a main reason for Robert to make it back to the juke. Robert liked playing with Tommy and his brother Ledell 'cause Tommy had some ways of singing way up high, higher than most men could reach, and he could do it with such ease, so relaxed like he was talking about the weather, but hitting notes like a hawk circling up in the sky, far, far above the ground. Tommy's singing was not quite a yodel, had a quiver that get to you, make you want to try to woo-hoo like he do but it ain't so easy as he make it sound. Robert liked that and, of course, it didn't take Robert but a couple of listenings before he had caught on to Tommy and then went on further down the road and take it different places 'cause Robert put more chords up in the music, make the falsetto be more pronounced not 'cause he singing higher but because he putting it on different places, not just at the end of a phrase, and 'cause he put it on top of different notes from the simple chords that Tommy use.

Of course, another reason Tommy interest in Robert is behind Tommy having the last name of Johnson, just like Robert daddy name (by now, we all knows Robert ain't got but one sure name and that's Robert, everything else depend on who telling the tale and when, and even some time Robert don't even use Robert), but anyway, Tommy coulda been kin to Robert through Noah. Robert asked Tommy one time he know of Noah, but Tommy said, no, he don't know of no Noah Johnson, but still in all, it may be so, seeing as how Crystal Springs ain't so far from Hazelhurst.

Robert particularly liked to second Tommy when Tommy would take to singing "Cool Drink of Water." When Robert would play behind Tommy, Robert could shadow him with the slide, make the guitar yodel just like Tommy do, especially when Robert playing with steel strings on his box and use a driving rod (or sometimes even his pocket knife) for a slide instead of a glass bottleneck, something about that metal slide scrapping on steel strings that whine like a haint in the holler at midnight. It gets so quiet up in the juke when they do that song, you could hear every note ringing clear and hear the steady flapping of Robert foot beating tme. Robert always would go out his way to hear a musicaneer he felt he could learn something from.

So anyway, Tommy he was standing up next to the stove, had his hands stretched out and was rubbing them together whilst he was relating about this woman friend he had.

"See, she likeded me by my playing, and one night we was up in one of them joints they got down there and she got into a fight with this feller, said he was trying to short her or whatever, and they got to cussing each other and all, and before you know, it he done jumped her like she was a man. Deedee, that were her name, Deedee she roll and tumble with him and probably woulda whipped him hands down but he was twice her size, Well, she must a bite him or something. He jumped up with blood all down the side his face, which is when he come up with a knife and said he was going to cut her so ugly, not even a murderer would be able to stand to look at her. Which is when me and my friend—brother Colt—intervene and suggest if he gon fight her, fight her fair. Either give her a knife or put his away. 'Course by now he so mad he don't pay me no mind and he slash at her, cut her arm good. That's when I plug him in the foot. I grabs Deedee and we high tail it out there, which all is how me and Deedee got to be friendly like. Never did lay down with her or nothing 'cause I was liking on another girl at the time, went by the name of Sandy, and it turn out Sandy and Deedee was cousins and all. I must of stayed down there a good six or seven weeks. Probably would still be there but Sandy she got killed up behind some guy she was tricking. Both of them was tricking at the time, I means Sandy and Deedee."

Just like all the others, by then, Robert was listening and sort of envious of Tommy who had done gone down to New Orleans and took up with them New Orleans womens, and everybody knowed them womens traffic in all kinds of hoodoo, say they could give you a drink of sweet tea and make you change you mind. Get you in bed and make you forget everything you knowed. So they all was waiting for the part where the woman had a dick.

"So one day it was raining and I was over to Deedee, this was right when I was fixing to make my getaway. We had done buried Sandy the day before and I was saying my goodbyes and all, would have left then but it was raining. It always be raining in New Orleans, I don't know how them people can stand all that rain down there. So I was telling Deedee maybe she should pack her leaving trunk on account it weren't healthy in her profession, and she say she know but she was used to it and all. So we got to drinking and talking about Sandy, and I don't know how, but we start into talking about tricking and stuff and Deedee she ask me if I ever see a dee-doe. I says, naw, I ain't knowed nothing about no dee-doe. Any y'all ever seed a dee-doo?"

There was a general murmuring as the mens tried the new word in their mouths: dee-doe. Robert was the first one to speak up to Tommy, "Is dee-doe some kind of fancy name for a dick?"

"Well, yeah and no. It's look like a full on hard on."

"So you laid your eyes on it?"

"Yes, sir. Sure as I'm looking at you, I was looking at it."

"What she do with it? I mean, she told you how she use it, how it go and all?"

"Yeah, she showed me. She had this strap she wrap round her waist and tie the dee-doe to it, and she be standing there with that thing just a sticking out and everything."

When Tommy had said that, everything got quiet, quiet, quiet. None of the five men assembled in that room could imagine themselves being fucked by a woman with a dick strapped on her. Hell, it made them uncomfortable just to think on such a thing. Again, it was Robert what was the first and only one to speak up.

"Tommy, I don't rightly know how to put this, so I don't mean no offense or nothing, but she show you or, I mean, she told you how that thing go? I mean, she say they be some mens who wants her to put that dee-doe, or what-so-ever you call it, to put that thing up in 'em, I mean stick it in they butt or what-so-ever? Huh?"

"Man, I don't know all that. When she strapped it on and I looked upon that, I couldn't think to say nothing. That shit was scary, and y'all knows I ain't no scary man, but brother, let me tell you, when you see a woman with a hard on dick strapped to her, it'll scare the shit out of you."

"What it made of?" Robert had asked, still curious as all get out.

"She told me I could touch it if I wanted to but I ain't wanted to. From what I could see, it looked like bullwhip leather, at least the black one did. I don't know what the white one was, 'cause by then I was fully sobered up and was anxious to get out there. I ain't cut out for all that crazy stuff they do down there."

All the fellers were thinking the exact same thing: get out of there. Get far away as you can.

Far away as you can, Robert repeated the phrase in his mind. Louisiana was another world compared to Mississippi. And now here Robert was walking through Louisiana where the womens got dicks.

MOTHER'S MILK
KEVIN JAMES BREAUX

"Don't blame me Mama for talking out my head,
I'm worried 'bout the movements you got and
those springs tremblin' on your bed."

Bed Springs Blues – Blind Lemon Jefferson (1927)

DECADE-TRAINED fingers plucked at the strings of his old Gibson, a hand-me-down from his grandfather to him.

Charly's voice was smooth as hot buttered rum. Loud and strong, he always finished his set with a song about that dear old man. Pop-pop always liked to joke that talent skipped a generation, but tonight Charly just didn't feel like laughing. He was spot-on in his performance, he knew it, but the crowd was just not feeling him. Not a *hoot* nor *holler*, no interest at all was paid.

Charly would have settled for a couple half-assed heckles even, anything to let him know they were hearing him. No, this dive, like the last three he played in, was filled with soulless men and women. *Creatures* he would call them in retrospect, only present in this hellhole for consumption and expulsion.

Stepping down from the five-by-five plywood platform the owner called a stage, Charly caught a whiff of a passing patron, a woman who had sat with her back to him the entire show. She reeked of stale beer and hot urine, or perhaps that was just the floor he smelled as his boots squeaked with stickiness with each step.

Charly spotted the proprietor moving towards him from behind the oblong bar. He was a kindly old man, dressed much too classy for this shit-hole joint, with a white dress jacket that nearly shined in the dim light. Gripping a wad of presidents in his left hand, he swung it out in an almost high-five motion in Charly's direction.

"You done good, boy. Don't let these beer swilling beasts make you think otherwise; hurricane stole their souls months ago. I tell ya, you got real talent in them bones."

"Thanks, Mr. Lieumeaux."

"That's fifty-five dollars there for you."

After shaking hands, the only person who had paid him any attention that night turned his back on Charly and walked away. It was time to finally go home.

CHARLY SAT on the heat-cracked eroding curb outside of his new dwelling. He sung a tune about the day he found this place, a hidden gem; he would praise it, in a tarnishing crown.

The Shady Grove Motel was abandoned no less than thirty years ago, visibly apparent by its 70's style frozen in time. Encircled by tall trees, and at the end of a long gravel driveway, the motel rested quietly just off Interstate 10, forgotten by all, save its new inhabitants.

Survivors of the hurricane, each and every one, these unfortunate men and women were simply happy to have a roof over their heads, no matter how run down and filthy the old building was. With no electricity, and pipes that only coughed out dust when the valves were opened, the displaced people of the Shady Grove Motel had found other ways to survive and stay entertained.

While Charly sang, many of the residents gathered in the courtyard to fill their bottles with water. Charly's words, a painful story of survival, touched all their hearts. They heard him, he knew *they* heard him.

This day was hotter than the last, still Charly sat on the curb, the shade that once sat over him slowly retreating from the rising sun. This was the longest heat wave Charly could remember. It seemed to be alive, stubborn with its unwillingness to leave. When his voice cracked, dry and strained, Charly stopped signing and stepped back into his dark, dirty, laundry-cluttered room.

"You should take better care of that golden voice, child," the sound of an old woman emerged from the dark corner of his room.

"Who's there?" Charly turned to his left, facing the wall across from his bare mattress bed.

"Your neighbor is who."

Charly could hear the old woman's voice from the other side of the wall, nearly centered with the cracked, amber, age-stained mirror that hung there.

"Neighbor?"

"Lived here *long* before you, child. Just never felt like talking to the likes of ya!"

As her voice elevated with frustration, her words began soaking in an old world accent. Who was she? he wondered, and why had he been so rude?

"Pardon me, ma'am, I meant no disrespect. What may I call you?"

After clearing her voice a moment, she answered. "You may call me Mother."

"Charly Bo Vaughn."

"I've listened to you sing every day, Charly. Your voice may taste like red wine, but it becomes bitter with its lack of soul."

"Excuse me?"

When she did not answer, Charly turned to his open door. Whoever this woman was, she had a clear opinion of his talent and surprisingly, it was the same way he felt.

"You need to reenergize your lyrics, spice them up, chile. If you're gonna hurt, then writhe like a worm on the blackest pavement in the summer heat. If you're gonna
burn—"

"I feel," Charly interrupted.

"There's too much misery in this world, why sing of it?"

Charly had been in the thick of it during that first week after Katarina. He knew despair; seen, heard, and tasted it first hand, and Mother's voice reminded him of the thousands he heard back at the end of last August.

"When was the last time you laid with a woman, Charly Bo Vaughn?"

"I..." He hung his head low, not able to see his reflection any longer as he spoke.

"It's okay, child, tell Mother."

"Been a long stretch."

"A new conquest could teach you to burn," Mother announced. "No more blues for Charly. No-no, all's you need is some fresh candy to go dirty."

LATE AT NIGHT, the Shady Grove Motel transformed into a treacherous place. The day-sleepers, those never seen during sunlit hours, stumbled from their rooms in search of sustenance. Drug addicts, criminals, and killers; these were the worst types of people imaginable. Given that these fiends wandered the motel complex after sundown, the innocent people, like Charly, could not sleep with their windows open.

Stifling hot, Charly felt like he was living inside a baking oven, tossing and turning atop his naked mattress unable to sleep. His throat, dry as sandpaper, and twice as scratchy yearned for something cool and smooth.

Tap, tap, tap.

A gentle knock rattled his door; however, instant fright pinned him down. He was unable to move. The last time he opened his door at this hour he had to fight off a heroin addict.

Tap, tap, tap.

There it was again, soft and unhurried. More prepared for the sound this time, Charly's finely tuned ears did not perceive the frenzied rapping of a strung-out junkie. Creeping quietly to the door, he peeled back a corner of the old newspaper he used to block the windows so he could see who was out there. It was a beautiful young woman.

"What do you want?"

"Mother sent me."

After unlocking the three deadbolts, he shoved open the door. The cool breeze outside slammed him in the face as the shadowy figured slunk in, her sundress a flutter. Gazing out, left to right, Charly saw nothing but the silhouette of the fallen street sign. Once lit with red and yellow florescent lights, the big arrow-shaped thing had been bent over by strong winds during the storms. Seeing it there at night, across the parking lot from his door, spooked him. It resembled a dinosaur bending over to snatch up an unsuspecting meal in its slathering jaws.

Caught in the clutches of the sight, Charly did not turn around until the young woman spoke.

"I like what you did with the place," she muttered sarcastically.

After shutting the door, Charly faced the girl for the first time, taking a good look at her. Although his room was dark, lit only by three pine-scented jar candles he bought at the dollar store the week before, he could see her as well as if a stage spotlight had been pointed down on her.

The young woman, probably a good ten years his junior, was wearing a loosely fit, gold-and-white print sun dress that was so bright in its luminance that it nearly seemed to glow. Offsetting the starkness of its color was the tone of her caramel skin. So low cut and slack was the top, it exposed so much of her abundant cleavage that Charly could safely assume she was not wearing a bra.

"Mother sent you?"

"Sure did," the dark haired beauty answered with an airy tone of voice.

Dangling from her left wrist was a string of black jewels that clattered against the object hooked by her index and middle finger only. A glass jug of milk. It had been many months since Charly had even seen, let alone tasted, deliciously cold milk. Oh, how he loved milk, more than alcohol at that, but none of the sleazy joints he played in had much more than stale beer and locally made swill.

"That really milk?"

Hoisting it up chest high, she nodded yes.

"Mother said this would be the perfect remedy for that ailing voice of yours."

Of all the things in the world he could imagine, there was nothing better than a glass of cold milk to soothe his burning throat.

"Mother was right."

"Then come get yourself some."

Matching his first step towards her was the darting-fluid motion of her left hand. Like a smooth stone skipping across calm waters, her tiny, blade-shaped fist crested the air from her side where it gripped her hip to her opposite shoulder. As his stride closed the distance between them, she peeled the thin dress straps off her shoulder one by one. His eyes glued to the jar of milk, nearly resting upon her breasts swelled with excitement as her dress shed from her voluptuous body to the floor.

"Who are you?" Charly asked her while soaking in every inch of her golden-brown skin. Whoever she was, she had a body that harkened him back to the days he hid in the bathroom with his copy of Tyra Banks's *Sports Illustrated* Bikini cover.

"Tonight, I'm yours, Charly." Her nose wrinkled when she spoke producing a playful sneer.

Hefting the heavy jug of milk up to her mouth, she wrapped her lips around its neck, first bearing her teeth so he could watch them sink slowly into the cork. After biting down, she tugged on it until it popped free, the sudden motion of its expulsion sent a ripple of motion down her body that made her breasts and stomach jiggle in Charly's ever watchful eyes. After spitting the cork out, she smiled.

"You want some of this, Charly?"

"Yes."

Tilting the glass jar forward made it gurgle and release, spilling thick white milk down her chest. Cascading over her collar bone, the cool liquid raced towards her large breasts.

"Hurry," she whispered through a shiver.

Fired like two pellets from an old shotgun, Charly's hands rapidly seized her breasts. Lifting and pushing the soft skin together, he formed an almost waterfall of milk, up and over her cleavage and into his welcoming mouth. This milk was the most refreshing he had ever drunk in his entire life. Cool, smooth, and tasty. Closing his eyes to avoid the splashing spray, Charly did not see what she did next.

Extending out past the tip of her left hand's index finger was a nail the length of an additional knuckle, polished sharp it mirrored that of a mountain cat's claw. As he lapped at the milk that flowed slowly over her hefty breasts, the girl traced her pointed fingernail just inches above her left nipple, scoring the milk coated skin. As the sliced, opened, flesh parted, sparkling red blood seeped out and mixed with the flowing milk running down her chest. Lost in the moment, Charly continued to drink, wholly unaware.

Moaning with satisfied pleasure, the girl almost laughed. Loosening her grip on the jug transferred its weight into gravity's heavy hands. Pulled free from her thin fingers, the glass container dropped to the stained carpet with a thud, not shattering, instead bouncing once before rolling off to the foot of the bed.

Startled by the sound, Charly opened his eyes to find them being sought out by the girl's.

"Who are you?" he asked again.

"Does it really matter," she said before pressing her lips gently into his, her hands at work on the bulge under his sweatpants.

"I-I just want to know you," he pulled his face away from hers to speak.

"You *will* know me."

Gazing down at her breasts, he finally spotted the self- inflicted wound.

"You're hurt."

"Cutting makes me feel. It alters every emotion, sensation; even orgasm into something much more real."

"But you're bleeding..."

"Yes, have you ever known a thing more poignant than blood? It can punctuate any statement."

"I don't understand."

Dipping her finger into the wound, she looked him deep in the eyes, sharing her insatiable hunger with him.

"Fuck me, Charly."

When the worlds fell off her tongue, she replaced them with her blood coated finger, licking it clean. It stained her stark white teeth.

With his large hands, he grasped the protruding crests of her hip bones, and spun her around. Nearly stumbling over her own spinning feet, the girl dropped forward, palms down onto his mattress.

"Don't think, just do."

Normally such a calculating man, Charly could not believe he was doing this. With his cock in hand, the flickering candle light illustrated the way to her glistening hole. All reason was gone, he just knew above all else he needed this.

Plunging himself into her felt like paradise, blissful and free. With each thrust, his problems and concerns washed away. Suddenly, the throbbing pain in his fingers had vanished and the scratchy ache of his dry throat was gone. All Charly felt was the warm wetness of her pussy, the soft fleshiness of her ass checks as they slammed against his lower abdomen, and the strands of her wavy, chestnut brown hair as he tangled them into a fist and pulled back on them hard.

"Fè mal m, fè m mal."

"What did you just say?"

"Harder! Don't you feel it, Charly? Harder!"

While sliding his hands over her shoulders and down her arms, he thought about her request. His mind was dropping down levels to where it had never been before, dark forbidden places. Thoughts were being painted like pictures inside his head, the media: blood and oil. When his hands reached her wrists, his mind was made up. Latching down his meaty hooks, he gripped her tiny wrists like two vices and with one violent, yanking motion, he pulled them back towards his chest and out from under her. No longer supporting her weight with her arms, she slammed face first into the mattress.

"Yes!" she chuckled.

Gazing down at her face, he could see the beauty grimacing through the entire affair. She looked like an angel, which made his feeling like the devil all the more intoxicating.

Increasing his force and tempo, Charly fucked his nameless partner harder and harder until the sound of their slapping flesh drowned out all other noises. When his eyes wondered past the curve of her back and the jiggle of her breasts, they found the quivering of her lips moving. What was she saying, Charly had no idea, and no longer cared. The man felt unstoppable. He was power turned into flesh and blood.

Spinning her over to her back, Charly wanted to look her in the eyes as he finished it off. Drilling deeper into her gave him a sense of superiority. She wanted this, he repeatedly told himself. When Charly could feel her muscles shudder with a tremendous release, he pushed harder still. Grunting through gnashed teeth, the girl finally screamed as her first orgasm reached its zenith.

"Bite me," she whispered.

"Huh?"

"Fucking bite me, *now*!" she scolded him for not doing what she asked the first time.

Bending over, he took a mouthful of her flesh in his mouth and bit.

"Not there, my boob," she moaned under her weakened breath. "Hurry."

Quickly repositioning himself, he bit down hard on her left breast, nearly overtop her self-inflicted scratch wound. As he squeezed his teeth together, he could imagine closing his jaws down all the way. He could feel himself tearing the flesh off her breast and just how exhilarating it would be to do so. Increasing his bite pressure more just made the sick thought easier to conceive. Charly wanted this woman so badly he began to feel as if he needed to consume her in order to be fully satisfied.

Growling in pleasure-filled pain, the girl tilted her red tinted face into his until their foreheads touched.

"Inside me, Charly, do it inside me."

"No! I don't even know your—"

"Give me my wish and I swear by God it will be repaid."

A hint of her salty blood was still on his tongue, his pulsating erection still in her pussy. How could he deny her? Grunting so loud, he knew the entire motel complex heard him; Charly felt like the energy being expelled from his body could explode with such force it would blow out his clenched teeth.

CHARLY WOKE the next morning to the sound of his cell phone's ringtone. Rolling over, he felt a puddle of sweat that formed at his back. Paying it little concern, his mind was on one thing only: where was she? Charly went to call out her name, thinking she might be in the bathroom, but no sooner did he clear his throat to yell did he remember that he still was not privy to her name.

"Hey! Ummm—you still here?"

No answer. She must have left. Shuffling groggily to the window ledge where his phone sat plugged into a solar power charger a friend gave him, he decided to see who was calling him first. Opening the clam shell of the phone, he was greeted by a shocking sight. Five missed calls, five voicemails. He never had so many at once. What was this all about, he wondered.

After pulling his pants on, he opened the door to let some much needed air into his small room. Outside the sun was shining and a cool breeze was blowing north to south. Poking his head out further, he took a long look at the door to his left, Mother's door. Charly considered knocking, but his phone had unexpectedly begun to ring again.

"Charly Bo Vaughn speaking."

"Charly, it's Patrick Lieumeaux, from the bar."

"Good morning, Mr. Lieumeaux."

"Morning, son? You ain't got no clock where you at?"

Dropping his phone from his ear, he took a peek at the hour, it was nearly three in the afternoon.

"Sorry sir, how may I help you?"

"You get my messages, Charly?"

"No sir."

"Well, let me break it down for you then. My older brother, he's got a big restaurant in Shreveport. He's having a blues festival and I gave him your name. He wants you, son."

"Really?" Charly could not believe his luck.

"Yeah, tonight, so I suggest you get yourself moving."

"Thank you sir!"

"Don't thank me..." he paused to clear his throat. "Just go do your best."

"Good bye, Mr. Lieumeaux."

Digging into his pants pocket, Charly withdrew a wad of cash. Just enough for the bus ride to and from Shreveport he surmised, having memorized most the fairs in a hundred-mile radius from his quarters. Clearing his throat, he sang a few lines, testing his voice.

"Baby don't go without me, cause I'm gone without you."

Not a crack or scratch, his voice felt strong and refreshed. Filling his chest was a newfound confidence; Charly could not wait to perform tonight.

THE VELVET BOX was an upscale restaurant and jazz club. Its stage was the largest Charly had ever seen, stretching the entire length of the back of the establishment. Feeling a little underdressed in his faded black jeans, Charly nervously hummed out the words to the new song he wrote on the bus ride to Shreveport while waiting back stage.

The trip had seemed particularly time-consuming, but Charly found the time prosperous, imagining himself up three new songs.

"Hey buddy, you're next," one of the staff pointed to him, and then the stage. "You got fifteen minutes max. Sorry, man, but we're going overtime as is."

Charly thought on what Mother said. She told him he sounded first-rate, but lacked soul. He may not have fully followed her words before, but he understood better now. After listening to the other blues musicians sing, he realized just what she was implying. These men all sounded great; they were skilled musicians, each with a laundry list of experience, but their lyrics only sizzled the flesh of the audience when they needed to burn.

"You ready?"

That was the question he kept asking himself. Was he ready to unleash his spirit? Was he ready to go dirty?

"Yeah, I'm ready."

Stepping out onto the spacious stage, Charly felt like a star. This was his biggest gig yet and he swore to himself he would only go up from here. Panning the crowd, he saw a hundred or more hungry people waiting to devour his music.

"I hope you' all ready for something a little dirty!" Charly shouted confidently.

Wanting to start big, Charly began with his most erotic new song. So steeped in sexual debauchery were the lyrics, he feared the manager of the restaurant would race out of his backroom where he was no doubt counting loads of money just to throw him out on his ass.

In near unison, the busy crowd quieted down. They placed their eating utensils down, awarded all attention to Charly. Singing with all his heart, he described in detail the night of love making he shared with a woman whose name he did not know.

Howling the last line of the song, Charly had never felt more alive and in tune with his music, "'Cause milk and blood fed my soul..."

The crowd erupted in a sweaty applause. Charly had done what he hoped. He pushed the temperature up a few degrees and the audience was feeling his heat. So riled up was the crowd that the manager did make an appearance, yet not to stop him, to give him additional time to sing! Charly kept going. He felt totally unstoppable, completely driven by something greater than himself.

Later that night, after the restaurant closed for business, Charly sat at the bar staring at an empty beer mug while two of the other musicians kept chatting up the owner, no doubt paving the way for future gigs. After a few handshakes, the owner was free of the chatty men and walking to the bar where Charly sat.

"You're good in my books, Charly, and after a concert like that, I am betting you're gonna be on the tips of many tongues tomorrow."

"Thank you, Mr. Lieumeaux."

"You need a place to crash tonight? My brother said you're between places."

"I would not decline your hospitality."

"Good then, stay the night, have the staff make you a fine breakfast when you wake," Mr. Lieumeaux offered Charly his hand. "I'll be in touch for sure."

CHARLY did not return home until mid-morning the following day. Refreshed from a hot shower and decent meal, he was all smiles. Strolling across the parking lot, he found himself on a direct line path to the door next to his, the room inhabited by Mother.

Mother deserved many thanks he felt, so Charly bought her a nice bottle of wine from the Velvet Box as his way of showing his appreciation. After knocking on the door a few times, he waited for an answer, nothing. Calling out, he expected her to reply, yet still nothing. Curiosity compelled him to push the flatness of the palm of his hand against the door while turning the rusty old door knob. Although stiff, the door creaked open. Before Charly's eyes could adjust to the darkness of Mother's room, his nose was assaulted by the stench of death. Coughing as he stepped over the threshold into the room, Charly tried his best not to gag or vomit, but the rank scent of decay was almost unbearable. Pushing the door all the way open behind him allowed the wind to swirl about the room and exhaust some of the stink, but not enough of it that Charly could take his tightly pressed hand off his face. As light seeped into the room, Charly realized it was easily three times the size of his, divided into four sections, the front room where he stood and two back bedrooms and a bathroom. Mother's room must have been one of the largest, as all the others he had seen were comparable to his in size.

No furniture populated the room, only trash; boxes and bottles. Cluttering the floor was a layer of dirty old clothing, which grew denser and deeper with each shuffling step Charly took further into the place. These articles of clothes appeared aged, some he dated back to the seventies by their style. Had Mother been living her all along? Had she been a resident of this motel for forty years? He could not believe the thought. As he reached the back of the first room, he saw several small wire cages lining the corner of the room behind several card board boxes filled with a black tar like substance. The cages where all but empty, filled with red and white feathers.

"Mother?" Charly called out one last time so not to startle her if she was sleeping in one of the back bedrooms.

Peeking into the first of the two bedrooms, his eyes adjusted to the shadow-dominated space. This room appeared to be a workplace, its walls lined with wooden benches. Although inquisitive, Charly decided not to venture into this room until the glistening of a glass jar caught his eye. On the nearest bench were two glass milk jugs, just like the one the girl brought to him the other night. One of the containers was empty, while the other was still full. Thirsty, and recalling just how delicious the milk was, Charly approached the bottles.

For some reason, his hand reached for the empty one first. Raising the glass jug up into the light that was trickling in over his shoulder, he spied a mouthful of the liquid at the bottom, but whatever it was, it was not milk. A viscous purple fluid clung to the bottom of the jug, and no matter what degree Charly turned the bottle, it did not move. Popping the cork, he took a sniff, instantly recoiling from an odor he would have sworn came directly from hell.

"Good God!" he choked.

After placing the bottle down, he rubbed his watering eyes clear. Suddenly, the room's other furnishings came into view. Hanging on the wall was a sickle shaped cleaver, its end coated in a mixture of dry blood and rust. Stacked five feet high were more wire cages, yet these were stuffed full with dead and decaying animals: cats, squirrels, chickens, rats. Charly thought he even spotted the black mask of a raccoon. The scent of death engulfed his senses. He knew he found it now.

"Charly," he heard Mother's voice behind him loud and clear.

"Mother?" he called out, but did not see her.

So spooked by her disembodied voice, he dashed out of the motel room, slamming the door shut behind him.

"Didn't mean to scare you, child."

"Scare me, I..." He huffed and tried to catch his breath.

"Do tell, Charly, how was your performance last night?"

"My gig? Oh, right," he wasn't sure why, but he felt compelled to answer. "It went great."

"Good then. My spell worked."

"Spell?" Charly did not like what she was suggesting.

"Oh dear, you thought all that clamoring was your own doing, didn't you?"

"Well—"

"Hush, Charly, let Mother explain. I cast an old spell on you, one to make you more popular. All you had to do was drink the blood from a woman's breast mixed with a little of Mother's Milk."

"What!" Charly felt his world tumbling over on top of him.

"You drank it, Charly, and it made you powerful. *You need me now.*"

"I-I don't need you!" Charly dug into his pocket retrieving his cell phone. "See this? Eight new messages, all people wanting to hire me for gigs."

"All because of my spell."

Feeling ridiculous with his cell phone held up to her closed door, Charly tried to reenter Mother's room, but the door was suddenly locked.

"You may have been right 'bout me needing to add some fire to my songs, but that's it! *This*, all this shit, it's wrong! I...I'm leaving."

"Go sing your new songs for your new friends, but Mother knows you'll be back."

THREE MONTHS LATER.

Charly stood outside the Velvet Box. He was not scheduled to perform until tomorrow night, but something worried him deeply. He had sold out every night, sung like an angel with lyrics the devil would approve. These people loved him; all was going as planned, until this morning. He woke up with a tingle in his throat that grew into a full-fledged soreness. The last time he felt this way was *that dark night*. Mother's words rang in his head, but Charly knew he didn't need her. All he needed was a little milk and the blood from a young woman's breast.

One of the college-aged waitresses, a beanpole of a girl arriving early for her shift called out his name as she approached. She did have a nice backside.

"We still on for our date tonight?" she asked coyly.

Charly flashed a big smile, realizing finding a solution was going to be easier than he originally thought.

"No doubt it would be a night to sing about."

ASK THE HEART
AKUA LEZLI HOPE

"You tell me you've had trouble and worry all of your life,
But you ain't had no trouble 'til you fall for another man's wife."

When You Fall For Someone That's Not Your Own
– Lonnie Johnson (1959)

LOVE was something Ava wanted to cross off her list. Not to take it off, but to say love was done, accomplished, fulfilled. She envied those for whom it was assigned. Where you were betrothed at thirteen, at least you got a shot at wedded bliss and there were fewer worries. The luck of the draw ruled no matter what.

She could remember only twice in her life when family or friends tried matches for her and both times they were so ridiculously wrong. The first time, the handsome friends whom she had paired, projected their unhappiness and tried to rope her in. The guy was an ugly, overweight nurse with a bitchiness they deemed a sharp wit.

"Why did you pick him?" she asked the female.

"Because he's nice and he's a nurse."

She was annoyed; because she wanted to be a doctor they gave her a nurse? She asked the guy friend why they chose this lumpy homeboy and he said—

"Because he's smart."

She chatted with the nurse and found him sharp-tongued and mean, ready to hurt for no reason. And he was gay and in love with her guy friend. She told her friends this and they told her that college had made her disgusting.

Her globetrotting aunt had tried once, inviting the whole family over to dinner. Ava found the surprise additional guest cold and unattractive, older and very self- involved. She grudgingly admired his ability to avoid the real world, which she so actively engaged. He was on his fourth or fifth degree. He, too, was sharp tongued, though not mean, because he, like her, didn't know what was supposed to happen. It was just a great meal in a hungry time. He didn't know it was a blind date. And he knew who he was—a gay black intellectual—as did she. Though she had a hard time telling her aunt that she wasn't being picky. He wasn't ever going to be into her and she didn't want to be anyone's "beard." Her parents, who were present, perceived his nature too, sat back and laughed at the whole charade; another story they would share in bed together and weave into their dense fabric of jokes and history. They knew their child and never attempted the impossible task of choosing her mate.

She loved them for this and more. How their secret love talk included song. Her father would sing: "It may seem funny honey, as funny as can be, but when I have four children, I want them all to look like me. When we move, way on the outskirts of town, I don't want anybody, nobody hanging around." In this, Ava heard the story of their lives. They were four, each of whom bore his mark. She had his eyes, cheeks, big head, and a version of his large mouth. Her brothers looked like him prettied, and her sister took other pieces. They lived in a house with a yard that was psychically if not physically far from the tall tenements and long concrete streets he grew up on.

Mondays might be stormy Mondays. Tuesdays were just as bad. Wednesdays full of worries and Thursdays oh so sad. The eagle did not fly on Fridays and Saturdays; he did not go out to play. He went out and mowed the lawn. He mocked the hypocrisy of those who sought absolution in occasional public contrition in church on Sunday, but he sang it anyway, the part about falling down on one's knees to pray after partying.

Long years before she understood how the blues made her, shaped her, Ava sang these songs in similar moments for comfort and release. She was delighted to learn that Alvin and the Upsetters, a local boy makes regional good, was going to play again, nearby, in the small city next door. Good, rocking blues.

Here she was, nearing forty, divorced and beyond the outskirts of town, in the boondocks where towns were tiny micro-bits of the megacity scale she had been born to. It was hard to understand where things were, where they were hidden, though the whole area of two cities and five towns was barely the population between her high school and its rival. Love and connection were hard to find, so were an espresso, bagel, crumb bun, or cannoli.

At the recent Sixties party featuring music that was really the Seventies, other members of the Association of Black Executives and friends had let their freak flags fly. She met a man, someone she never thought existed in this man-barren backwoods. Comfortable in his aging body, he moved with seductive ease. His easy touch on her shoulder was familiar and electric, certain but not presumptuous. She relished it. His arms and legs were long, as she preferred. His tenor was warm, and when they danced close, he smelled delicious and sang on key.

When she was leaving, he pressed her for her number and she gave it happily. He hugged her for just the right length of time pressing his length against her, enfolding her, giving her a quick shot of sweet affection. When she told her brother-friend, to quiz him about the guy, he sucked his teeth and rolled his eyes.

"Ron? That dog was sniffing around you? He's married. Got kids. What an effing dog!"

She was hurt, though no promises had been made. She didn't realize how far she had skipped down her daydream road. The town was too small for such shenanigans.

"Was his wife at the party?" she asked Kwame.

"Nah, he never brings her anywhere other than church."

That behavior was so disgustingly old school, Ava thought as she settled herself at the small, round wood table on a spindly wooden chair too small for her in her coat. She looked around to gauge whether she could grab another chair to hold the volumes of cloth swaddling her against the winter that would not let overdue spring arrive. She had never been in this part of the small city next to hers. It was old and odd in an old urban bar sort of way. Kingsbury reminded her of the kind of bar found below or near an elevated train, storefronts huddled and squeezed together, sputtering neon, beckoning respite and refuge, the faint perfume of booze, tobacco and pungent coffee curling out the door, sharp in the cold night air.

She had read about this joint in the one free alternative newspaper that filled the Frills of New York sub shop where she grabbed her workday lunch. Kingsbury was a treasure on the blues circuit mentioned again and again for various acts making their way up and down the hills, lakes, and mountains that are New York outside of the City. When she lifted her eyes from her bustling and de-layering to look around, the hand-worked warmth of dark wood comforted her. It was almost coffeehouse cozy. The large main bar was substantial with the curve of its big lip to her side and ahead of her; a lit platform with drum kit and microphone stands, waiting.

A grey, grizzled man ambled over; his half apron tied twice and pad in hand, signaling he was her waiter. *Great*, she thought, *so this is how it works*.

"Hi! Something to drink?"

"I'm cold. Do you have anything to eat?"

He handed her a plastic encased folder to consider.

"Can I get a coffee and amaretto to begin?"

"Together?"

"No. Gee, would you have espresso?"

"Yeah. We just got a machine." He flashed a grin of pride.

"Then change the coffee to espresso and the amaretto."

"I'll be right back to get the rest of your order," he promised.

Espresso was rare in this part of the world, only slightly more hard to find than a decent cup of coffee. Ava felt rewarded for her efforts. She had picked the time the only group she knew would be there. Alvin with his Upsetters extended the tradition he was born into. She corrected her thought of Upsouth. That was her downstate urban ignorance talking. There was a black, northern, rural life and continuum undocumented and under recognized. She had bumped into it one day after work when Alvin was shouting the blues in a repurposed storefront on the main street of her small town.

Her coffee and amaretto arrived and she sipped and shivered, ordering bits to eat: onion rings, fried zucchini, baked and refried potato skins which arrived thickly crunchy, fresh and fragrant, all in time to settle and warm her before the music worked its anticipated magic.

As she lifted a cheese and scallion filled potato skin to her eager mouth, a black woman caught her eye. They exchanged smiles and nodded. The woman headed her way and she went through a quick mental calculus as she quickly chewed. Would this be a bother? But so much had passed in the ready smile and direct gaze. So many black folks would nod, and then drop their heads, or the corporate folks would avert their eyes after a mumbled hello. And weren't they already sifted, to be in this place, in this small upcountry city, to hear their own music?

"Hi! Hope you don't mind if I join you?"

"No, this is nice, and then I won't feel guilty about having an extra chair," Ava said as she helped the woman take off a layer of clothing and placed it on the chair.

"Thanks. I'm Rayna."

"Nice to meet you. I'm Ava."

"What you got there?"

"Warm ups and a bit of cheer."

Rayna laughed heartily and Ava relaxed. She wouldn't have to fend any guys off, she wouldn't be alone when the blues came and opened up desire and expectations. Rayna's laughter opened up something too. They chatted about where they lived and worked. Rayna, a marketing expert, consulted mostly from home to be there for her kids, though she traveled more than she liked. Ava, a marketer, too, understood the challenges of freelance though not Rayna's industry.

"Do you come here often?" Rayna asked, having helped herself to one of Ava's potato skins, vowing to return it when her order came.

"No, this is my first time."

"Mine too! I just wanted a bit of real culture, live culture. I grew up with the blues. My turntable is busted and the stuff I love best is not on CD."

Alvin and the band stepped up to the platform and began with a rousing, swinging song of loss. Lost job, lost car, lost woman. He was part of a long line of bluesmen; Utica was part of his lineage. Maybe the segregated past held a decent living in its constraints. There were places where blacks had to go, or they went no place. Perhaps that was part of the fading glory and hell of the past: having a skill and knowing you would have an audience for it.

Then as he sang of being a stranger in his hometown, Rayna touched Ava's forearm and squeezed. Ava smiled at her. They were strangers in his hometown and knew how those words held true.

When the first set broke, the live music was replaced by recorded music.

"Wow what a nice transition," Ava shared.

Rayna laughed. "Yes, nice." She popped a stuffed mushroom cap in her mouth.

"Those look good. What's in them?"

Rayna pursed her lips, shiny with oil, her tongue flicked her cheek and returned to tasting the inside of her mouth. "Minced onions or scallions, spices, breading, stuffing, red peppers. Here." Her long fingers flew up to Ava's surprised mouth and popped in a mushroom half. Her arm grazed Ava's breast in the delivery. Ava noticed the length of her reach, long arms.

"Yum, delicious, tastes fresh."

"Surprising, right?"

"You've got quite a reach."

"Long arms, long legs, but not so tall, just 5'5". How tall are you?" Since they had met with Ava seated, she realized her height had been obscured.

"5'9" in bare feet."

"Nice for you, you could always reach the top of shelves."

Ava laughed at the gentle teasing and how comfortable Rayna's pretty, dimpled face and warm, relaxed voice made her feel. Ava's height, achieved before high school, had always been a problem. Despite her baby face, she was seen as older than she was because her height and breasts had arrived years before the other kids got theirs.

"What are you drinking?"

"Amaretto and espresso."

"Wind you up and slow you down. I love amaretto too, but if I have any it will make me sleep. Want to split an order of sweet potato fries with me?"

"Sure. Thanks!" Ava felt she was indulging herself, but sharing more fried yummies made the small transgression on her usual healthful eating permissible.

The next set began. Slow wailing contrasted deeply with the first set: *umchuck umchuck umchucka Um*, like lifting spadefuls of dirt or pounding railroad ties, melodramatic pauses where a hush falls and noisiness leaves the music the bass reduced to single-line footsteps and the drum just rim and brush, and then stopping, and an insistent line plucked, a plea moaned oh, oh, oh. If there were room, it was the kind of music to dance real close, to feel the thick press of another's desire, to roll meat against your hip bones. Oh oh to clasp and cling and dip and grind, riding a thigh, getting a knee up there, if you were in sync and sliding back up, your buttocks pulled, clutched, as you roll and your breasts and stomach, your softness, pressed against a hardness.

"And oh oh oh oh oh please please please don't go."

And then all the instruments rush in howling and Ava wanted to laugh at the revelation that while the words sang of leaving, it was an ode to orgasm, as much about entering and joining and not getting enough, wanting more. Could a man really be unsatisfied? There was only one she could not outlast, and it was because he was huge and uncomfortable and hard to accommodate unless she stayed fluid and aroused. He left her walking funny for the first time in her life, one fall in Brooklyn, and he left because she didn't love him and wouldn't pretend to. She sighed remembering. Rayna touched her arm.

"Are you parked near here?"

"No, I'm three long blocks away, you?"

"I'm right outside. Want a lift?"

"That would be great. I hate the cold."

The rain had turned to snow that should have been long gone and was falling in big slow flakes. Rayna slipped her arm around Ava's and shivered, guiding her to her car.

"It was great to meet you."

"Same here." The car was a few doors down.

"The benefits of arriving late," Rayna laughed, unlocking the door for Ava before running to the driver's side and jumping in.

"Too cold too c-cold" she sang as she fiddled with heat controls.

"Where's the seat belt?" Ava leaned sideways, arched, searching the side for the seat belts.

"It's a double." Rayna ran her hand across Ava's chest, and then up to somewhere against the door and pulled down a strap and fastened it. Ava was not sure it was intentional and held herself still.

"Which way?"

"Straight ahead for one block then make a left and go down two." When they got near, Ava said, "There, that blue Honda straight ahead" and Rayna pulled in neatly behind it. "Thanks so much for doing this, for hanging out," Ava said, trying to find the seat belt release.

Rayna turned, pulled Ava's coat open and thrust her hand inside, cupped a breast and thumbed a nipple. Ava felt shock, fear, and a thrill. Rayna flicked her friend's bra up with a small grunt and pulled her left breast out, squeezing it and tugging her nipple, which rose in hard, rapt attention. Rayna turned, leaned over, pulling Ava's coat open wider and brought her face to Ava's chest. The cold shock of her fingers was replaced by the warm softness of her lips and the deeper warmth of her tongue. Ava's discomfort and surprise aroused her. She felt excited, disturbed by her excitement and deeply pleasured.

Rayna's sucking had begun in silence. Now she began to smack her tongue against the roof of her mouth and sigh, "Ummm umm good."

"What are you doing?" Ava panted.

Rayna unbuckled herself and was now halfway across Ava, still strapped down. Rayna moved the strap out the way and freed Ava's other breast.

"This is the one I saw, the nipple that pushed through all those layers." Rayna squeezed her right nipple. Ava groaned and closed her eyes. She felt herself lowered. Rayna now straddled her and the car's CD player sang *Please please please* as Rayna sucked one and caressed the other. Then her hand went down Ava's pants and this made Ava move. Ava reached to stop her, but not in time before Rayna's fingers touched her wetness, her palm flat against her hair, her fingers strumming, poking. She pulled her hand out and licked a finger.

"Uumm."

She put her hand back pressing the lowest part of Ava's stomach, twirling her hair. Ava shivered from her knees to her hips. She felt her thighs clasp and her arms were numb. She was aroused and lit and didn't want to be, and her own reluctance, plus Rayna's seemingly psychic understanding of which keys to press, opened her. Ava saw light though it was dark. Her face burned with embarrassment and she squeezed her eyes tightly. Rayna's hand stopped drumming against her pubic hair, her fingers pressed the bone and combed through the mound of flesh petals, pushing in, knuckling her bone.

Ava was in a timeless space and the music that Rayna had worked her to, she slowly realized, had softened, brightened. No more wailing guitars or throbbing basslines.

"I-I-I—" She stretched her shoulders, arched her back, trying to sit herself up.

"Oops, sorry, let me help you there." Rayna had been rummaging through the glove box and paused to press the lever to raise the seat. Ava realized she didn't remember being lowered. How had this started? The bustling meant it was over, but what was next?

"I'm not gay," Ava said.

Rayna laughed that same bell song of a laugh that disarmed her. "Neither am I." Then in a theatrical tone, "I just don't know what came over me."

"Well, I know what came over me—you did."

"And I know what came on me—you did," Rayna mimicked.

They both laughed, though unequally. Rayna's was hearty and Ava sounded nervous and false to herself.

Rayna finally found what she'd been searching for: wet wipes.

"Ah, one more sniff before I remove the evidence." She held her fingers to her nose and inhaled and sighed and inhaled again, and then began to wipe.

"Why did you do that?"

"Why did you stay still?"

"I don't know."

"Neither do I."

"You know if you had kissed me, I would have split."

"A kiss is corny. Besides, my kisses belong to my husband. I wanted to taste you, to feel you pleasured. Your arousal is so visible. You've got those big, stretchy buttons and your color changes."

"I blush when I feel embarrassed."

"I can see it. Very cute. Look, I'm glad you didn't slug me. I'm glad you let me have my way with you." Rayna unwrapped another packet and assiduously wiped each finger.

"But you're married."

"So?"

"Does your husband know you're like this?"

"Know what? Like what? Skilled and seductive? What makes you think this isn't my first time?"

"Is it?"

"Yes and no. First time as a grown up with a husband and kids. You should meet them."

"Meet them?

"Yes, see how normal I am. How this was just a notion."

"Rayna, I don't know what to do with any of this."

"You've got my card."

"So now the talking is over. We've smoked our cigarettes and rolled over." Ava quipped.

They both laughed.

"Did you ever smoke?" Ava asked. "I did."

"Me, too," Rayna said. They laughed together again.

Ava squeezed Rayna's arm. "Good night."

Rayna leaned over and kissed Ava's cheek, her left eye, the side of her mouth and the top of her neck with little suckings that left red rings Ava saw in her bathroom mirror back home. *Now what the hell is wrong with me?* she asked herself. But she had been awakened. She undressed quickly and rummaged through her drawers for relief.

"No!" she yelled at the cats who came through the opened bedroom door. "Out!"

She found her dick stone and egg rock. Egg rock was for straddling, it started out cold, but between her thick thighs it would return her heat to her. She had time. She needed to work out what had happened. She took the dick stone with her in the shower.

"My baby my baby I-I-I love the way she-e walks/when the girl gets sleepy I love the way she baby talks."

She arranged herself on her wide bed, her towel hot and damp beneath her, and she pulled it up and taut between her legs, strapping the stones to her.

Cmon cmon Cmon baby do want to go the music drawled and she felt the stone slide relentless and unyielding but now small inside her wet widening. *This is what I want hardness inside me throbbing.* "Hardness," she chanted, and then hissed, "hardness hardness harder harder."

THE DINNER INVITATION two weeks later surprised Ava. She had set everything aside. Her discomfort, her questions, her arousal and had buried all her wondering and feelings in work. She had a strategy to devise, a campaign to develop, a client to convince and all the proofs and language had to be precise. The call at work felt like she stumbled while skipping. She didn't fall but almost did, and her heart raced. She calmed herself: dinner friends, husband, children. A new context would help put everything in perspective. Knowing a man was married doused her ardor every time, seeing this woman married, no, being seen in the married woman's married context would strip whatever this was away.

Saturday night was hard. Ava was tired from the long work week that had just ended. She had dutifully bought and dressed three bottles of wine. While she loved semi-sweet local wines like organic Eye of the Bee and Golden Crown by Four Chimneys, she decided to be a bit more conservative for dinner, Wiemer's Pinot Noir, Dr. Frank's Semi Dry Riesling, and for desert, Wagner's Ice Wine. She was glad she had done so; this investment early in the day meant she had time to dress, apply makeup, and wrap her head. She debated over a dress or pants. At work she wore a uniform of her own design, black or dark brown lined suits of wool, pantyhose, pumps, and long sleeved T-shirts in black with the occasional blue or brown. She decided on a flowing dress, knee-highs, and low-heeled black boots. She twirled and smiled at herself in the mirror.

She had printed out the email with instructions. "Horseheads" was another strange place name. The area was full of references to Native Americans, every river, many streets and towns, with no one ever speaking of them directly. Horseheads was an incomprehensible jumble of country, rural and suburban that went up and down hills, into hollers and straddled both sides of the long, unfinished highway 86/17.

Rayna lived in a bit that had a couple of streets of long, low, ranch homes, modern, but incongruous to Ava's eyes, the split fences, wagon wheels in yards, huge stones on broad lawns. The long driveway was paved with white pebbles that crackled beneath her car wheels. She thought she was late, but seeing no other cars in the drive, decided with relief that she was not.

Inside, the long, wide living room was a glow, a fire crackled in the fireplace, a big sectional facing it.

"Glad you made it." Rayna smiled, dimpled, totally relaxed while Ava felt shy, nervous, as she held the bottles out in front of her.

"Why thank you so much, you shouldn't have."She gave Ava a hug and kissed her cheek and Ava felt Rayna's tongue flick her cheek. Rayna stepped back quickly and giggled. "Let's put this here," she said, putting the bottles down, taking her coat, stroking Ava as she pulled it off.

Ava stiffened. "It seems quiet for a household with children."

"They're with their grandparents for the weekend."

Rayna hung Ava's coat in a closet now visible, a built-in on one side of the doorway, picked up the bottles and instructed, "Follow me to the kitchen and meet my other half."

"Your home is huge and lovely," Ava said, surprised at how it seemed to unfold before her and that the kitchen actually took time to get to. She was glad Rayna held the bottles because she knew the aproned man at the stove.

"Ava, I think you may have met my husband, Ron. Ron, here is Ava."

He paused from stirring and turned and smiled. "Ava! Yes, we've met."

"Nice to see you again, Ron." Though she felt exposed and blushed, she knew because she felt the tips of her ears heat up. It was more than just words. He was so nice to look at, so relaxed and limber. He held himself erect, arms at his side, and when he turned toward his cooking, he moved quickly and with assurance.

Rayna chided, "Stop fiddling. You know it's delicious. Look at what Ava brought us."

"Very thoughtful," Ron complimented, "red, white and sweet."

Rayna walked around the large island separating them from the stove. She hugged him around the waist. His butt was just below her breasts, her head was only as high as the bottom of his shoulder blades. Her hands went under the apron.

"I can't cook like this," he complained.

"You don't need to cook anymore. It's done, let's eat."

Ron sighed and made a funny face. "I'm not sure what happened when you two hung out," he paused and Ava steeled herself for what might come next. She wasn't sure either. "But she's been incorrigible ever since."

Only me, Ava thought. *How do I get into these things? All I did was share a table. Ron, who I danced with and desired, Ron who goes on forever, is the husband of my first female masher? Why didn't I know this and did she know I've met him? Did she know this when she and I met? They don't have the same last name so there was no way for me to know.*

"C'mon let's eat. The table's already set."

"Which would you like first—your red or white?"

"Well what are we having?" Ava asked. "And aren't there others coming?"

"The Babcocks cancelled last minute, said they couldn't get a sitter," Ron shouted as Rayna guided Ava to the dining room.

Ava admired the modern chandelier of rag bits, glass shards, plastic bottles, and sprays of tiny white bulbs. The long, light maple table was carved spirals and scrolls, the legs and ball feet were similarly inscribed. The walls were pale and at the far end of the room a huge Chiwara's spiral horns arched into space.

Still nervous, Ava's hunger and appetite quieted her musings. Her favorite fish, wild salmon with tamari, maple syrup, and ginger was uncovered before her. "My favorite!" she exclaimed.

"So I heard," Ron laughed, not as fully or deeply as Rayna, his tenor was a bit high. When he spoke, he pushed his voice down, but when he laughed it flew up, boyish and young. What else had he heard? Ava struggled to remember talking to Rayna about food, but perhaps it was a conversation she had had with him. They ate the fish, salad, snow peas, wild rice, and tiny dumplings filled with shrimp. Ava wasn't sure what they were, but they were for the sauce Ron had worked on. They finished the bottle of Riesling and had begun the Pinot Noir.

"Are you ready for desert?" Rayna asked, carrying small glasses for the ice wine.

Ava had done most of the talking; remarking on the art and other features, and Ron and Rayna offered up children stories. Ava relaxed and enjoyed the special occasion of good cooking that was not her own.

"Let's sit by the fire," Rayna said.

"Yes, I worked on that."

"He's such a fireman." Rayna laughed and paused from her table clearing to rub his shoulders. Ron leaned back into her hands, rubbing the back of his head between her breasts.

Ava watched, not sure whether this was an intimacy she should see. Ron led her through the doorway and she saw that this floor formed a circle. She asked for the bathroom.

"Which one?" Ron asked Rayna who chuckled, "The little one, the nearest one!" and then said to Ava, "He just finished a project in our master bath and wants to show it off. But you just need to go, right?" They all chuckled.

Refreshed, Ava tried to find her way alone to the living room. "Hello?" she called.

Ron appeared and draped an arm around her, his large hand laced his fingers through hers, squeezed, and then he rubbed her arm. He sat first on the couch while she stood before it, gazing at the fire.

"You're so charming," he said.

"Thank you."

"Come sit down," he patted the seat beside him, but when Ava went to sit down, Ron pulled her on to his lap.

"Ron..."

"Shhh."

"Ron."

"Yes?"

"What are you doing?" Ava stood up and he pulled her back down, hard. She felt him grow between her buttocks.

"Rayna wants this," he said as he adjusted himself behind and beneath her, pulling her dress up. He squeezed her tightly in his arms, each hand held a breast and his elbow pressed her ribs.

"Ray," he called, as he squeezed. Ava wriggled and his legs clasped her.

Rayna came in. "Oh, desert!" she purred. She pulled Ava's dress up further and began to lick Ron's fingers where they held Ava's large breasts. She pulled Ava's bra up, and then pulled her nipples through the cage of Ron's fingers and sucked them, licking his hands. Ron bounced and squeezed Ava with his legs.

"Rayna told me about you," he said, punctuating each word with a thrust. Ava felt his hardness grow up her back.

"Then I told her about you." He dropped his hands, using one arm to prop up her breasts, presenting them to his wife. His other hand went behind her, she felt his knuckles against her buttocks, rubbing and rolling and realized he was stroking himself. "You've made us so happy."

Rayna was now on her knees before them, her hands squeezing his thighs. Then she pressed and spread Ava's. She leaned in and gnawed his legs, leaving damp spots on his pants and Ron groaned as if in pain, deep and guttural.

"Wait, wait, wait," she commanded as he began to bounce Ava.

Rayna grabbed a remote from the side table at the side of the couch and pressed some buttons. Ron squeezed and heaved and sunk his head at the side of Ava's neck and began sucking her shoulder.

"Ah ah," she gasped, noticing that they were moving in time to the music.

"I've got the right string but wrong yo-yo."

Rayna pulled his arm out from his pants and put his huge hot hand on Ava's diaphragm. She then pulled Ava's arms out. They had been behind her; her hands had been under Ron's behind.

"O baby take a ride in my Cadillac take a ride take a ride take a ride."

"Now missy, something for me," shoving Ava's hand under her dress, Rayna guided it. She had no panties on. Rayna stood over them, taller than them both now and shuddering over Ava's hand, and then crouched while her orgasm flowed. Rayna sucked Ava's fingers and returned her hand to gather more. Rayna caressed Ava's breasts and sucked her husband's tongue. Ron cried and spasmed, bucking Ava off onto the rug. Rayna wriggled on top of him.

"Help me angel, I'm almost there. Help me, baby" Ron pleaded, kissing her stomach wildly and squeezing her melon-shaped buttocks and Rayna said "No!" To what, Ava wasn't sure, but saw Rayna was now seated on her husband's face, her skirt covering herself again and him. She unbuckled his pants and freed him. Rayna held him with both hands as if he were a hose with water turned full on. And it seemed, as she pulled him out, there was a long black train, gleaming, and a dark tunnel in her hand, and she took him in her mouth.

"You can help," she muttered, smiling and burbling over her mouthful to Ava.

But seeing them locked and moaning broke the spell. Ava was no voyeur and the distance, small as it was, gave her some slight perspective. This was a mess. They had used her neediness. It would be a story to not tell the grandchildren, and as much as she would have enjoyed Ron enabling her, knocking on her walls and stretching her to fit, she would want to know that when he trembled he trembled for her. She would want to know what each moan meant.

She waited, watching the fire while they wailed and rocked.

"That's it, that's it!" Rayna sounded choked. The strangling sensation alarmed Ava so she turned to look. Rayna was now face-to-face with Ron, and her skirt bunched up, exposed Ron only partway inside her and they cried together.

"*Ugh Ugh arghhhhh*," he barked. Rayna laughed and squealed as he slid out.

They kissed passionately, noisily, and he sat up with Rayna on his lap. She grabbed tissues from a cut crystal tissue box.

"I've got to go," Ava said.

"Please, please stay awhile. We can try this again," Rayna said.

"You've been so good for us," Ron added.

"Ron's too big for me. I thought there was nothing for us to do, and with you, we've found a way."

"Great," Ava said flatly. They were both around her now, Rayna's breasts in her back, and Ron's coil pressed against her stomach.

"Thank you," Ron murmured, pulling them both close and nuzzling Ava's neck.

She started to say something and thought better of it. She just needed to get out of there, away from them and be on her way. She pulled away and Rayna rubbed herself against Ron, and stroked his crotch, while Ava found her coat in the closet and let herself out.

The driveway crackled loudly as she backed out, frightening her. It sounded like something was breaking. Ava couldn't see more than a few yards ahead. She worried about unseen deer or rabbits leaping out and her slow response time. As she tried to clear her head and retrace her way out to the highway, fog walked across the road and tumbled like cloudy boulders and gates in lines marking the highway home.

SHE HAD TO GO AND LOSE IT AT THE ASTOR
D.L. KING

*"She didn't know exactly whom to blame
And she couldn't say just how or when she lost it
She only knew she had it when she came."*

*She Had To Go And Lose It At The Astor
– Pearl Bailey (1959)*

"OH, MY BABY'S goin' out on her first date. Oh, I just can't believe it. Harold, go and get the camera. Babydoll, you look beautiful, simply gorgeous. Take the picture, Harold!"

"Ma!"Minnie squirmed in her mother's embrace.

Not being enamored of her mother's taste in clothes, she'd worked for a month and a half to get the money to pay for this dress and she sure didn't want it wrinkled and tear stained before she even got out the door. It wasn't exactly that her mother's taste in clothes was bad, it was just—conservative.

Minnie had found the perfect dress for a real sophisticated evening of dinner and dancing at The Astor. It was a beautiful, dark green silk with a demurely scooped neck and low, low, low back, all the way down to her, well, never mind. It had long, fitted sleeves and the dress hugged her every curve. She'd got a pair of pretty, red stack heels to wear with it, too, and a long necklace of red beads, twisted at the end and worn backwards to show off the hollow of her back. A sprig of holly on her barrette, pulling her hair back from her face topped everything off, making her just the image of a Christmas fantasy.

She sat down at her dressing table to touch up her lipstick, Ruby Kiss, it was called, and her mother laid a gentle hand on her shoulder, gazing at her in the mirror.

"Harold, you go on back to your paper, now. Minnie and I have something important to talk about."

Minnie knew the "sex talk" was coming. It wasn't like her mother hadn't already told her about the birds and bees, but she knew, dressed up like she was and ready to go out for the evening, her mother would want to drive home the point.

Once her father had closed the door and left them alone, her mother turned to her. "Minnie, men just want one thing." Minnie turned to look at her and started to speak. "No, I know you think he's different but, Honey, he's a man and he's gonna take one look at you and think about that one thing. You gotta trust me on this; I know. You don't know much about life yet. We kept you as pure and innocent as we could. You spent all those years at that convent school 'cause we didn't want you associating with riff raff. Now, I'm not saying Mark isn't a good boy..."

Minnie's shoulders slumped. Mark was a *man*, not a boy! Her mother was so old fashioned. And just the mention of that school set her teeth on edge. She was lucky to have gotten out of there alive, what with all the punishments she'd had to endure. The paddlings in Mother Francis' office had been just too humiliating. Hands on that big walnut desk, arms bracing her body with her legs spread, skirt stuck to her blouse with a safety pin and her panties pulled down. That nun had the wickedest paddle. Wide, with holes in it. It was made of solid oak. And boy did she feel it when it landed on her bare bottom. It seemed she was always getting caught passing notes in the chapel or laughing during the health class movies.

Once, she found a dirty magazine in her father's closet. There were lots of pictures of naked women, but she also found a few pictures of naked men. She'd cut one out and brought it to school to show Emma, her best friend, but Emma had passed it on and by the time Sister Jacqueline grabbed it, six girls had seen it. They all had to go to Mother's office. This time they'd been made to spank each other. They had to line up, one behind the other, with their skirts pinned up and their panties down and spank each other's bottoms. And if a girl didn't do it hard enough, she got punished even harder by the girl behind her. Minnie had been at the end of the line and Mother Francis spanked her—with that paddle—really hard—she really loved that paddle. Minnie secretly believed she loved seeing the girls' naked behinds, too, almost as much as she liked making them cry. That was probably why she became a nun in the first place.

Her mother was still going on about boys and being careful and not sitting with your legs open. Minnie was automatically *yessing* her at each pause in her mother's monologue.

Finally, she heard Mark's knock on the door. Before she could reach the handle, her mother said, "Minnie, you look so lovely tonight; you don't want to spoil the effect with your old wool coat." And she placed her own sable cape over Minnie's shoulders.

"Oh, Mom!" Minnie said, stroking the soft black fur. "Thank you so much." Her mother reached around her to open the door.

Mark wasn't the most handsome guy she'd seen but he certainly was very dashing in his tuxedo. He held his arm out and she curled her hand, and then her whole arm around it and smiled up at him. Somehow, her father had appeared by her mother.

"Bring my Minnie back by midnight," he said. "I trust you'll treat her like a lady, son."

With a "Yes, sir" they were out the door and down the front steps to the car and driver waiting at the curb.

Minnie wasn't nearly as innocent as her mother thought. She had big plans for the evening. She was tired of being a girl. She wanted to be a woman, after all, Mark was a man and she was pretty sure he could be trusted to act like one. Once in the enormous back seat of the car, she placed her little red-and-black beaded bag on her lap. It held everything she'd need for the night. Her Ruby Kiss lipstick, her compact and mirror, twenty dollars in case of emergency, and a dozen individually wrapped condoms—ribbed, for her pleasure, of course—whatever that meant. She hadn't been sure how many a girl needed for an evening out, but was pretty sure she was safe with an even dozen.

Once the car pulled away from the curb, Mark wrapped his arm around her shoulders and said, "Aren't you the vision of Christmas Present?" He leaned in for a kiss and she let him. She opened her mouth and sucked on his tongue while his hand dived into the back of her dress and snaked its way around to the front and to her naked breast.

She melted at the unfamiliar feel of his strong fingers stroking and squeezing her tit, making her nipple hard with longing. As he withdrew his mouth from hers, she felt him squeeze her nipple in an almost painful pinch, and as he did, she felt moisture seep from between her legs.

"Oh, now look at what you've gone and done, silly," she said. "I can't go into the Astor like this." She looked down and framed her ripe tits with her hands. "One's all pointy and the other's not!"

"Well, Miss Davis," he said, "Allow me." And he kissed her again, this time gnawing and sucking on her bottom lip while both hands toyed with her tender young nipples. Once she began to squirm in her seat, he sat back and said, "There, that's better."

She looked down at her chest and saw both nipples standing up hard against the soft fabric of her dress and giggled. She put her hand in his lap and said, "Why, Mr. Ford, you're so naughty! Now I look like I'm freezing to death, when that couldn't be further from the truth."

"Let me see." Again, Mark reached a hand into the back of her dress, this time lower down and snaked it around to her front.

She grabbed his arm and said, "Don't! You'll stretch it out. Let me." And she hiked up her skirt, over her waist.

"And you call *me* naughty. You're not wearing any panties!" His hand cupped her hot, wet pussy and stroked the hair there. Soon a finger found her opening and gently played in it and stroked her folds. "You're right, you're not cold at all," he said with a sly smile and a wink.

Minnie laughed and grabbed his wrist and removed his hand from between her legs. She smoothed her dress back down and said, "There'll be plenty of time for that later. I don't want to get all mussed before I even walk into the lobby!"As the car glided across the Brooklyn Bridge, she took out her lipstick and compact and fixed her face.

The car came to a stop and the chauffeur opened the door to let them out. She hadn't noticed how attractive he was earlier. He tipped his cap and winked as she placed her arm in Marks. The doorman, with his white gloves, although not nearly as handsome as the chauffeur, was no slouch either, as he opened the door and bent at the waist as they passed. She could feel his eyes following her as she walked into the lobby.

She'd only been inside The Astor once, when she was a little girl. It was as grand as she remembered. Mark led the way to the ballroom where the tables had been laid with their gleaming service. Pretty crystal snowflakes adorned each centerpiece of pine and red roses and more crystal snowflakes hung from the ceiling, over the dance floor, in the center of the room. The band was at the head of the room and people were already dancing to a swinging jazz number. Once they reached their seats, Mark removed her cape and hung it over the chair. She put her bag on the table and they went off to dance.

He nuzzled against her neck and kissed her earlobe. "I reserved a guest room for us," he whispered. "I thought you might want to freshen up later." He placed a key in her hand and she shivered and sighed. "I have one too. That way we won't have to go up together, if you know what I mean," and he winked that sly smile at her again.

The waiter served the meal and he looked good enough to eat, himself! The food was so good she insisted on meeting the chef, who came out to say hello. She'd always thought chefs were supposed to be fat, but the chef at The Astor looked more like a movie star, even if he was her father's age.

She asked him if he'd give her a tour of the kitchen and, though it wasn't usually done, he winked and said, "Allow me, Miss." She gave Mark a kiss on the cheek and said she'd only be a minute as she slipped away from the table and let the chef lead her out of the room. "It's very hot in the kitchen," he said.

"That's all right," she replied. "I like the heat."

By the time Mark had finished his Scotch, he was beginning to get worried but, just as he rose to go and look for her, she appeared. The waiter and the chef each held a door open for her to reenter the ballroom and Mark couldn't help but notice their sly smiles.

When she reached the table, the band began to play a torch song and Mark led her to the dance floor once again. As he held her tight, he let his hand wander down to stroke her soft skin just above her bottom. The feel of his hand sent tingles up her spine and spasms into her pussy. She pressed herself against him and felt him hard against her, in turn. His hand moved down to cup her bottom. His fingers played against the bend between her leg and her rear end and she laughed. "What was the number of that room, again?"

She caught the eye of a gentleman in the elevator who pressed the penthouse button. He had the same sly smile that Mark had. Wasn't it strange that every man she saw was so handsome and sexy. Usually only a few guys caught her eye, but that night, they all looked good. She pressed the button for five and he said, "You should see the view from the penthouse!"

"I thought you'd gotten lost," Mark said when she opened the door to the room.

"Nope, just looking around," she replied. She drank in the sight of Mark: tie untied, white shirt unbuttoned down to his waist, socks and shoes off, lying on the big four-poster bed. Looking him in the eye, she slowly made her way from the door to the bed. She ran her fingers through the hair on his chest and he sat up to kiss her.

"You sure this is what you want?" he asked.

She laid her bag down on the table beside the bed, reached down and took hold of the hem of her dress and, in one fluid motion, lifted it over her head and off. There she stood before him, in nothing but her garter belt, stockings and shoes. Her breasts were high and shapely, topped by the little hard points of her nipples. Her waist was tiny, flaring into wide hips, which curved into the most beautiful ass. A neat patch of black hair covered her sex. She knew exactly what she looked like. She'd been practicing for this moment for weeks. She might have thought her hips were a little too wide or her breasts a little too small, but deep down she knew he'd think she was perfect.

He pulled her down with him and threw a leg over her, holding her fast to him. Clamping his mouth over hers and thrusting his tongue into her, he wrapped his hand around her leg and drew it up his body, opening her up to his exploring fingers. She felt him split her behind and reach down between her legs, fingers skittering through her slit from the back of her ass to her clit. She'd never felt anything like it and thought she might swoon but then soon relaxed into the feel of his fingers and mouth.

"Hey," she said, "aren't you gonna take your clothes off? I don't want to be the only one naked in this room." He laughed and let her up. He began to un-tuck his shirt but she couldn't wait and reached to unbuckle his belt and unzip his pants while he still had his hands on his shirt. He was still trying to remove his cuff links when she lowered his pants and freed his straining cock from its confinement.

"It's so hard," she said, wrapping her hand around his girth.

"All because of you," he said. "All for you." And he kicked his pants the rest of the way off and shrugged out of his shirt. "Minnie, you're a vision." With one hand squeezing a tit and the other exploring her dripping interior, he said, "I don't know how long I can wait to be inside you."

She lay back on the bed and luxuriated in his attentions. The feeling of his hot mouth closed over her straining breast, the nipple almost painfully hard, so hard that his tongue, teasing it, felt like little electric shocks, shocking her body and racing through her, down to her pussy, where his fingers continued to manipulate her. She was so wet down there. She didn't think she'd ever been wetter.

"Wait a minute, honey," he said and started to pull away from her. "I gotta get something."

"No. Don't stop," she begged. "I got it right here." And she reached over to the bed table and her purse and pulled out a condom.

"Why, Minnie, you minx. You planned this all along."

"Who, me?" she asked, batting her eyelashes at him. "I just like to be prepared, is all." She handed him the little foil package and watched as he rolled the piece of rubber down his cock. He kissed her hard and stabbed her mouth with his tongue as she felt the tip of his cock pushing against her pussy lips.

"You're sure? This might hurt a little. But you're really wet. So—you're sure?"

She told him yes, yes she was sure and grabbed his cock with her own little hand, pushing it into her until he took over and carefully slid himself all the way inside her. He felt deliciously large and filled her up completely. They stayed like that for a bit, as close as two people could be in each other's embrace, before he began to move inside her.

They rocked and rocked and rocked against each other and she thought it was just about the best thing she'd ever felt until he touched her with his fingers, just above where his cock entered her. Then it was all sparks and fireworks and pretty soon she screamed out her pleasure. He looked at her and asked if she was all right. When she said she was better than all right, he said, "OK, here I come, then," and it was as if his body turned into a machine, pistoning in and out of her.

She could feel the tension build between them. She was pretty sore, but she felt the now familiar signs of her own climax approaching again. Briefly she wondered if they would come together, and then she felt the fireworks explode behind her eyes and could think of nothing else. His fucking became erratic and there was real purpose behind his thrusts, and then she felt him explode.

Her heart was still racing a mile a minute but as she began to relax and the sweat began to dry, she turned to Mark and kissed him gently on the lips. He looked like he was about to drift off to sleep.

"What time is it?" she asked.

He lifted his wrist to his face and said, "About 11:45."

Minnie shrieked. "I promised Daddy I'd be home by midnight. Don't you remember? We have to go now. Now!" she repeated when he didn't jump right out of bed.

"OK, Babydoll. You got it. But don't you think you should put your clothes back on first?"

Racing across the Brooklyn Bridge, she knew she was going to be late, at least a half hour late—probably more like an hour late. Well, she'd been in trouble before. But she sure had had a great time at The Astor.

As soon as the big car pulled up to the curb outside her house, she opened the door and jumped out, not waiting for the chauffeur to open it for her. Mark followed her onto the sidewalk and looked up at the stoop where her parents were opening the door.

"Minnie!" her mother gasped, placing a hand to her chest and looking like she was going to faint.

"Damn it, son, I told you to treat her like a lady!" her father said. "And you," he looked straight at Minnie. "You had to go and lose it at The Astor!"

Minnie could feel her face flush hot from embarrassment. How on earth did they know? Was it written all over her? Did she look different? Was her dress on crooked? She'd fixed her hair and makeup before leaving the hotel room. She was sure she looked all right. She looked over at Mark. Did he look different? Was his tie straight? Shirt buttoned right?

"Daddy, what do you mean?" she asked.

But just then—before he could answer her, the chauffeur got out of the car and walked over to her. He placed the sable cape over her shoulders and said, "Sorry Miss. The waiter brought it out when he thought you'd left it at the table. I should have given it to you earlier. I hope you weren't too cold."

Her mother hugged her daddy. "Oh, thank god," she said, "she didn't lose it at The Astor after all!"

ONCE WASHED UP and ready for bed, she emptied out her evening bag; she put the lipstick and the compact on her dressing table, the money in her drawer and counted the condoms. *Next time I'll know better. I didn't need this many. Why, I only used four...*

THE SUMMER OF BOBBY
JOLENE HUI

"I hear a lot of buzzing, sound like my little honeybee
She been all around the world making honey
But now she is coming home to me."

Honeybee — Muddy Waters (1951)

IT WAS SO HARD TO BE GOOD—especially in the summer when my skin was so sweaty. I was constantly wet. Bobby worked nonstop. I missed his company and when I was left alone, I wandered. He encouraged my adventures and asked me about them. Unlike most men I'd been in relationships with, Bobby wanted to hear every detail about my encounters.

I wasn't working the summer when things became too difficult to juggle. I was a corporate technical writer and my company had closed for the season due to a lag in business and the need for the execs to have an extended vacation. At first the thought of an unpaid furlough kind of irked me, but once the first week was over, I felt like going back to work would be the most difficult part of the summer. I quickly took to the non-working lifestyle. I stayed up late until the early hours of the morning and rose around noon. Some days I'd spend hours drinking iced tea and watching my cat play with her stuffed catnip-filled mice. Being able to breathe and to sleep was an amazing feeling. No hassle of the fluorescent bulbs, people in suits annoying me, and no ergonomically shitty desk to suffer through all day.

A true young teen of the nineties, I was ingrained with the grunge sound. When I was younger I was in love with Kurt Cobain. His lyrics wilted me to the core and made me wish I were older so I could rescue him from that bitch Courtney. When their song "Where Did You Sleep Last Night?" made an appearance on the *Unplugged* album, I listened to it on repeat for days. It was like I was sensing my own destiny. A cover of Leadbelly's "In the Pines," the song was haunting and beautiful, filled with so much emotion I cried the first time I heard it. I could not even comprehend the lyrics, as I was still a virgin and could only imagine what sexual jealousy and pain felt like. Nonetheless, I could feel it Kurt's suffering through his singing.

During that unemployed summer, I listened to the music of my teens. I was feeling nostalgic and, somehow, I was feeling inspired by it. Aside from just breathing, I spent the remainder of my time cooking and often dancing around the house to the music of my past. However, the most important memory of that particular summer was the sexual promiscuity that kept me satisfied in the workless lull. Stabilizing my summer was my boyfriend at the time, Bobby. I did everything for him, even though he was so busy working I hardly saw him. He kept me sane and I kept him fed and warm at night when he was around.

Bobby and I had an explosively spicy sex life. The thought of his dark cocoa skin rubbing against my olive flesh made me wet with desire. In the summer he usually wore sleeveless shirts, leaving his thick, toned biceps exposed for me to touch and lick at my leisure. His hair was corn rowed, easier to take care of in the summer heat. I loved my men in all colors, but Bobby was who lit my fire until it nearly exploded with everlasting sparks. When he smiled, his straight white teeth lured me into his mouth. When he was angry, his stern eyebrows made him sexier in a different way. He was always intense, the way he swaggered, the way he spoke slowly and evenly, the way he carried himself. He was a strong, proud, and unbelievably sexy black man.

Bobby was a real man. The sexiest man I'd ever seen. I couldn't control the skipping in my heart each time I saw him enter a room. Testosterone dripped off his skin. Days after I met him I couldn't imagine loving anyone as much as I loved him.

Not having to dress in boring corporate attire, I'd taken to wearing little dresses in the summer heat. I went through my men like the sweat soaked my dresses—incessantly and all the way.

First there was Joshua, with his blonde hair and blue eyes, Joel was also a J but opposite in looks. He was Jewish, with dark brown curly hair and a stereotypical large nose. Steven's piercing green eyes swept over my thin limbs and round booty. Paul had smooth olive skin that caressed me when he was on top of me. Christopher H, Christopher F, Christopher D, and Christopher S were all a blur of sweat, arms, and legs. There were many more. A few were nameless. All were a cure for my summer boredom and my way to make Bobby carry me into the bedroom, peel my damp dress from my body, and fuck me until I couldn't see straight.

After weeks of working, Bobby would come home.

In the dark he'd insist, "Tell me what they did to you."

I'd tell him my adventures and he'd take my panties off followed by my little nightie tank top. He'd rub my nipples and slide his fingers down my stomach to my clit. He'd kiss my stomach, pulsing two fingers inside of me and rubbing them along my swollen nub when he pulled them out. Then he'd stretch his nude, ripe, body on top of mine and kiss my face. "Baby, you're mine. Don't you forget that."

His fingers in my pussy, he'd expertly mingle his tongue with mine until I came all over his hand. When he fucked me, he always did it with such tenderness. He grabbed my waist with his cum-soaked hand and slipped his cock inside me. He worked it smoothly inside and outside of me until I came again. I moaned and scraped my fingernails down his back.

When we pulled apart, he kissed me again, leaving kisses on my forehead and brushing my black bangs aside. He got out of bed and put his clothes back on.

"I'm going to Cleveland. I'll be back in a week," he said. This was all very typical for him. I pulled my naked body under the sheets and blew him a kiss.

Bobby's uncle was a contractor who had jobs all over the country. Bobby was one of the best electrical engineers his uncle had ever worked with so he contracted with him to come along to get the buildings wired quickly, effectively, and efficiently.

He insisted he didn't spend any time with other women when he traveled. I, of course, would not judge him if he did, considering the amount of men I'd entertained in the times he was gone. The amount of work kept Bobby from really doing much else. He said picturing me with other men while jerking off while he fell asleep was what he liked the most. The one time he'd hired company he said he was disappointed and felt guilty. He wanted to save his lust for me, he said.

"Don't forget to make good stories for me." His parting words always made me smile and gave me and filled me with a sense of adventure. I fell asleep dreaming of what kind of casserole I would make for dinner and who would be my next adventure.

JOSHUA'S blue eyes beckoned me from the corner of the bookstore. I'd never been picked up in the cookbook section. Then again, I had never been picked up in a bookstore before. His long fingers flipped the pages anxiously but with style. He was dressed casually in loose jeans and a polo shirt. The clothes clung to his toned muscles in all the right places. I couldn't tell if he was a rich white boy or just clean cut and attractive. Either way, he was turning me on by just flipping through a Crock-Pot cookbook.

"So what are you cooking me for dinner?" I couldn't stop the words from pouring from my lips.

He smiled. "Crock-Pot cooking generally takes hours and hours. How long are you planning on staying over?"

I drove, following him closely until we pulled into a duplex. As soon as we got inside we started kissing and touching. We fucked quickly on the living room floor. I panted and screamed like an animal. His sheathed cock pounded me from behind.

"Do you want me to make you dinner?" He asked me, in a matter of fact way.

I smiled, not knowing how to reply. My lovers and I rarely shared more than a few words and they didn't have to do with domestic duties or niceties. Ordinarily I would have left after a quick peck on the cheek, but something made me stay. "Sure. What's on the menu?"

He shrugged and walked into the kitchen in his underwear.

I followed him and said, "It can't be something in a Crock-Pot because you left without buying the book."

He shook his head as if I had just told a terrible joke. I stared at his body while he took out all the kitchen supplies: a large wok, a cutting board, a knife, and a spatula. I didn't say a word as I watched him slice up veggies and chicken. He poured peanut oil into the heated wok and threw in the chicken.

"Yum, that smells really good," I said. I was usually the one who did the cooking so this was a special treat for me.

Putting my arms around him, I liked how he felt while he stir-fried. His arms worked to lift and toss. I peeked around his abdomen to watch him add some noodles. My stomach growled at the smell of oyster sauce. Maybe it was my Asian heritage, but the smell of stir-fried oyster sauce excited me. I kissed Joshua's back while he worked away.

I was delighted when we sat down to eat. I hadn't even realized I'd been hungry. The chicken almost melted in my mouth. It tasted marinated even though it hadn't been. All the flavors were perfect.

"Where did you learn to cook?" I asked him.

"I taught myself," he said.

I didn't mean to eat and run but I had to before I was tempted to stay any later. I wanted to fuck him again, but I nearly ran to my car after kissing him gently on the lips and running my hands across his pecs.

During all of my adventures I was always expected to come home at night. Whether or not Bobby was home, he'd call me to wish me sweet dreams. I knew to be home by midnight for a call. I never brought anyone back to the home Bobby and I shared.

The night after I ate stir-fry with Joshua, Bobby called me at midnight on the dot.

"Boy do I have a story for you," I said softly into the phone.

"Save it 'til I get back to you, sweetie," he said.

"You sure you don't want to hear it now?" I offered, even though I was too tired to tell him.

"I want to see the story coming from your lips," Bobby replied.

I slept soundly that night. I fell asleep much earlier than usual, a warmth spreading throughout my body that lulled me into dreamland.

Joel touched my hand a couple nights later in the grocery store. I was on the hunt for chocolate chip cookie and cinnamon bundt cake ingredients.

"Whoops, sorry," I said. He pulled it away immediately.

I don't know what I was thinking, baking so much in the hot summer, but I had to keep myself busy or I'd have been prowling around town even more than I already was. I felt like a cat in heat. Bobby brought it out in me.

"Did you want this particular bag of flour?" I asked. I topped my question off with a wink.

He laughed. "Nah, I think I can take the one next to it. I think my mom will live."

"Ah, shopping for mom?" I put the bag in my cart.

"You know Jewish moms...always baking."

I laughed. "I don't know. I'm Asian, not a mom, and always baking." I wasn't sure I wanted to pick anyone up who lived with his mom. "Do you live with your mom?"

"No, no, no," he said. "Just running an errand for her. Why?"

My cheeks flushed when I pictured us wildly going at it in his bed. "I just wouldn't want to go home with you to your mom's house. That's all."

He grabbed me by my waist and pulled me away from our shopping carts. In seconds we were in the grocery store restroom where Joel had to slip a quarter in the door for us to use the facility. He lifted me up against the wall that was, surprisingly, clean. I lifted my dress and he slid his condom-covered cock inside me. A mere ten minutes later I checked out with all of my baking ingredients.

At midnight, Bobby called me. "Tell me what you did today." His voice was smooth chocolate on the other line. I talked him through the events at the grocery store. He moaned. I could hear his masturbation sounds on the other end of the line. I plunged my fingers into my soft core when I finished my story. All that was left were the moaning noises coming from deep within me. For minutes we moaned to each other, heavy breathing, panting, wet sex noises coming through on both lines. We came together, screaming into our respective phones.

"Good night, baby," he said.

"Love you, Bobby," I said. I wrapped my arms around my body and fell asleep.

The rest of the men fell into my life like pieces in an extremely large jigsaw puzzle. Quick fucks and baking goodies consumed my life. Bobby wasn't sure when he was going to be home. He thought in maybe a week or so. When the phone rang one night at ten I was startled. Bobby never called me that early. I answered it to hear Joshua's voice on the other end. I hadn't recalled giving him my number.

"Hey, sexy," he said.

"Oh, hi." I knew I clearly sounded surprised.

"Wanna come over for a late dinner?"

I was shocked, not sure how to answer him. My automatic instinct said yes, but I knew I needed to be home by midnight. Should I push the time limit? Should I go with my gut? The feeling in the pit of my belly that lusted for the clean cut blonde?

"I'll be right over."

As soon as I hung up the phone I knew that I was in too deep with this one.

He answered the door in an apron. His blue eyes were rimmed with dark circles but he had a smile on his face. It smelled glorious.

"I made roast beef and wanted to share it with someone," he explained.

Before we got to the roast beef, I put my arms around his waist and thrust my nose into his neck to get a good whiff of his scent. He kissed my lips. I kissed him back, taking notice of the way his tongue darted around with mine in my mouth. The first time we were together had been urgent and dirty. This time was different. It was slower, more deliberate, more of an exploration of two lovers who were in a long-term relationship. I felt like I knew him intimately, like we'd been together for a while and needed to learn each other.

Slowly, we took each other's clothing off. I slid his apron off around his neck. Took his shirt off, unbuttoned his pants, and pulled them down to his ankles. My face at his crotch, I kissed his package through the material. He was already hard, bursting against the boxer briefs. I put my fingers inside the waistband and tugged them down, freeing the swollen staff. My lips encircled him and sucked him. We proceeded to pleasure each other for hours. It felt so delicious I had no idea how to stop. My stomach gurgled from the smell of the roast beef floating from the kitchen. In the bedroom after we'd both gotten off a few times we reclined on the bed, staring at his dark ceiling.

"Wow," I said.

He put his arm around me and buried his face into my neck. We awoke at five and ate dinner while it was still dark outside. When I left I felt sad. I waved to him while I drove away and went back to my empty apartment.

Bobby had only left me two messages. The first was a "where are you?" message. The second was a "baby, I'm coming home tomorrow" message. I knew I had let him down. And I knew that our end was coming. I had not slept where I should have last night. I would not lie to Bobby, but I know that I had messed up. Something changed between us. I didn't want to share where I'd been last night. Never in our relationship had I strayed for the entire night. I soaked in the bathtub to wash Joshua off my body.

I stayed up sipping iced tea and making banana pudding all morning. In the early afternoon Bobby came home. He carried me to our bedroom. Without words he told me he was leaving. He fucked me tenderly and rolled off of me without making any noise. We lay in silence. I was still in my pink flowered dress.

"Did you ever hear the story of the ghost of Linda Sue?" Bobby traced my breasts through the thin material with his fingertip.

"No. Tell me." I kept my eyes closed and relaxed under his touch.

"Well, legend says there is the ghost of a beautiful woman who haunts the forest. The men working out there hear her wailing every Friday night. They say she roams the pine trees at night, looking for the body of her husband who was killed. His body was never found. Only his head was found in a wheel on a road leading out of the trees. It was suspected that one of her lovers did it out of jealousy. She committed suicide because of her deep sorrow."

I kept my eyes closed, picturing the woman in a long flowing nightgown, her dark skin glowing in the moonlight.

"I'm going to be working in those forests, you know," Bobby said. He sat up. His butt touched my thigh.

The woman dissipated and all that was left in my mind was the glowing moon. "I'm going to miss you, you know," I said, meaning it.

"Baby, you know I'll come back," he said. "I just need to go where the pine trees are for now." He turned around and kissed my forehead tenderly. Then he was gone.

I spent the rest of the summer longing for Bobby and wondering how I could have betrayed him. He was in Seattle where the business had been permanently moved. Joshua and I saw each other twice a week until I started working again. We were just a brief summer fling. I never talked to Bobby again, but I still get a sense of sorrow like the one I felt when he left that day. He haunts me just like the ghost of Linda Sue. Whenever I feel inclined to bake a sweet dessert, my heart throbs and I remember that passionate summer.

CAN'T BE SATISFIED
GARY PHILLIPS

*"I don't want a woman who wears a number nine
I wake up in the morning, I can't tell her shoes from
mine."*

Goin' Away Blues – Charlie Campbell (1937)

HE RESTED the semi on the bleached gravel among a row of others at
the truck stop off the highway. Shutting the rig down, he re-checked
the pressure gauges assuring him the refrigerated trailer was working
properly. The driver rubbed a hand on his tired face, dried sweat and
road grime working its way into his stubble. Roosevelt Hopkins took
a quick glance at his features in the rearview, idly flicking a finger at
the baubles dangling from it.

He got out of the truck, stretched, and walked toward the diner
called McKinley's Manor, home of fine eats and cold beer. He entered
to the smells and sounds of the business of feeding strangers.
Hopkins took a stool, nodding down the way at another trucker he
recognized from this route. Perusing the menu, he was pleased the
café had smothered pork chops and greens. He'd love to eat heavy,
something satisfying on his hollow stomach, but he had to make the
port by six in the evening so no time for a nap after such a meal.

"Get you something to drink while you make up your mind?"

Hopkins looked up at the waitress. She wasn't a kid, but she was
pretty in a way a woman past forty could be. Darker than his
complexion, she had full breasts beneath the military-pressed white
shirt she wore, the diffuse presence of a black bra evident
underneath.

"Water would be just fine."

She pointed with the eraser end of her pencil over her shoulder.

"We've got a barbequed half chicken as the special today, and that comes with sliced carrots and candied yams. Now look this is real Q, sugah, not a roasted bird with store bought sauce splashed on."

Her voice had him imagining a smoky club, laughing low, sharing drinks and tongues. He spun back to reality. "Cool. I'll figure out what I want."

She smiled briefly with practiced ease and scooped ice chips into a large plastic tumbler. Hopkins studied the menu and settled on a tuna melt and fruit, tempted as he was to have fries. Not for the first time he lamented being old enough to worry about his waistline and cholesterol.

"To be young again," she said, putting the water and ice before him.

For a moment, he wondered how she knew what was on his mind, and then understood she was looking at a man and woman cuddling on one of the benches in a booth by the door. Both not too far past the legal age for drinking, tattoos decorating their bare arms.

"You ain't ready for your rocking chair yet."

The smile again but this time it seemed less automatic reflex. "Aren't you sweet."

He chuckled and gave her his order. Today's folded sports section had been left on the counter. Hopkins read the ball scores and about athletes' woes until she returned with his food.

"This is your first time through here, isn't it?" she said. There was no name tag on her shirt.

"Had to do my friend's run," he said. "Play cousins we are. He's having some elective surgery but he's got to pay the bills like the rest of us. The time or two I've been through here before, it's been at night."

"I work the night shift a couple of times a week. Funny we never synced up." She went away as more customers arrived.

Hopkins enjoyed his lunch, playing out various pleasurable ways he might "sync up" with the woman. Could be this was merely harmless flirtation on her part, just something to pass the time during the days of the same. But it beat worrying about some baller's knees going out.

Afterward, he put his money down and she said, "Come on back, okay?"

"Will do." He walked outside regretting not pushing himself to ask her which nights she worked, but it wouldn't have been the first time he misread the vibe, and he didn't want to look like a chump. For all he knew she was a part-owner and wanted to sucker him back only in regards to having the cash register sing the ca-ching chorus.Stepping away, Hopkins heard two men coming around the near corner of the diner.

"That's a sweet sled, that's for damn sure."

"Yeah," his companion agreed, working a toothpick between his teeth with gusto. "It'll need some work but could be nice once it gets going."

The two walked away talking about the car, and curious, Hopkins went around the way they'd come. Behind the diner were wood pallets stacked by the screened back door, a half drum for the 'queing, a locked dumpster, and some plastic buckets that once contained allotments of industrial strength butter.

There was a short cement path leading to a circle of cement bordered in overgrown grass and weeds. An old-fashioned car port, virtually bereft of its paint, was over this. Reposed under the car port was a two-tone, white on blue, 1957 Plymouth up on blocks. He got closer. The car's color was dulled but his cursory inspection of the body indicated little rust or dents.

"You've been a good ol' wagon, daddy, but you done broke down."

Hopkins turned to see the waitresses he'd been talking to standing in the rear doorway of the restaurant. She was smoking a cigarette and came down the short steps to walk over to him and the car.

"One of the Eighty-Eight series," he said. "Hi-Fire V-8's in 'em they were called."

"Rocket 88. You know about cars?"

"I know about ones this vintage." He squinted at her as some of her smoke drifted by his eyes. "Whose is it?"

Hand on her hip, her other fingers around her cigarette. "Mine, slick."

"You keep it out in the open like this?"

She took a puff. "No, most of the time in the last eight years or so it's been in a garage and under a tarp." She pointed at the interior. "Take a look."

He opened the door, and looking inside, the aroma of leather preserver hit him, triggering a pleasing sensation. "You've kept the seats and dash in good shape," he complimented, straightening up.

She lifted her brows while taking a last drag on her cigarette. She exhaled and flicked the butt onto the concrete pathway. "A friend was working on it but he had to stop a few weeks ago. Clarence, the owner," she jabbed a thumb at the diner, "let him work on it here 'cause there was the room and my friend had removed the tires and chained it up."

She paused, then, "Friends are something, ain't they?"

Hopkins frowned and looking under the car as she indicated, could see a heavy chain wrapped around the rear axle leading to a stout iron ring embedded in the circle of cement. A padlock gleaming off-yellow affixed the chain to the ring.

Hopkins said, "Can't leave a fine car like this."

"My friend made some progress before he took off with the tires and the keys to the locks."

"You broke his heart, huh?"

"I do it all the time." Both hands on her hips now, head cocked to one side. "Why you care?"

"I like to put my nose in all sorts of tight places."

She showed strong teeth. The café's owner, a heavyset man in rolled up sleeves and suspenders, came to the back door, scowling.

"I'd like to take a look at the car if I could."

She was walking back to work but stopped, turning her head part way around. "Be back Thursday, 'round nine at night, the Scimitar Lounge, down the road a'piece here." She went back inside and he watched the sway of those hips as she did so.

Hopkins had a hard time taking the grin off his face as he powered up his friend's rig and drove away.

THE BAR she told him to meet her at was on Sixteenth Street. Hopkins strolled in and was surprised there was live music in the form of a lanky youth with his guitar and portable amp on a small raised stage off to one side of the place. He was doing justice to a rendition of an Albert Collins song, "Cold, Cold Feeling."

He spotted the waitress sitting at the bar in a simple dress, legs crossed showing a conditioned thigh. She was talking to the bartender, a tall, lean individual with an old-fashioned bowler perched on the back of his head.

"What's your poison?" she asked, touching his arm when he sat next to her. She wore a luminescent peach-colored lipstick that complimented her dark skin.

There was just enough plunge to her neckline that in the half-light made her breasts seem larger than he remembered. If he wasn't careful, he was going to break out in a sweat.

"Vodka tonic, the house vodka is fine."

"That's the only kind we got, pardner," the bartender said. He smiled good-naturedly at Hopkins and made his drink.

"How you doing, you make your delivery on time?"

"I did, thanks for asking. How's your work?"

She made a sound. "Work, you know."

His drink was placed before him. He clinked his glass with hers as she held her drink aloft.

"Here's to not being satisfied."

Hopkins reacted. "That's a crazy toast."

"Yeah?" She sipped from her drink, eyes like a waiting jaguar on him. "You don't want more?" Her foot was out of her shoe and she rested this on his lower leg, moving it around some.

"I want plenty," he said huskily.

"I know you do." She moved her foot go a higher on his leg, digging her toes in.

Later that night, they were in the Rocket 88 up on blocks. It was a cool evening, but they were generating enough warmth. She lay partly against the rear door on the back seat, her legs open and dress pushed up. She rubbed her midnight blue nailed hand on her mound. She slipped a finger inside her pale panties and rubbed her clit, moaning.

"Do you want me, RH?" she said between breaths.

"My head's about to explode, baby." It was roomy in the rear of the car and he had no trouble unbuttoning and removing his shirt.

"Which head?" She took her finger from between her legs and placed the tip on his willing tongue. "You better get over here and fuck me."

"Yes, ma'am."

It was almost light before they two excited the car after their thrashing and sleeping in the vehicle.

"Doesn't that hurt?" He asked her as they walked away, she carrying her shoes over her crooked fingers of one hand.

She turned into him and put her free hand on his withered member inside his pants. "Not as much as I hurt you."

"I need more of that hurtin'."

She kissed him.

That weekend Roosevelt Hopkins had to do a haul with his friend's truck again but was able to make it back to town the following Tuesday. He'd brought his tools and went to work on the Plymouth. Some time ago, it had been explained to him, the gas left in the tank had been dumped and the fuel lines blown clean.

Old gas tended to become gummy and had to be disposed of in the process of rebuilding an auto. A reconditioned engine block had also been installed by the last mechanic working on the vehicle and Hopkins located the heads for the car in the trunk. Those he had to send out two towns over to get redone. But locating a mechanical fuel pump, alternator and so forth wasn't too hard given the Internet and the number of old car clubs and enthusiasts out there.

He and Clover, that was the woman's name, Clover Stovall, were going to get in the car when he got it running and take off down the highway. Since being laid off more than two years ago from the brewery where he'd driven a delivery truck, Hopkins had made do with hustling freelance jobs like filling in for his buddy.

Hopkins didn't want to get sucked down in debt at his age trying to finance his own rig, but this catch as catch can approach to making a living was wearing thin as well. He needed a change and so did she, Clover had told him.

"I don't care where we go, as long as we put miles between this place and the next and the next after that." They lay spent in her bed, night sounds rustling through the compact bedroom in her compact apartment. They were on the second story over the Shelby Domino and Tonk Parlor, and unofficial after-hours joint.

"Your boy just got twenty-five on the bones," Stovall said, caressing and licking Hopkins' chest.

He laughed at her joke about the domino game happening below. They could hear the muffled excitement of the players through the floorboards.

"You gonna be ready?"

"Like I got something holding me here."

"That car's gonna be our ticket, Clover." It gave him a chill to say her name.

She had her hand around his member, going up and down slowly and surely as he stiffened. "I was going crazy until you got here, RH. You know how much this means to me?"

"I know how much you mean to me. I needed this second chance."

"Hmmm," she murmured, taking him in her mouth.

Head thumping against the headboard, heart hammering, Hopkins looked down at her bobbing head and put both of his hands gently on the back of her head.

She decreased her rhythm momentarily and whispered, "Go on, RH. Put it deep in my mouth like you do my pussy." She increased her actions again.

"Ughhh," he exclaimed and thrust his hips as she noisily gobbled him. "Oh, yeah, shit..."

Hopkins was consumed. Down below the domino player who was in the third house, ahead in points, pushed his hat back some with a touch of his long fingernail to the underside of his brim. He smiled a rattler's grin as he plopped down another tile for fifteen.

"Damn, son, you can't do no wrong tonight," an old man, a regular, groused as he considered his hand.

He spread his arms. "What can I say?" The game went on but soon the outcome was clear as the winning player poised a tile over the lopsided cross on the table of the previously played dominoes.

"Get it over with," the old man said.

His hearing, keener than any man's or woman's, picked up Hopkins who joyfully announced, "I'm comin', Clover, I'm comin'." He slammed down his winning domino at the same instant Roosevelt Hopkins loosened in his lover's mouth.

"That's game," the victor pronounced to a round of groans and cussing.

ON A HOT Sunday afternoon, a breeze billowing the fabric of the light summer dress she wore, Clover Stovall handed a rusted key to Hopkins. "Unlock our future, Roosevelt."

He took the key and crouching down, grasped the lock and let it go, surprised. He looked up at the woman.

"What's wrong?" She rubbed her fingers in his short naps.

"Felt...felt like it had a pulse."

She clucked her tongue. "Don't be silly."

"Yeah," he half-heartedly agreed. He reached out, hesitating, and then took hold of the lock again. It was warm in his hand but certainly, he told himself, not alive. He hadn't paid much attention to the padlock while getting the car back together. But it now occurred to him up close it wasn't done up in imitation gold plating, but was the real thing. Nor was there a smooth, machine finish to the lock. Rather it appeared to have been forged and shaped long ago. Not that he was an antiques expert, but this shadowy notion flooded through him.

"Damn," he muttered, inserting the key in the lock's key slot. Behind him, he didn't see his lover putting a hand to her stomach, anticipation afire on her pretty face. As Hopkins turned the lock, Clover Stovall responded by licking her bottom lip, her hand going lower.

Hopkins stood and undid the chain from around the rear axle.

"Start the engine, Roosevelt. Start this goddamn car," Stovall demanded, wide eyes fixed on the Plymouth.

"I will," he said, "but we gotta do it right. I'll turn the motor over to pump the fuel and oil out of the sump. Have to do that for several cranks to make sure—"

She latched on to him and kissed him fiercely. "Just do it. Shit."

After his precautions, the car running like a sewing machine, they took the Plymouth for a test drive.

"Front end could stand an alignment," Hopkins noted, taking a curve onto a country road. "But we can worry about that later."

"That's right." Clover Stovall sat close to him on the bench seat, her hand on his thigh. She turned on the radio, catching a news program in mid-broadcast. She turned the knob and found an oldies station.

"*When I start drilling, I'll have to give you Novocaine,*" Dinah Washington warned in her sirenic voice on "Long John Blues" from the dashboard speaker.

Her hand rubbed his thigh and then rested on his zipper. Spellbound, Hopkins looked from her to the end of the road where it narrowed down among a mass of poplar and maple trees. Coming out from under a leafy overhang was a man in a bowler Hopkins at first couldn't place—then did. He slowed the car.

"What's he doing here? What's going on, Clover?"

"We better get out." Her body language matched the sudden arctic tone of her words.

Hopkins shut the engine off and got out. The woman scooted out on the driver's side as well. She had her shoes in one hand and went to stand next to the bartender.

"Explain this to me," Hopkins said, more hurt than angry.

"Hard to sum up in a few ticks, pardner," the bartender began, gesturing with the bowler in his hand. "Old folks hoodoo tales they spouted in their rocking chairs from way back when. Conjure ways handed down and down, intricacies inside of other intricacies," he said, his long fingers proscribing a symbol in the air between them.

Hopkins advanced. "You're not taking her or this car from me."

Clover Stovall shook her head from side to side. "'Fraid it's not for you to say, sugah. This is all been writ before you and me came along."

The bartender smiled slyly and put a hand around her trim waist. "Ain't she something?"

Hopkins made to strike out but was forced to grab at his chest as a lancing pain attacked his heart. He got wobbly on his feet, his vision blurring and breathing as if his windpipe was now the size of a straw.

"You used me to break some kind of spell," he managed to wheeze at the pair.

The bartender hunched a shoulder in his suit coat. "Well, yes, see it could only happen at a certain cycle of the earth and Beelzebub yank my toe, you happened by during the—what they call it—window of opportunity."

There were others before him, Hopkins realized. Because of particulars of the spell he had no knowledge of, the men before him had or could only complete part of the task. Who knew how many years she and the car had lured fools like him.

The bartender and the woman laughed, and Hopkins, now on his side in the dirt, didn't have the strength to stop her from plucking the solitary key from his numb fist. Impotently he watched the two embrace. The bartender made a show of putting a hand under her dress, and then they departed in the car intended for his escape and rebirth.

He rolled over on his back, hearing Hi-Fire V-8 rumble away as the car took the two farther and farther away. His edging toward death's shroud lessened as the wielder of the power over him left. He was already forgotten by the two schemers, he figured.

Hopkins was glad his friend was superstitious. He kept a crow's foot, black cat bone and purported piece of the box that held Stagolee's revolver hanging from the rearview mirror of his truck. When, in an off-handed manner, Hopkins had told his friend about this incredible woman he'd met who liked to go barefoot and about the make and model of the car, his friend had convinced him to keep a charm on his person. It was on a small chain he'd given Hopkins.

Hopkins had scoffed, but to placate his play cousin, had attached the piece of silver, shaped like some sort of flower he didn't recognize, to his key chain. Soon he was able to rise and dust himself off and walk back to town. Soon too he was on the road in a borrowed vehicle, looking for the man he met who still kept the old ways, who said he was maybe Rawhead Rex. Others swore he went by the name of Uncle Monday.

No matter. He was going to find him, her and the car. He was going to be satisfied.

MIDNIGHT SPECIAL
VICT?R J. BANIS

"Mama, I got a hot dog and it ain't nevah cold
It just right to fit your roll."

Mother Fuyer—Dirty Red (1947)

HOT SPRINGS, ARKANSAS - 1949

"HE HERE. He at the back door," Sukie say.

It was early. They wasn't open for business yet, most the girls just laying around by the windows, fanning themselves, sometimes calling out to men on the street below, but more friendly like than serious. Rufus busy cleaning the bar. Marilou be in her office, checking yesterday's money when Sukie come in without knocking, slid inside all quiet like and push the door shut behind her.

"He at the back door," she say, looking as scared as maybe she seen a ghost. Added, like it make everything clear, "He been shot."

Marilou stare at her like she musta made it up. Knew who she meant, 'course. They be talking about him jes a little bit ago, nobody hardly talking 'bout nobody else. Wasn't expectin' him to turn up here, though.

"They lookin' for him all over the place. How he get here an' nobody see him?" she say, and, "He gonna get us all kilt, an' he ain't careful."

"You want me to send Rufus? Tell him to git?"

Marilou thought on that for a minute, rolling her eyes up at the cut glass chandelier like she thought she find some message wrote up there, telling her what to do. After a bit, she give a great sigh and heave her big ole self out of the chair. "Ought to shoot him mysef," she say in an exasperated voice. "Mens. Always tryin' to git that ole rib back, isn' they? You hasta help me."

Sukie shook her head, eyes wide in her coal-colored face. If she had the nerve, she say no, but one dark look from Marilou an' she jes shut right up. She know better than to sass Marilou when she say like that. She follow Marilou meekly through the bar, where Rufus hardly give them a glance—women's business, was what he figured, too early to be customer trouble—and down the hall.

"Huh?" Marilou say, opening the back door and seeing nobody there.

"In the bushes," Sukie say, "I tole him to hide hisself, lessen somebody come along and see him."

"Where you at?" Marilou demanded in a sibilant whisper. The Azalea bush next the door groaned. She stepped off the stoop and looked into the bush. A pair of eyes, wide and bloodshot, blinked back at her.

"Mighty glad to see you, old gal," he say, and she say, "It ain't mutual, tha's for sure. You wantin' to get me kilt, tha's what you comin' round here for?"

"Didn' have no place else to go," he say, breathing heavy, the words coming out slow, like they been penned up too long. "They after me like a dog."

"Tha's the truth," she say. "They lookin' all over the place for you, every policemans in two counties."

"They ain't found me yet. You gonna help me, or what?"

She took her time over that, didn't answer him direct, either, but she say to Sukie, "We best take him up the back stairs."

It was two flights up, supporting him between them and him not able to do much more than shuffle his feet. He stank, too, of sweat and blood and dirty water from some place he been hiding. *Prolly down by the crick*, she figured, it was a crick kind of smell. And fear, you could smell the fear on him worst of all, hung about him like a fart round a hound dog.

In Marilou's room, the biggest bedroom in the place, which suited her position just fine, she propped him by the door, Sukie helping him to stand. Marilou went to a big old wardrobe against one wall and, putting her broad shoulder again it, rolled it out of the way. Behind it, another set of stairs, narrow and steep, went up to the attic

"I never knowed this was here," Sukie said, surprised out of being afraid.

"Wasn't supposed to know. Never tole nobody about it. Rufus, he probably 'member this attic. Or maybe not. I fix it for mysef when we had that trouble couple years back, figure I might need me someplace to hide. Git him on the cot, there."

Except for the cot and a pillow on it, there wasn't much else in the room but a bucket for a toilet, flies making a racket around it, and another bucket full of dirty water. The blind was pulled down tight over the one window. Across the way, at the Gypsy Casino, the neon lights flashed on and off, on and off, green and red splashes leaking through the window blind, dust thick everywhere. The room like an oven. Not a breath of air stirrin'.

They wrestled him onto the bed. He give a weary smile. *Look like a death head grinnin' up at me,* was how she saw it. Behind her, Sukie slip out the door and disappear down the stairs. *Jes' as well*, Marilou thought, *she be too excitable.*

"Much obliged," he say in a weary voice. "'Preciate it greatly, I surely do."

"Don't be getting' too grateful, an' don't you be thinkin' you stayin here either," Marilou say. "I leaves you rest till morning, tha's all. Be way quieter then, 'bout four, five o'clock, jes 'fore the sun come up. Can't keep you here past that. Daylight come, it too dangerous."

"I unerstan'."

"Jes so you do. Don' mean to be hateful, but I got my own skin to think of, me an' the girls. Them girls all depends on me to look out for 'em."

"Everybody know you good to your girls. You always good to me, too, honey. I know that. I's a mean bastard sometimes, wasn' I?'

"They's worse ones, I 'spect. Men, they all mean, you ast me. Somepin about that sap you all got down there. Don't matter much. Runnin' a place like this, you see some bad ones, is all."

"You always my favorite, though, I swear it. Never mean to treat you bad. Jes the way things happen. You right, I reckon, it's the sap." He paused and say, like the idea just popped into his head, "You wanna take a ride while I be here? For ole time sake?"

She snorted. "Listen at the fool. Can't hardly crawl up the stairs, two women hepin' him, and he layin' there thinkin' 'bout poontang, if that ain't jes like a man."

"I ain't dead yet, girl. If we was careful, I could..."

"'Sides," her eyes narrow, "I ain't got what you like down there nowadays. Not what I be hearin', anyways."

"Ah, that shit." He coughed. "People talkin queer shit, tha's all it is. You oughts to know that. Do women all the time, since I's knee high, always like it jes fine an' I 'spect the ladies do too. Most of 'em acted plenty grateful, seem like. That other stuff, tha's just prison business, it all you got to do when you in there. But I always thinkin' 'bout women when I doin' it, and tha's no lie. I swear it, most the time, I thinkin' 'bout you, honey, an' you wantin' to know the truth."

"You always was full of it." She looked pleased anyway.

"Don't you pay no mind to that shit, is what I'm sayin'. Jes somepin a man gets used to when he inside, is all."

"Maybe. Tha's what you say. What you did, last night, though, you didn' get used to that in no prison."

He tossed his head back and forth on the pillow, like he was trying to get something inside it to come loose. "Fuck. I oughtn' of done it, I know that, it was like I jes go crazy all a sudden. I don't know where it come from. Just somepin got into me, come over me out of nowhere. Like the devil done took me over." She looked unconvinced. "Tha's the truth. I never even thought of nothin' like that before, I swear it. It was like somebody else doin' it, like I wasn' even there."

"Uh huh. Like the devil do it. Don't make no difference, I'm tellin' you, they gonna burn your ass for it, make no matter where it come from, burn the devil's ass too an' he say anything. Been different if'n it a colored boy. You mighta got away with it if he colored, nobody mind much about a colored boy. But a white boy..."

"I know, I know. An' they finds me, they string me up for sure."

"'Cept, they finds you here, they be stringin' me up with you."

"I jes didn' have nobody else to turn to, you know what I'm sayin'?"

"You already say that. Won't hep my neck none when they puttin' a rope round it."

"I'm goin, I swear it. Soon's I can."

She study him over good. "Don' look to me like you goin' anywhere, an' not on your own. How'd you git here, is what I like to know?"

"I git here, is all. An' I be goin', too. I go right now, an' you say I got to. Jes get me down them stairs, an' you won' see nothin' but my ass on the way out the door."

"They be shootin' your ass they see you, make no matter whether you is goin' or comin'. You jes has to wait here till mornin', is all. I have the boys bring you down later on, 'fore it git light, they carry you over by the railroad track."

"Long as it okay with you, is all I'm sayin'."

"An' I ain't saying it okay, neither, I just saying tha's how it be."

"Tha's okay, then, tha's the best thing, what you say. We wait 'til morning, then I be outa here. Ole Rufus'll hep, won't he? He wouldn' turn me in, would he?"

"Rufus know to keep his mouth shut. He don't want strung up neither. You didn' jes make trouble for yoursef, fool, you make trouble for every darkie round about here. Everybody scared."

"I understan. I ain't wantin' to make no trouble for nobody. They put me by the tracks, is all they got to do. I can manage the rest of the way. Once it start to get light, I jump me a freight, be long gone, won't see me no more 'round these parts, I swear it."

She looked at the wound in his side. It had stopped bleeding but it looked ugly, all red and puffy. *Prolly,* she thought, *it infected already. For sure he wouldn't be jumping no trains. Mos' likely he'd end up under one. Or he jes lay there an' die where they leave him. Wasn' no worse than what'd happen to him if they catch him, though.* Nothin' she could do 'bout that, 'bout any of it. She like him well enough, always had. He be her first, and they say you always sweet on your first. Not sweet enough she wantin' to get herself kilt, though.

He closed his eyes, breathing heavy. She thought maybe he pass out, till he say, his eyes still closed, "You ever hear tell of the Midnight Special?"

"Tha's a song, isn' it? By that Lead Belly."

His laugh turned into a cough that left his lips looking like he been eating berries. "Huddie Ledbetter," he said, smiling around his pain. "He the king of the twelve string guitar. Shit, that boy could play a guitar an' tha's no lie. An' sing. He sing like the angels, didn' he?"

He hummed a snatch of off pitch melody, ended up with, "Haah." She thought that was a groan, but he did it again, and say, "Used to grunt like that 'tween verses, ole Lead Belly, say it the sound the men make on the chain gang as they bringin' the hammer down."

"S'at so?" She figure his mind was wandering. He looked feverish, and he be feelin' hot when they carry him up. She brought him a tin cup of rusty water from the bucket and held his head while he drunk it down. She hoped he didn' die 'fore she got him out of the house. They burn the house down, they find out she shelterin' him here, and her with it.

"It's a train," he say out of nowhere.

"What you talkin' 'bout? Wha's a train?"

"The Midnight Special. It a train be taking the prisoners from New Awlins out to Angola prison in the middle of the night. At midnight. So's nobody can see 'em, I guess." He silent for a minute. "There's a hell hole for you, Angola prison. I's there. Lead Belly too, jes not the same time as me, I mean. Worst place on earth. You get solitary, they put you in a metal shed out in the sun, like to bake you to death. Going to Angola same as goin' to hell, is what they say. Them as been there."

"Didn' s'pose it no country club."

He was quiet for a spell again, and she was fixing to leave him, when he say, "They's a thing men tell at Angola. They say you see the Midnight Special, you see its headlight shinin' on you in your cell at night, it mean you gonna be free by the morning."

"Huh. Well, I don' know nothin' 'bout that, but I am tellin' you, for sure you gonna be free of this whorehouse, by morning, an' tha's the Lord's truth. You git yousef some sleep now. I send the boys up when it be time. Not for a spell, though, too many people 'round." She hesitated at the door. "You be wantin' some food? Or a whiskey? I send Sukie up with a bottle, an' you want one. You allus fancied your whiskey, seems like."

"Nah, that's okay. 'Bout whiskeyed out. I gonna sleep, is all. Wouldn't mind me a cigarette, though."

She found a pack in his pocket, lit one for him, put it between his lips. He puffed greedily. She waited, and when he began to snore, she took the cigarette out of his mouth and stepped it out on the floor, and went back downstairs.

SHE WAS sitting down in the parlor next to some pecker-headed redneck, jiggling her titties for him and pretending he was Diamond Jim Brady, Booger man playing some fine stride piano over by the bar, place jumping now, when she spot Sukie hanging back in the doorway. Sukie saw her look and give her head a jerk.

"Where you goin'?" pecker head asked when she stand up. "I got somepin down here hot to handle. I was thinkin' we'd mosey on upstairs for a spell."

"You sit right there and keep that ole thing of yours hot for Miss Marilou," she say, "an' I'll be back 'for you even knows I is gone."

"He up there yellin'," Sukie say, rolling her eyes toward the stairs. "Best quieten him down, 'fore somebody outside hear him."

She climbed the stairs, out of breath by the time she got to the top. "Getting too ole for this shit," she muttered, pulling herself up by the railing, stride piano trailing after her like cigarette smoke. She heard him callin' her name 'fore she got halfway up: "Marilou. Marilou."

"What for you be makin' all this racket?" she demanded, slipping into the room and closing the door firmly behind herself. "You wantin' to bring every sheriff deputy in the county up here?"

He was halfway sitting up on the bed, his brow shiny with sweat like it been waxed and his eyes a-glittering. He smell all gassy too, or maybe that the toilet bucket. Green and yellow splotches leaking through the blind. Piano tinkling faintly below. Away in the distance, a siren wail. She hopin' it not coming here.

"I seen it, Marilou," he say, all excited. "I seen it."

"You seen what?"

"That old train. The Midnight Special. I seen its headlight."

"You out of your head. Them tracks half a mile from here, three quarters more like, plus the blinds is down tight on the window. Ain't no way you seein' no light from no train, not clear up here."

"I seen it, I did. It was a-shinin' right in my face. I'm goin' free, I tell you. I be free by morning."

He dropped back down on the bed again, eyes closed, breath rattling in his chest. She look down at him, at the face use to be handsome, ugly now from pain, way she didn't want to remember him. She feeling scared, and sad too, wondering how he come to this, on the run, hiding away in an attic. Dying, most likely. Even he git out of here, they have the dogs looking for him by now. Dogs be better off than him.

She had to go, couldn' stay up here. White man waitin' for her downstairs. *His kind gits impatient they don't git what they wants when they wants it.*

More sirens on the street. Didn't seem to be coming here, though. Room hot as a stove. Lights flashing behind her. Music down below. That ole bucket stinking. All of it wrong, seemed to her. Wasn't no way for a man to die. Man ain't had no chance to live happy, seems like he ought at least die happy.

She be knowing him a long time too. He wasn' a bad man, not like some she could name. Brought her flowers once, she remembered that like yesterday. He be sweet to her too, most the time.

What chance he have, though, a colored man in a white man's town? What chance any of 'em have?

She see the moment he go free.

TRICKED
ZANDER VYNE

*"But if I can't sell it, I'm gonna keep sitting on it
I don't see the need to give it away."*

I'll Keep Sitting On It If I Can't Sell It
— Georgia White (1935)

THE FIRST TIME I saw her in the flesh, I knew she'd be trouble. But, trouble is my business so I didn't worry until later.

I'd driven in from the City of Angels, losing myself in a long stretch of desert nothingness, finding it again in the bright neon sunburst that is Las Vegas.

I knew just where to look for her—as far on the wrong side of the tracks as one could get in Sin City. In my line of work, it pays to be cozy with bad people and worse places.

I had pictures, so spotting her wasn't difficult.

I'd thought this would be a routine job. In and out, done. A dog, a steak, and a hefty paycheck waited for me at home.

Then I saw her, Sky Harlow, and I wasn't so sure I'd called this one right at all.

She wasn't what I'd expected. Say chippy from sleeze-ville Vegas, and you didn't picture this Snow White, Goth princess, siren-witch. She belonged on the screen or in a painting, not walking the boulevard. The girl in the pictures I'd seen was younger, fresh-scrubbed, but I could still see her under the makeup. Smoke and mirrors was her game, just like mine. Like always recognizes like.

I rolled my window down. She leaned in, femme fatale, kitten-with-a-whip gorgeous, and agreed to come with me to a cheap motel off-strip. Five hundred bills had more to do with her trust than my good looks.

I sat in the room's only chair, careful not to touch the armrests. The place reeked of stale smoke and paid-for sex. Outside, I heard loud voices, car horns, and the screech of tires. I focused on her. It wasn't hard to do. Sky was a vision of succulent flesh on display. A lock of hair fell like a raven's wing over her left eye whenever she looked down—innocence defiled, and liking it.

She perched on the edge of the bed, her knees almost touching mine. I drew away and, spreading her legs, she showed me that she wore nothing beneath her slinky red skirt. Her cunt was smooth and had a tender pink center. Nothing I hadn't seen before.

"Please, don't do that."

My hands cupped her knees, pushing them together. Her skin was hot and I pulled away, as if burned. Maybe I was in hell. I was dizzy.

"Then get talking, Mister. I haven't got all night."

She crossed her arms over pert little breasts. They spilled fetchingly over tight black leather—a corset that hugged her tiny waist like a lover's hands. She really wasn't my type. I liked my women tall, cool, and blonde. Classy. Sky was raw sex, blood and razors, stings and nettles with an angel's face.

"I want you to talk. I want to know about you, about your life." I wasn't lying. I'd been paid to find out, but looking at her, I really wanted to know who the fuck she was. I cared and had no idea why.

"What're you? Some kind of reporter?" Her eyes narrowed into black-rimmed, violet slits—cat's eyes, hoyden's eyes, liar's eyes.

"I'm just someone with cash enough to indulge a healthy curiosity. What more do you need to know?" I made my tone harder—bullets on brick. It worked.

"Alright, so what do you want to talk about?" Her voice went soft as butter melting.

She pulled her jacket around her even though it had to be pushing eighty in the close room. Her small movements produced the scent of her perfume—flowery—poppies and opium. I inhaled it like a drug and that's when I knew I was in deep shit.

"Tell me about the men you sleep with."

She laughed. "We don't do a lot of sleeping, Mister."

"Alright, tell me about the men you fuck."

"Well, I don't always fuck them. Sometimes they want me to suck them or just watch them jerk off. Maybe show them my tits or talk dirty to them. Do you like that, Mister?"

"Do you like it?"

"Sometimes." She looked me right in the eye. I liked that.

She frowned, and I could see her youth in the expression. She had a dimple in her chin and baby-fat still clung to her cheeks. The rest of her body was all woman, the stuff of every bad boy's wet dreams, but scrub away the makeup, and she was little more than a child. Old enough that the law usually didn't hassle her—she'd assured me of that in the car on the way here. She didn't tell me, but I knew she was twenty-five, not much younger than me.

"Tell me about the times you like." My cock was rock hard and I crossed my legs to hide it.

She leaned forward, her tongue taking a slow trip along the curves of her upper lip—pink on slut-red glitter. "Well, I have one regular who's very handsome, very clean. He always talks with me first, almost like you're doing, and then he watches me play with myself."

"Do people ask for that often?" I imagined her spread out, fingers buried in her pussy, and almost came in my pants.

"Sometimes." Her voice went stainless steel cold.

"I'm not judging you."

She smiled—coquettish, but wary. "I don't care. You paid me so it's your dime. But, it's pretty fucking strange you giving me five hundred bucks just to sit here and talk. You want me to talk nasty to you? Is that it? You want to hear what bad girls like?"

I ignored her questions mainly because the answer was yes, but I had a job to do. "Don't other clients sometimes have odd requests, ask you to do things you don't understand?"

"Of course." She leaned back into the pillows, curling onto her side to face me.

I listened. Let most people talk and they'll get around to telling you what you want to know, you won't even have to ask.

"Weirdest one was a guy who wanted me to suck him off while he sang 'Danny Boy.' He was Irish. Cried when he was done. I didn't ask for the story. He was in enough pain."

Her voice was girlish now, soft, and sweet. This girl was a chameleon. All she needed was an idea of what a customer wanted and she became it. She couldn't quite get a handle on me though, which was the way I wanted it.

"How much did you charge for that?" I imagined her in a dirty room similar to this one, on her knees in front of some old Irishman and wanted to slap her then fuck her silly. Hell, I'd even sing.

What the fuck was wrong with me? This was a job, nothing more to either of us. She wasn't a hooker with a heart of gold, and I wasn't the tough-but-kind private eye. This was no movie. It was life—rough and real, and vicious as a pit-bull in a room full of kitty cats.

Her matter-of-fact voice brought me back. "I did it for fifty. With no fucking, I didn't even have to clean up after." Her heels snagged the bumpy orange bedspread as she sat up again, shrugging her shoulders.

"And, did you like doing that?" I really wanted to know.

"Not especially. But, in a way, I was helping him. He needed me. And, I needed the money so it's all good." She shrugged her shoulders and drew her knees to her chest. I saw a flash of bare ass before she remembered my instructions and smoothed her skirt down, pretty legs dangling over the edge of the bed.

The image of her naked curves burned a hole in my memory. I kept flashing on it and my palms itched. I wanted to touch that perfect white skin. Instead, I lit a cigarette.

I managed a smoke ring, though I was beginning to feel slightly buzzed and was fighting a growing urge to get up, walk out, and end this now. I found a loose thread on my cuff and worried it with my fingernail.

"Does your pimp make you earn a certain amount every night?"

"I don't have a pimp. I stay away from the popular places and no one messes with me." She cocked her dimpled chin at me, purple eyes flashing. Proud and pissed off—a dangerous combination, one that made my heart and cock throb in unison.

"How'd you decide to make this your profession?"

"I didn't decide. Life did."

"Tell me about it. Don't you have friends, a family? How about a boyfriend?" I stubbed out my cigarette.

"I don't have or need anyone, Mister, and the last person I told my life story to said it was—what was the word?—oh yeah, predictable." She voice was brittle. Her expressive eyes had gone dark. "Now, you've about used up your five hundred and that doesn't even come close to covering this kind of soul-searching shit anyway."

I almost felt bad enough to stop, but not quite.

"Just one more thing. Are you happy? Sexually?"

"I don't see what I do for a living as having anything to do with my own sexual happiness, if that's what you mean. The two are separate, business and pleasure."

"You mean it's never good for you?"

"Well, it's not all bad. Like I said, some of my clients are very nice." She stood up on platform shoes—wet looking, black leather with stiletto sharp heels.

I stood too. I was unsettled, antsy. I stepped closer so she wouldn't see that my dick was a pole down my leg. I felt her warmth, breathed it in, and drowned in the violet pools of her eyes.

"Tell me how it is, fucking so many men in one day."

She arched her back, her nipples kissing my shirtfront—leather on linen. Her breath was sweet, her tone naughty. "I love it."

That was it. I slammed into her, knocking her back against the door with a thud, my hand jammed between her legs. She was wet and my fingers slipped easily through her folds as her leg lifted and curved around my waist. I jerked her head back; handfuls of black hair filled my fist.

"I love this," she said, sliding my zipper down, taking my dick in her hands and rocking into me, her fingers hot and slithery, just like the rest of her.

"You love the business, huh?" I groaned as she jacked me off, my thumb and forefinger catching her clit and giving it a twist. I shifted to give her better access to my raging prick.

"You didn't pay for sex, Mister. You paid for talk." She leaned forward and kissed my jaw, right where I could feel a tick of tension throbbing. It calmed, but the rest of me remained taut, coiled, and agitated.

I cupped her cunt and the swell of it wet my fingers. They slipped up inside her. I held her, just like that—pinned to the door, impaled on my hand, my nose touching hers.

"So, this is pleasure?" I breathed in the scent of her—pussy and honey, bee-stung flowers and nitro.

"Yes."

She didn't beat around the bush. I liked that.

I spread her wide with my thumbs, cock poised at her pink gate. Then I remembered. She was a whore and I didn't have a condom. Fuck.

She laughed and reached into her corset top, pulling out a foil packet. "This the problem, Mister?"

She tore the packet open with her teeth and, with expert fingers, rolled the latex sheath over my cock, winking as she snapped the tight ring at the base. It stung. I liked that too.

"Now, fuck me. Fuck me hard, fuck me fast, and shut the fuck up."

I did it. I slammed into her, wanting to hurt her, and love her, and somehow make her remember me as something more than a cock. I stopped asking myself why and just went with it, sinking into her over and over again, reaching down to fiddle with her clit until she writhed and moaned, and became just a girl, just a girl who wanted what I was giving her.

I didn't say another word. I was quiet, purposeful, hard like she wanted it—hard as concrete, hard as my heart, hard as her life. I fucked her. She fucked me. It wasn't pretty, or romantic. It wasn't the sort of thing you see in movies or read about in books. It was real.

We almost fell as we came, shattered and clinging, panting and grunting. My knees shook. I laid my head against the door, tucking it next to hers, and closed my eyes.

Jesus fucking Christ. This girl knew what I needed and somehow, in the middle of it all, I knew what she needed too. I lifted her from the floor and let her wind herself around me. I held her, and soothed her, petted her and kissed her. I loved her.

When it was all over, she gently unrolled the filled condom—tossing it in the trash—zipped my pants, and smoothed her skirt. Her hair had fallen away from her forehead and those huge violet eyes looked right into mine as she reached around to finger the gun I had strapped to my side.

"So, you going to tell me the real deal about why you came here and just who the fuck you are?"

It was like ice water in my face, her tone, her look. It was true; I'd come to do a job, but somehow I'd gotten here, to a place where the job didn't matter anymore for the first time in my sorry life. Sometime between the money changing hands and cumming, I'd seen inside this girl, and didn't want to hurt her. Trouble was. somebody else did. Somebody a lot meaner than me. I couldn't tell her that though, no fucking way.

So, I shook my head and took her hand from my gun, kissing her fingers as she wrapped them around mine. "No can do, Sky. Just believe me when I tell you, that meant something to me."

She jerked open the door before I could say anything else. "Fuck you *and* your something, Mister."

She walked away, hips rolling, her finger forming the universal punctuation to her statement.

She didn't even look back.

I DIDN'T make it home. The dog went hungry and the steak rotted in my fridge.

I checked into one of the fancy hotels on the strip. I poured myself a whiskey, spilling some on my trousers. My hands were shaking. Once upon a time, I'd have ordered an expensive call girl for the night, to ease my tensions, but tonight I sat alone.

I drank, unseen behind a wall of glass. Garish lights in rainbow colors flashed up and down the street as I thought about my newest problem—Sky.

I rummaged in my bag, pulling out the letters and pictures, putting everything else in the file aside.

The first letter was yellow with age, handwritten in an old woman's shaky hand:

Dear Dr. Jonathan Soames,
My girl Tashia bore you a child. I tried, but had to give her up.
She got eyes like yours. It's my time and I thought you should know.
You all she got now.

Iris Hughes

Sky's grandmother had tried to do the right thing, letting Dr.
Soames know about his illegitimate offspring. Probably just heard
Doctor and pictured Marcus-fucking-Welby. I guessed Sky's mom
hadn't wanted her mama to know the truth, about her life or her
sugar daddy.

The second letter was a couple of months old, on fancy letterhead,
the kind of stuff I couldn't afford:

Dear Dr. Soames,
I've enclosed the full report on your daughter. As we discussed on
the phone, she supports herself by prostitution. She goes by the
name Sky Harlow and works the strip in Las Vegas by the Suncoast
Motel. I've enclosed pictures and directions.
Her mother, Tashia Hughes, died shortly after giving birth to her
(see enclosed death certificate and burial information). As you
know, her grandmother raised her until her death when Sky was
sixteen.
As far as I have been able to trace, you are the girl's only living
relative.
I wish you luck, whatever you decide to do.
Godspeed,
Dick Jones, PI

I knew Dick. He was a straight-up shamus. He'd done his part,
cashed his paycheck, and probably forgotten all about the good
Doctor and his hooker daughter.

As for me, well, I didn't have any paper trail. Guys like me never
do. That's why the Doc ended up in my office. Offered me $2,500 to
find out who'd miss Sky when she was gone and a lot more to tie up
all the loose ends.

Now I worried about what would happen when I got back to LA,
about the next hatchet man the Doc would hire to do the job if I only
dropped the dime on Sky for the change. How they'd do it. When.

I worried over Sky and why not? Nobody else would, not even the
cops, not that types like us would ever knock on their door.

But, what could I do?

I'd done some checking. The Doc had an heiress wife and twin girls almost the same age as Sky. He had a Bel Air mansion, memberships to country clubs; he golfed with the Mayor and lunched with the famous. He had a lot to protect.

I imagined what would happen if I came back empty-handed. What would happen to me and to Sky. I spun different yarns in my head, trying them on for size, all night long. The endings were mostly the same—dead people, sorry people.

I thought about going to Sky, spilling it all to her. Would it be better for her if she knew the score, knew what was coming? Would she hate me? Could we make a clean sneak? Would she want to?

I was tired. I slept when the sun rose.

LATE the next day I drove down that long, flashy strip, watching floods of humanity mingle in the heat and insanity that is Las Vegas. Some smiled. Some looked pissed off. Other than the shimmering lights, gaudy in the bright daylight, it could have been anywhere. Same faces. Same shit. Different day.

Most days, I do what I do because every day *does* bring something new—a new set of problems, a new puzzle, and a new reason to exist. Every time my door opens, it's an adventure. Sometimes it's as simple as helping an old lady catch the neighbor trying to poison her cat, sometimes it's a lot more complicated.

This was one of those times.

I came to that place at the end of Las Vegas Boulevard where the lights fade to desert emptiness, and the street splits—left to the City of Angels on-ramp, right to the bad side of town.

I'd thought it over all night and, in the end, turned down the only road I could.

COME FOR ME, DARK MAN
ANNE TOURNEY

"If you want to make me lose my mind
If you want make some time
You gotta bone it like you own it"

Bone It Like You Own It – Denise La Salle (1976)

LONG before she gives herself up, the woman hears the song. Its notes are alien, yet instantly familiar. The melody sets off a deep low burn, like a stolen gulp of whiskey, or the scent of a lover's body as he moves forward with his eyes fixed on her mouth. She begins secretly buying records, hoping one of them will hold that song, and soon she's a captive to the music. The rich, raspy voices fill her bedroom, bringing elements of another world—dust and sunlight, hunger and heat, liquor and lust. Their sinuous tonality is like nothing she's ever played on the upright piano in her parlor. The notes sink into her flesh and deepen the curves of her body; they flow through her blood vessels and set up a hard thud between her legs. Her house rocks like a backwoods juke joint. She packs up the records and hides them in the attic, but her sacrifice can't drive away that original melody. They call it the blues, but when she hears that music, she hears red—cunt red, lush and infernal.

Night after night she wakes up from a parched sleep. She hears the whistle of a freight train rolling by, so close that its juddering motion rattles the windows. She has heard that imploring cry for so many years that it never wakes her anymore, but tonight the call has changed. Could that be her song, warped into the train's low moan? Her heart pounds, her breath catches in her mouth, and her fingers stroke the sweaty groove between her breasts. Her flesh feels unfamiliar. Her pulse is offbeat.

Come for me, dark man, mutter the gears of the train.

Grace hears the song for the first time on a sweltering May afternoon. She doesn't think much of the singer at first; there are so many men drifting through town, trying to get a meal in exchange for a few hours of work, or an afternoon serenade. Looking out the window over her kitchen sink, she often sees hobos walking along the railroad tracks that border her backyard. She tries not to meet their eyes; she's afraid that one of them will demand an act of charity. They are everywhere these days, these poor drifting men. Does anyone consider the poverty of a woman who's lost her husband, the deprivation that she feels at her core?

On the day she hears the song, Grace is hanging her clothes out on the line. Not much laundry anymore; she hardly ever changes her dress, never wears stockings, and doesn't even bother with underwear most of the time. She's decided to wash her sheets today, and she's made herself a cool tent under the damp cotton. That's where she's sitting, with her bare legs gleaming in the grass, when the man steps into her yard.

"Your husband should fence you in," he says.

In spite of the heat he is dressed in a dark suit, red with dust at trouser cuffs. He wears a narrow tie, and a pair of ancient boots. Over his shoulder hangs a guitar. She can't see his face under the brim of his black hat, but she feels the full burn of his stare. She must look like a fool sitting there on the ground, sprawled out like a little girl, her laundry basket abandoned. The man is appraising her, surveying the length of her legs, the curve of her hips.

"My husband's in the house."

"What's your name?"

"Grace. What's yours?"

He doesn't answer. Her face goes hot, as if she'd made a gross blunder, although she hasn't said anything that she wouldn't say to any other man. Grace jumps up, swatting grass off her skirt. In the gloom under the brim of the man's hat she sees only the pale caramel sheen of his skin, the weight of his full mouth. His lower lip is cleft in the middle, like a plum.

"Could you spare some food? I can do odd jobs. Play you a song."

She turns and walks toward the house, half hoping he will leave her alone, half hoping he will follow. When she opens the screen door, the familiar squeal sounds like a cry of panic. He stays outside for a few moments, standing behind the screen. She reaches out to open the door, and then he is stepping inside, filling her kitchen.

"Fix me something to eat," he says. Somehow, now that the door has closed behind him, he isn't a beggar anymore. Grace's heart pounds. She keeps her back turned while she makes him a sandwich. She hears him set his guitar down on the kitchen table, pull out a chair, and sit down.

"Your husband upstairs?" He begins tuning the guitar.

"My husband is dead. He was killed in France."

She doesn't know why she didn't perpetuate the lie she'd told earlier. She could have said that her husband was napping. Out of work, like everyone else. Sleeping the day away, as Grace often does.

"You get lonely here by yourself?"

"No."

"What do you do for company?"

"I have friends all over town," she says. Another lie.

"What do you do when you need a man?"

"I don't need any man." Grace rubs the damp tangle of hairs at the back of her neck.

"You can bring me that sandwich now," he says.

She sets the plate down on the table beside her guest, but he doesn't touch the food. He sits with one long leg crossed over the other, regal and composed. He hasn't removed his hat, and his face is hidden as he strums the guitar. She feels a strange pang of jealousy for the instrument, with its scarred, deep-waisted body. His right hand spans the guitar's belly; his left grasps the slender neck. He plays a few chords, then reaches into his shirt pocket and pulls out a broken bottleneck. Grace puts her hand to her throat, covering the soft spot above her windpipe.

"Listen now," he says.

Then he plays, using the broken bottle to coax dangerous, sexy sounds out of the strings. She has never heard anything like that guitar's throbbing wail, the sliding pitches that seemed to shudder through her flesh. He's playing in E minor, the dark key. She feels a pull deep in her body, as if the music were being drawn out of some underwater cave where her desires live. The music has a driving rhythm that mounts slowly, like the approach of a train—faster, faster, leading up to the tantalizing space of time in which a person could jump on board if she wanted to, before the train disappears.

Come for me, dark man, dark man come down,

You're gonna give it to the dark man when that train rolls into town.

Gonna hop on board the train, meet your master in the car,

Better get down on your knees, 'cause this train is going far.

The words make her nipples prickle under her cotton dress. They make her feel wild and sad at the same time, as if the wildness were some part of her that she has been mourning for years. Through her vertigo, she senses that some transaction is going to take place with this stranger in her kitchen. When the song is over, he will want something. She will want something. A bargain will be made.

When the song ends, the stranger sets his guitar on the table. He stands. Grace is shaking. He takes her by both hands and holds her slender wrists. Her rib cage rises and falls like the withers of a scared horse. He lets go of her wrists and lowers his hands to soothe her, the way a master would calm his frightened beast. His fingers are embedded with grit. Wherever they travel, she feels the ancient accumulation of experience—on her shoulders, the small of her back, her hips and buttocks. Then under her skirt, on her inner thighs, and in the wet, wet shallows of her cunt. He brings his fingers to her mouth and makes her suck her own juices. She tastes herself, tangy and musky, on his tobacco-stained skin.

One hand around her throat, the other gripping her hair, he pushes her to her knees.

"I know what you want," he says.

"How?"

He cups her face in one hand, lightly stroking the curve of her jaw. Then he slaps her. She gasps. His palm is as rough and hard as raw wood.

"Don't ask questions," he says.

But she knows what he means. Grace has always wanted more than the tentative caress, the polite fumble in the dark. He unbuckles his belt and pulls the strip of leather out of its loops. He folds the leather in half, the way her father used to hold it when he punished her. Grace catches her breath, remembering the bite of her father's strap against the backs of her thighs, the way her buttocks burned for hours afterward. She once asked her husband to give her that secret pleasure, but when she saw the stark confusion in his eyes, she never asked again.

"You like my belt. I see you looking at it."

Grace nods.

"You need this belt?"

"Please," she whispers.

"One day I'll use it on you."

The stranger lowers the belt behind her neck and holds it loosely with one hand while he unzips his fly with the other. She closes her eyes. He feeds her his cock, using the strap to guide her head. His hips move like the train she heard when he played the guitar.

Come for me, dark man.

When he comes, he tastes of a soul-deep bitterness. He tastes of rust and wild fennel and leather. He tastes of the bent notes that he played on his guitar. He tastes like her own blood.

"I'm going to come back for you," he says. He lets the belt fall and fills his hands with Grace's hair.

"When?"

"You'll know when it's time. You're going to hear it. Listen for the train."

He replaces his belt, packs up his guitar, and then he is gone. He never touched the food she made for him.

In the nights that follow, Grace has dreams that leave her weak with shame and wonder. One night she dreams that she is standing naked in a boxcar, her hands tied above her head, while the man with the guitar gives her what she needs. A "licking," was the word her father used, and that's exactly how the blows feel: like tongues of fire. Again and again the strap strikes her thighs and ass, until the heat spreads through her entire body. The dark man orders her to stand with her legs spread apart, and his belt laps her pussy a few times for good measure. God, how she craves this cleansing. She opens her mouth to cry for mercy, but the word that explodes from her lips is *More*. The waves of fire turn into a tide of pleasure, and she wakes herself with her fierce cries.

Grace's nightgown is bunched up between her thighs. She touches the damp cloth, half expecting to find blood on her fingertips, but it's only the wetness she released when she came.

GRACE brings in a little money mending and altering other people's clothes. Anything to keep herself occupied. Over and over, the needle pierces the fabric. Its gleaming head rises through the cloth, then disappears again. The sound of the thread penetrating the rough cloth is as harsh as a lover's gasp. All sound is amplified. She can't touch her piano anymore without craving that music; after the first few bars of Hayden or Scarlatti she has to get up, go to the phonograph, and play another one of those records.

That music. That lewd music, rough and sweet at the same time, like a dripping honeycomb. Unfit to play in her house. What would her husband do if he was alive to see her standing weak-kneed in the kitchen, listening to some stranger play a dirty song on a guitar?

Filthy. Immoral. She can't wash her memory of the scene. She sees the stranger standing in her kitchen, blocking the afternoon sun like an eclipse. She has to stitch that day together piece by piece, because once she heard him play his guitar, she lost the threads that hold minutes together.

Grace drives the needle into her finger. Sucking hard, she makes the small pain blossom. She has an urge to penetrate her own flesh. She could pierce her earlobes and wear gold earrings, like the women who weave and sway along the streets in the seedy parts of town, using their bodies to beckon men. But what she really wants is a harsher assault. Hard leather, hard hands. The steel tip of a boot in the small of her back.

A drop of blood, welling out of her finger, falls onto the hem she's stitching. She wonders if other women have the same desires. Doesn't all desire come from the same well? In the pit of her being that well opens like a shimmering eye, brown as primeval water, like the eyes of the man with the guitar.

FORGIVE ME for wanting him the way I do, Grace prays. *Forgive the weakness of my flesh and the irresolution of my will. Forgive me for abandoning you when you have not abandoned me. Forgive me for leaving you to serve another.*

What is it like, to be immersed in a master? It's like the dusk that comes over Grace just before she faints. First she steps into a ghostly gray borderland. Then cotton fills her head, blood darkens her vision, and she falls. Kneeling on her pew at church through the long communion service, Grace begins to sway, and she knows that she's about to go under.

Grace murmurs prayers as she waits to take the host, but she is not thinking about the body of Christ. The dark man offers her the sacraments she has always longed for: the thunder of a heart running off its rails, the redeeming pain of leather against her flesh, the deadly radiance of the soul's eclipse. As the congregation shuffles up to the altar to take the bread and wine, the choir sings a new hymn.

Come for me, dark man, dark man come down,
You'll be swingin' on that freight train when my dark man comes to town.

Rosy mouths open, releasing the words like ravens. Bile swells in Grace's throat. She lurches out of the pew, half-falling into the aisle. Heads turn. Bursting out of the chapel's doors, she inhales deeply, but the soft air can't eliminate the thick taste of her longing. She sits down on the stone steps and lowers her head. Through the folds of her skirt the smell of her own musk, wild and feral, rises up to meet her nostrils.

Wherever she goes, that song follows her. As soon as she hears the notes, the wall she has built with faith and self-reliance crumbles. Lately she hardly recognizes herself. Her pupils are so dilated that the blackness edges out the fragile blue iris. Bruises wind around her arms like serpentine bracelets. That's where his fingers held her wrists, when he pushed her onto her knees. All up and down her street, her neighbors whisper. She gives them plenty to talk about; she's been telling everyone about her conversion.

"You can't know what it's like," she tells any woman who will listen. "When you hear the song the first time, that's only the beginning. When you look into his face, and he comes down on you like a thunderhead, it's like nothing you've ever known, but everything you wanted."

They look at her with curiosity, then with fear.

"You won't know what to call him, not at first. You can't call him by the name of any lover or god, because his love isn't like anything you've ever known. After he touches you for the first time, your body will know exactly what to call him. You can't call him anything but Master."

"Come with me," she begs them. "Please just come. We could catch the train together, when it's time."

But the other women back away. They know that Grace has lost her mind—or something else. Even as they hurry back to their homes, they feel Grace's hunger, under the thin silk of her refinement.

WHEN he needs a woman, they are never hard to find. In the houses along the railroad tracks, there is always a housewife or widow whose desires have been shaped by the moan of the train whistle. She is waiting for music that she's never heard, anything to disrupt the pattern of her days. She doesn't know this yet, but she will give up her body and soul for a song. One afternoon, when she's alone in the house, a man will step out of the tangle of wild grasses along the tracks. He will be tall, dressed in a dark suit, boots, and a hat. He will calm her with his battered elegance, seduce her with the same song he's been singing for years. The song has never been recorded, and if you ask about it in any juke joint, no one will have heard of it. Only his women know.

After weeks of waiting, it's finally Grace's turn. She finds herself hiding in the woods beside the freight yard, her heart hammering. From a distance she hears the snort and sigh of the train, and she thinks she has an eternity to decide. Before she's ready, the beast is rolling by. She doesn't know anything about hopping trains. She has no idea what to do.

Come for me, dark man, warble the frogs in the grass.
Come for me, dark man, echoes a mockingbird in a mulberry tree.
Come for me, dark man, cries her thundering blood.

Then she remembers skipping rope as a child, picking up the rhythm of the other girls' chant, waiting for the moment to jump in and catch the arc of the rope. She waits until a boxcar door yawns in front of her. She fixes her eyes on the ladder. She runs, a bit too fast, and her hands slip on the rungs, her ankles turning in the gravel before she regains her grip and hoists her body up the ladder into the car. As soon as she wobbles to her feet, she is thrown forward into the darkness. The boxcar wall rises up to meet her, and she falls hard.

She's alone in the car, with the profane light slanting in across her hands, and the masculine smells of steel and dried piss all around her, and the thrust of the machine's giant gears. Face-down, with her cheek resting on the floor, she watches the crackerbox houses beside the tracks. She sees a woman standing behind a picket fence, a woman watching the train. Then a second woman flashes by, and a third. Pretty maids all in a row—women joined like paper dolls, linked across the years by their desires.

Come for me, dark man, dark man come down,
Gonna give it to the dark man when that train rolls into town.

As the train presses on to the borderland, its kneeling passenger sways back and forth, semi-lucid, so far from her ladyworld. The train will never stop. He will never come. She has become simple-minded in her longing. She is foolish, probably mad. She has left her home, her town and church, and hopped this train like a hobo, all because of a song.

Just when Grace is about to crack, wondering if she'll break her neck if she leaps out of this car and runs for her life, the train slows down. Stops. With a grating yawn, the boxcar's door slides open— time is speaking of its true breadth. The setting sun captures him in silhouette, angel of darkness, just before he climbs into the car. In this annunciation, he is splendid and terrible to see. Over his shoulder hangs the guitar.

"You came," she says.

He looks down at Grace, crouching at his feet, then he slides the guitar off his shoulder and places it carefully against the wall. She wants to ask him to sing for her, but she knows better.

"Take that dress off. I want to see you."

She strips, then huddles naked on her knees, her arms extended in front of her. Her hair sweeps forward, cloaking her face. Her back is an ivory arc, the bones of her spine barely forming a ripple in the convexity. Swelling from the deep indentation of her waist, her buttocks are full and milky white. Her deceptively delicate hands— hands that can reach over an octave on her piano—are arched as if to fix her to the boxcar's gritty floor.

His boot presses down on her hand. Not enough pressure to break the bones, or even to bruise them, only enough to flatten the fingers. Grace's fingers cave under the boot's insistence. The cold steel tip glides down her arm, lifting pale hairs in its wake, then rests on her skull. Particles of dirt dig into her forehead. The boot moves on, the sole coming to rest on Grace's neck, with its graceful cords and silken hollow. His instep bears down on the slim column—the density of his being comes to rest on the most vulnerable part of her body.

Finally he lifts his foot, then steps around to face her, offering Grace the toe of his boot to kiss. She presses her lips to the leather. In the infinite maze of the leather's cracks, dirt has mingled with tar and blood, hardening the boot into a hoof.

"Are you going to take me?" she asks. Her desire rings in her ears. Her skull resonates with the notes of his song. Tears burn in the corners of her eyes.

"Hush," he says.

He steps out of sight again, and his boot begins to explore her spine. Inch by inch it claims her back, conquering each vertebra with a tap. She flinches as the metal touches her buttocks, dips into the hollow between her thighs. The point sinks into the wet groove. She gnaws her lips. Her ass rises, and a desperate growling whimper comes from her mouth. Like a cat in heat she flattens her chest and belly against the ground.

The boot withdraws. Grace panics. Then his hand grips the nape of her neck. His fingers dive into her hair, and she is pulled upright, onto her knees. Behind her, he straddles her legs. His left hand holds her hair, while his right strokes her throat. Down the throat, across her collarbone, then under her breasts. He handles the soft flesh roughly, twisting each nipple, stretching the nub until the breast rises from its cradle. She grinds her teeth.

"Don't ask me to take you," he says. "I'll take you when I want."

He gets down beside her, bracing her hips. His hand passes over her stomach, then goes between her thighs. He parts her lower lips and pushes two fingers inside her. His inspection continues from the inside—first her cunt, then the tight hole behind. His fingers are coarse and soft, warm and cold. In the beginning she thought he was evil, now she realizes that he is everything at once.

He smacks her bare rump with his palm. She moans. No gentle kiss, no hand stroking her lightly, has ever made her moan like that.

"Use the belt," she begs.

"You'll get what you need when you need it."

He pulls a bandanna out of his pocket and ties it around her eyes. In the scratchy darkness behind the cloth, she inhales the smells of him: dust and whiskey, tobacco and wood smoke. He pushes her onto all fours, and she hears him undressing, pulling off his boots. Naked, he mounts her, holding his forearm firmly across her throat as he enters her. He is her lover now, murmuring in her ear, singing the words to the song in a low voice as the train supplies a slow percussion that matches the thrust of his hips. She'll have her pain soon enough, but for now there is only the friction of his cock, keeping time with the engine's rhythm.

Grace screams. There's no more pretense about what she is. It's something much older than love, this roaring need. She cries out like a woman falling, her howl merging with the train's whistle. Her journey is underway. This train runs only one direction: into the night.

HEAVEN IS A BLUES CAFÉ
HZAL

"What you got in your mind ain't gonna happen today
Get off my bed, how in the world did you get that way?"

You Can't Sleep In My Bed — Mary Dixon   (1929)

I WAITED *until dark fell before going outside. The last time I was here I was just a kid. My great-grandmother had died and for the first time in years most of the family had come back to where they had migrated from. That was back in the thirties. Most of what I remembered was this place where the men slipped off to, a blues house, and they would always come back drunk and cussing making the women folk upset.*

That was fifty years ago, 1938. Now, I was living on the land my great- grandparents owned. Nobody else from the family was coming back so I was more or less chosen since I was the only one not working and had no family. It had been over a hundred degrees today and there wasn't no way I was going outside. Even now that the sun had gone down, I was still sweating. The warm breeze of a night wind slipped across my face. I walked out to the dirt road and just started walking. Like last night I just started walking down the road no destination in mind. I did the same thing in the city. I would just wake up some times in the middle of the night and start walking. I was a night creature.

"AIN'T you one of the Gany's?" I had been in town two weeks and no one had never said more than "Hi" or "Good morning" or "Good evening" so at first I didn't respond just looked at the woman standing in front of me, brown and pretty, nearly as tall as myself.

"I said, ain't you one of the Gany's? You sho look like'um."

"Yes," finally came out my mouth but I was still stuck on her eyes.

She pleasantly stared back, not the least bit shy.

"Excuse me, sir, but are you buying that hammer?" the store clerk barked.

"Oh yes, yes", I said, still focused on the woman asking about my family.

"I can wait," she said and went and stood by the door.

"And can I get a pound of six inch common nails, ten feet of screening, and three two-by-six flat boards."

"That'll cost you sixteen dollars and twenty three cents."

Outside the hardware in the sun, her honey skin color looked even prettier and her eyes had that almost hazel color. The braids she was wearing folded over her shoulders. Her breast rose slightly as she breathed and her hips swayed like small waves as she walked out the door in front of me. We stepped off the front entrance of the store onto an area that, in my mind, was private but was really the space between the hardware and the barbershop.

"I saw you last week but I was with my brother," she stopped talking as if trying to get me to understand something.

"So what's your name?"

"My name is Theresa but everybody just calls me Terry."

"My name is Seko."

"Seko? What that mean?"

"Nothing. Just a name my momma gave me."

"So what you doing back here?"

"Well, the family got some land down here and wasn't anyone available but me to come down, so here I am."

"So what you been doing walking back and forth to the hardware or just out walking around at night down these dark roads?"

"You seen me out walking at night?"

"Seen you a couple nights ago. Followed you for a while."

"Why you do that?"

"I didn't know who you was at first, but after a few minutes, I knew it was you."

"What was you doing out."

"Same as you. Restless. You know the night it was calling so I went out. Besides, walking helps me."

"Yeah, it does. So where you going now?"

"Well, I got some chores."

"Anything happening tonight? I know even in the country yaw got to cut loose."

"Depends on what you call cutting loose."

"Dancing and drinking, listening to some good music, a blues house."

"Ain't no more blues house and most of the boys just go down by the river and drink their hooch. Sometimes the girls join them but not too often."

"Sure there's a blues house. I heard the music. Them cats' was really jamming."

"Must a been somebody's radio. Ain't been no blues house around here in years. Not since Anit was killed back in the forties at Snoots Blues Café."

"Are you sure? Either I'm crazy or I had a bad dream. I went across the field behind my house and followed this old pathway and saw some lights. Then I heard the music and went over there. I watched from the trees as cars drove up, people got out, and I saw this one guy with this red and white guitar go in. I heard him playing, tore the place up. I don't know why I didn't go in but I went home satisfied."

"You sure you wasn't drinking or something?"

"No, I don't let myself drink too much. I got a bad habit once."

"So, that's why the family sent you down here to the country."

"Yeah, sorta. Damn, girl, I don't normally talk this much. You wanna come over tonight? I mean, if I ain't being too forward."

"Yeah, but you got to come and get me. I'm about a half a mile from you. West of you. Our house is the pale green one. There is a big rock out front with a rooster painted on it."

"Oh, yeah, I saw that house. I saw a couple guys down by the barn."

"That was probably my brothers, Frank and B.W."

"So, I'll see you tonight?"

"Come around eight. My brothers will be gone by then."

"Is something wrong with your brothers I need to know?"

"Well, to be honest, my mom and dad died a couple years ago, and they running things and they even try running me. Just come after eight, ok?"

"Ok, but I ain't trying to get into trouble with your brothers. I never mean to hurt anybody."

"You don't look like the hurting kind. Let me see your eyes." Terry looked in my eyes and smiled. I smiled back. I wondered what was really going on with this girl. She seemed not to be anything what I thought a country girl would be like. I guess I should have found out more about this girl. She was fine, sultry; full of Southern heat. When she took my hands in hers and rubbed them, I felt an urge hit me to fold her over and pop her right there. I said "See ya later," and she moved away from me like we were being forcibly disengaged. I could still feel her presence until the afternoon sun drove her away.

It took me no more than thirty minutes to walk to her house. Frank and B.W. were gone just as she had promised, for some reason I felt relieved. I thought about meeting them and wondered what they would think about some guy they didn't know taking their sister back to his house for what, a rendezvous, some Friday night good time. Terry came to the door with a soft, beige-colored sun dress and sandals. I felt like I had just been trapped. I was more than a willing victim. We didn't talk much on the walk back to my family's house. I had put two chairs and a candle on the porch. I had repaired the screen door and fixed the broken steps. I was always good working with my hands, came natural. My uncle had always said before he died that I was just like my great-grandfather, the one that built the house and the barn and the fence and hot house and even some of the furniture. The bed I slept in was a hundred years old.

We sat on the porch after eating the fried chicken and greens I had cooked.

"You did a good job on that chicken, and how did you know I loved fried eggplant?"

"I didn't but I thought you might. I seen all them green tomatoes on your porch and ain't much difference between them and fried green tomatoes."

Terry filled my head with all the stories she could think of about the Old South she grew up in. I told her about Cleveland and how living in the city is. Concrete and people and hustling and the snow and the freedom we enjoyed much different from the South.

"Yeah, but the South has changed. Yaw just think yaw got a little more freedom but we got room. We got land to grow things on."

"I been thinking about that. It is nice not to hear sirens and worrying about getting shot or mugged all the time. It got a little scary sometimes. My momma used to worry about me all the time when I would be walking at night."

"Well, we got different things down here to scare you. Snakes and gators and things that walk at night."

"Things that walk at night?"

"Just things."

"My momma said I was a night creature that why I walk at night. Now, what gone get me down here at night. A haint? A spirit?"

"Shhh, don't talk so loud about that kind of stuff, you might wake something up."

"Are you kidding? Ain't nothing out there that aint real flesh and blood. Just like that blues place I told you about. It's real. I been over there a couple of times."

"Did you ever go in?"

"What?"

"Did you ever go in? You said you was hiding in the trees and looking at people go in and how good the music was, but you didn't go in to party with the folks on the inside."

I just found myself staring at Terry, trying to figure out what she was saying. What did she mean by asking a question like that?

"I didn't go in cause I didn't want to. I'm a stranger here, remember."

"Yeah, you're stranger than you thought. Did you think you could just walk up there and nobody would notice it? You didn't get an invitation, you just showed up."

"An invitation? What the hell you talking about. Who the hell are you?"

If what happened next would have been told to me by somebody else, I would have called them the biggest liar God ever made. Terry walked off the porch onto the road and started singing and people started coming down the road and from out of the fields. I sat on the porch with my mouth wide open. A car was coming, driven furiously with the dust from the dirt road flying around like a storm. The car slowed for the people in the road, and then stopped right in front of my house. All I saw was the red guitar sticking up in the air in the back seat. The driver of the white convertible Cadillac smiled and waved his hand at Terry. He called out to her: "Anit, come on girl. Let's go. It's time to party. Tell your friend to come on too, he's invited. We gone get down and dirty tonight. Gone play some of them grind'um out blues."

Terry came back on the porch and took my hand and we got into the Caddy. Most of the people had already faded into the woods.

The ride was quick and nobody was saying a word. The driver parked the Caddie on the side of the house. We entered in and the music started pumping as we walked past the door. The driver had retrieved his guitar and gone to the bandstand. Everything grew quiet and I felt Terry's hand grip mine tightly. A long wail leaped out of the red guitar and everybody including me screamed "Yeah!"

"My name is Red Leaf and tonight I'm cutting the head off the limit of the blues. Tonight we gone go somewhere I done visited before. Do you wanna go? Let me hear it if you wanna go...Open yo gatdamn mouths and scream my name if you riding with me..."

We all screamed our lungs out—"Red Leaf, Red Leaf...take us man, take us!" I ain't never experienced no shit like this. The red guitar was still wailing that single note like a mad siren. I ain't never screamed for a man at a concert, and I been to plenty, but this was different. Then I felt her on me, from behind. She felt like a snake the way she was moving on me. Red Leaf brought the mike to his mouth and began to sing. I noticed that many of the women had a look of lust in their eyes as they bored into the partner they was dancing with.

Red Leaf:
When the day started you was on my mind
Now that sun done gone down I know it's you I got to find
I got to release what I'm feeling
Sweet little thang you got my head reeling
Now here we are together
And I'm tight as a piece of leather

I moved in on Terry as she pushed her right leg forward. I took her around the waist and we did a buck shuffle back and forth. I hadn't given another thought to what was really going on. At the end of the first hour we were so wet from dancing and grinding we had to step outside. The stars seemed to be jumping to the music.

"See that big red star up there? That's Betelgeuse."

"How you know that living in the city? I been to Atlanta and the sky in the city don't look like the sky in the country."

"You're right, but when I was in school I took a class in astronomy. I thought it might be fun. Anyway, it was different, but that was the one star I remember because it was red."

"You're not like other guys. You're different. I'm surprised you're not scared. Do you know where you are really?

"No, you going to tell me?"

"Maybe you'll remember after a while just like I did."

I watched Terry as she returned to the house where Red Leaf was snatching heads off the limit of the blues.

Red Leaf
What you got to give, give it me now hot and loaded give it to
me, take your hands off me if you gone play, or tell me come here
baby let's play get down under this dress and do your best make
me holla tonight make me holla its alright it's alright o yea o yea
what you got to give me give it to me now hot and loaded hit me
hard from the front and from the back take off my head baby and
play music down into my soul work me work me with that blues
thing you playing with between your legs...

I found Terry inside jumbled up with a group of men and women all dancing sensually to Red Leaf's wailing, begging-to-let-loose the animal of passion.

She caught me by the eye and turned her shoulders so that the bones of her clavicle were defined. I had not noticed the fine tawny hair on her but it was there glistening under the light. Wet like the morning dew waiting for a hot wind to come and dry it off. The driving rhythm drove her and the others, and I pounded my foot to the drums, to the bass, to the guitar, to the piano, to the stomping feet working through another pulsating blues rhythm. Somehow the blues sanctified all that was in the house. Except for the bathrooms and one other room, all the walls had been removed and the second floor was gone, leaving the beams of the rafters exposed. The colors of the walls were black and all the trimming was done in red. The floors were a dark hardwood and four large speakers hung from the ceiling and two large bass reflectors bounced on the floor as the dancers gyrated.

And I noticed that the crowd was both young and old and the dress ranged from over-revealing to sexually subtle. Corn liquor flowed freely and I took my share, reaching deeper and deeper into the barrel the blues poured from. I kept the cup to my lips. Terry supported me in my endeavors to stay upright. Red Leaf had taken a much deserved break and had just returned to the stage as Terry helped me in and out of the bathroom. Taking the mike in his hand Red Leaf said: "As all of you know, there is one here who is special to me above all the rest. For more than a generation I have been singing to her, and so now, again, I swallow my pride and bare my defenseless soul, expose myself and cast these timeless blues at her feet. Anit, welcome again."

I watched the crowd divide itself. I felt her hand release mine. I heard the door shut and the lights went down as Anit/Terry made her way to the foot of the stage.

Red Leaf began a mournful tune with a lazy beat that wrung around Anit's neck as she raised her arms as if in anticipating being saved and the feeling of sanctification returned from around the corner it had recently retired to. My eyes swerved in my head from the alcohol and from the event. Then I saw what I thought for a second was a friend of mine who passed away three years ago, but that was not possible since he died in Cleveland and that was hundreds of miles away.

Red Leaf:
When you find your way you'll find me waiting
With a guitar in my hands and words in my mouth

I'll beg you like before put down your body here
All you got to do is say it say forever, say forever
Heaven is a blues café
Heaven is a blues café
I'll take the dust off your feet
I'll take loneliness from your heart
Take a red leaf from the garden of my love
And place it on your heart bury it there
And I will appear
Anit, Anit remember this was once our road
Here we come again..."

I don't know what happened to me. Years ago, me and a guy that I thought was a friend fought over a girl, my girl, and I killed him, not on purpose but he died never the less. Terry, or whatever her name is, had me or the liquor had me, but one thing I would never allow, I would not allow anybody to take anything from me. Somehow, in my madness I had laid claim to Terry and I wasn't about to give her up. I made my way to the front and grabbed her from behind, picking her up and headed for the closed door.

That was the last thing I remembered until I woke up here in jail. I had been charged with murder. I explained to them the whole story as I've explained it to you. They said the blues house had been empty for more than twenty years and it was just a falling down structure whose roof had caved in. It was there her brothers found me and the naked body of Terry. They beat on me and probably would have killed me but a sheriff out hunting heard my screams and took me in. The thoughts of her sweet body come to me, and I feel her riding me out in the back of that blues house while Red Leaf was swinging past dark clouds looking for the sun that sanctifies all blues singers. I feel her hot lips and the sound she made while I sucked on her nipples. I hear the gasp I made when I finally pushed into her wetness. Moisture had escaped down her thigh and we gripped each other in the dirt seeking to justify a memory of something that had gone terribly wrong. We screamed, she screamed, I screamed. What were we screaming for? Was it because Red Leaf had set upon us with his guitar to stop us, or was it the crowd, filled with a blues rage touching us in an attempt to devour us with the sound of misery, or were we just *lost in time* in a house that refused to die as long as the past would continue to return again.

So I sit here, full of amazement and wonder what did I really do that was wrong. When she asked me if I was afraid, I should have said hell yes but if that had happened then I wouldn't be telling you this story.

"Tell me Sherriff Bet, is what he says true?"

"Well, I don't know about the blues club part. If we hadn't found him, her brothers would have killed him for sure. We had been looking for the girl for about three days when we heard him screaming. The boys had sawed off one of his hands and were getting ready to emasculate him, but we saved him from that."

"Well, tell me this isn't very similar to what happened over in Red River County. I remember having to go down and cover that story for my paper. Some guy from up north met some girl and claims that they went to a blues café. Girl turned up dead, blood was everywhere, but none of the blood was the girl's or the guy."

"Yeah, that part we ain't figured out yet. I mean, the girl here also had lost a lot of blood but none of the blood in that house was hers—and there was a lot of blood. The oddest thing of all was the words written in blood on the wall: Heaven is a Blues Café.

RED EYE
LISABET SARAI

*"Bought me a coffee grinder, got the best one I find
So he could grind my coffee, 'cause he had a brand new
grind."*

Empty Bed Blues – Bessie Smith (1928)

HE WAS THE ONE. She knew it, the first time she felt him slide into her. Everything was right. Perfect fit, glorious fullness without pain. Every movement woke new nerves, sent new sensations shimmering through her. Bent over the seat, digging her nails into the faux leather covering the armrests as her body shook with his thrusts, she couldn't see his face. She didn't need to see him; she knew what he was thinking, knew what he wanted.

She arched her back, letting him bury his flesh more deeply in hers. She clenched her inner muscles around his hardness, wanting to swallow him, to make him part of her. He rammed his cock into her again and again, one hand over her mouth to stifle her cries. She writhed against him, each stroke a shuddering, prolonged delight that nudged her closer to the ultimate pleasure.

He was not gentle like the men she had dreamed about before she knew him. He was not tender. Still, she had no doubts that he was meant for her. In the darkened cabin, he read her body like Braille. He knew how to tease every nuance of pleasure out of her wet and open flesh. While one hand held her gagged, the other toyed with her nipples through her blouse, twisting and squeezing the swollen nubs. She worried briefly that he'd tear the fabric, until the seething flood of sensation washed her worries away.

Above the susurrations of the passengers shifting in their seats, the coughs and the snores and the faint babble of movie sound tracks, she could hear the slap of his balls against her bare thighs and his open-mouthed panting. The steamy jungle smell of her cunt rose around them. She was sure that someone would notice, would turn around to check the empty rows toward the back of the section. His palm smothered her moans. Then the pulse of his come inside her swept her into a whirling climax. The engine whined in her ears. Gravity released her. She floated weightless, shaken by spasms of pleasure so intense that they practically stripped her of consciousness.

When she came to herself, she was on her knees, her face buried in the cushion, the seat belt buckle digging into her cheek. There was no trace of him, save for the burning in her cunt and the used condom she found under the seat. She pulled herself to her feet, smoothed her uniform down over her torn pantyhose, slipped back into her sensible pumps. She was still shaking.

She peered through the dimness toward the front of the plane. There was a man's head there in 16B, silhouetted by the lighted No Smoking sign on the cabin wall. He leaned against the headrest, seemingly asleep. She could almost believe it had been a dream. But her thighs were sticky with her own juices, and when she pressed them together, delicious echoes of her climax sparked through her.

Later, an hour before landing when she came down the aisle with drinks, he had grinned and slipped a card into her hand. "Email me," he had said. "If you want, that is." His expression made it clear that he had no doubts about her decision.

So it had begun. He was a fortyish media hotshot with a cedar-and-glass ranch house in the Hollywood Hills and a condo on Central Park West. He had lots of excuses to fly cross-country. He had a wife in LA, a suspicious wife who checked his cell phone bills and tried to read his email, a wife too expensive to divorce.

She was twenty eight, a single girl from Iowa City, brought up on the Bible, Nora Roberts and Danielle Steele. The airline had based her in Minneapolis. Her schedule changed from month to month, but whenever she was assigned the red eye, she'd let him know. He'd do his best to arrange a trip east to coincide. Business class. Sixteen B.

It started with her standing at the door of the plane, proper and well-groomed, inspecting boarding passes. He'd tower over her, giving her a proprietary grin that liquefied her bare cunt. She'd learned not to wear underwear when he flied. His scent made her knees buckle even as she welcomed him aboard. "Sixteen B," she'd say, handing back the slip of cardboard. "Down the right aisle, sir." His fingers would brush hers, sending electric sparks to her cunt.

Sometimes he'd murmur his instructions, sotto voce, as she came through with the drink cart, forty five minutes out of LAX. Sometimes he would email her beforehand, sharing his fantasies. "I should crouch behind you as you're checking the boarding passes. My fingers would be buried in your cunt, my thumb stuck in your ass. Then we'd see how cool and collected you really are, Ms. Perfectly Poised Airline Hostess."

Alone in her neat apartment, she'd still blush, reading his messages. Her nipples would harden to aching pebbles. Her pussy would grow so wet that she'd be slithering back and forth on the vinyl desk chair. She'd close her eyes and remember how it felt to have his cock, or his fingers, or both, inside her. She couldn't wait.

At the same time, he scared her. Or rather, her need for him scared her. More than once she was tempted to call in sick when she was assigned to the red eye. What would he think, boarding, finding himself welcomed by some other young lady in the trim navy uniform? Would he miss her, really? Would he make a pass at someone else?

Ultimately, she couldn't bear to give up a chance to see him. To touch and be touched by him. It might be weeks, even months, before the next opportunity. Typically she'd be at the airport hours before the scheduled departure time, hanging around in the staff lounge, drinking cup after cup of weak coffee and replaying their last encounter. Once, he had laid her out on an empty seat, binding her wrists with the seatbelt while he slurped hungrily at her cunt. On another flight, he'd locked them into the bathroom, and then made her kneel on the commode and swallow his cock. He had even fingered her to climax in the galley, while the other stewardesses chatted on the other side of the curtain.

She was amazed that they'd never been caught. People—the passengers and the crew—were all so oblivious. For everyone else, the flight was just routine: stressful, exhausting, part of the job, something to be gotten through. For the two of them, it was a ritual.

"It's been six months," he had written to her yesterday. "Our anniversary. I think we should plan something special." She'd followed his instructions, giving herself an enema, gasping at the nasty, delicious relief that came from emptying himself. She bought a tube of personal lubricant at a pharmacy on the far side of town, her cheeks blazing red even though she knew she'd never see the cashier again. As she waited for the first passengers, just inside the door, she was suddenly, irrationally sure that he wouldn't show up. That he'd leave her, empty and hungry, suffering through endless five hour arc across the continent.

But no, there he was, elite level frequent flyer that he was, one of the first people up the jetway. Her heart revved like a jet engine. Liquid trickled down her naked thighs.

"Good evening, sir." His smile lit up the entire cabin. Calm certainty washed over her. Of course he was here. He was the one, the one she had been waiting for.

"Good evening, Miss. How are you tonight?" He hovered over her for an endless moment and she had a fleeting notion that he'd kiss her, though he never had, not on the lips at least. *I'll remember that later*, she thought. *I'll imagine his mouth on mine.*

"Very well. And you?"

"Excellent. Looking forward to the flight." He gave her a conspiratorial grin that nearly made her laugh out loud.

"Sixteen B?" she asked, a bit boldly.

"Of course."

"You know the way."

"I do indeed. I'll see you later." He gave her butt a soft slap as he passed. She desperately hoped that no one noticed.

After the folks crammed into economy had gotten their pretzels and the business class passengers had finished their chicken breasts in cream sauce, the lights dimmed. The flight was smooth, no turbulence predicted until eastern Pennsylvania. Their steel cocoon hurtled through the darkness, over the blankness of the plains where she'd been born.

She moved silently through the aisles, headed for the rear-most lavatory, the larger one that was handicapped accessible.

"Leave the door unlocked," he wrote. "Lift your skirt to your waist and bend over the toilet, holding onto the invalid bars. Put the lube on the sink. And wait for me."

When she'd read his instructions, she had imagined what it would feel like, to be so exposed and vulnerable. Since the lock was not thrown, the indicator lights would show that the lavatory was free. At any moment, someone might slide open the door and come face to face with her bare bum. How could she possibly do such a thing, even for him? Still, she knew in her soul that she'd follow his instructions to the letter. She didn't sleep, the night she got that message. She sat up, naked in her single bed, staring at her own pale, lush body, wondering what she was becoming.

Now, actually arrayed in the indecent position that he had dictated, she felt oddly calm, though there was an undercurrent of excitement. He was in charge, even if he was still lounging back in 16B sipping his Scotch. She would wait for him. She trusted him to come. To take what he wanted and give her what she needed. And if someone else discovered her lewdness, well, perhaps that was his intent, to show her how much she craved the exposure and the shame.

A steady stream of cool air from the ventilator played over her buttocks. She could almost believe it was his fingers, stroking, testing her readiness. No one had ever touched her, there in that most private spot, let alone entered her as he promised to do. She was simultaneously terrified and eager.

Five minutes. Ten. She became agitated. How long? She felt the plane shift, a kind of hiccup in the air. Could they were descending, two hours early?

All at once she heard of squeak of the door sliding open. She stopped breathing. There was no gasp of shock, no outraged shriek. His scent wafted into the small chamber. The door scraped shut. The lock clicked. She released her pent-up breath.

He laid his hand lightly on her naked rump. "Lovely," he murmured, his fingers drawing small circles on her flesh. Bending over, he planted a kiss on each cheek. "Thank you, Alison."

Her heart surged. He rarely used her name. That was part of the game, the conceit that they were chance-met, lust-driven strangers, that this was the first time that he'd partaken of her body. Perhaps tonight would be different. Perhaps they were moving toward something closer, more substantial, something beyond fantasy.

He did not say anything further. He simply stroked her ass, and looked at her. She felt the heat of his gaze sweeping over her like a spotlight. She didn't need to see him to know. It was, as always, as if she could read his thoughts. She arched her back a bit, offering him the swelling globes that he admired so much. He reacted with sudden, stinging slaps, one to each cheek. Her startled cry turned into a moan as the heat raced from her burning butt down to her pussy.

"Minx! Are you so eager?" He slipped a finger between her splayed thighs and into her soaking cunt. She bucked against him, unable to control her reactions. "Seems as though you are. Well, I won't make you wait any longer."

His hand left her sex for a moment. It was unbearable. She heard him pick up the K-Y. The tube made an obscene spurting sound as he squeezed out what sounded like several tablespoons. Then his fingers were back, lightly stroking her pussy lips and circling her clit. She squirmed, rubbing against him, halfway to coming already.

Then other sensations distracted her from the hungry buzz in her cunt. He traced one slippery finger down the crack between her cheeks. It settled against the whorl of her sphincter, swirling around that sensitive spot, slathering her with lubricant. At first he concentrated only on the entrance. Even that was nearly too intense to bear. He massaged her clit and her rear hole in the same rhythm, circling, spiraling down, and then slipping his digits into her, front and back. His finger in her anus reawakened all the shameful pleasure of the enema. She clenched down on him, struggling for breath. He probed deeper, then added another finger, stretching and loosening the rubbery ring of muscle.

He knew that she was virgin there. He took his time, adding another finger only when she was rocking backwards, keening, urging him deeper, silently begging. He pulled out, and she thought that she'd weep. Then she felt delicious pressure against her slippery hole and knew that it was his cock, much thicker and harder than his fingers, seeking entrance.

He hovered there, rubbing the bulb against her, easing her open. All at once he jerked his hips, forcing his bulk halfway into her rectum. She whimpered at the sudden invasion, edged as it was with unaccustomed pain. He thrust again and buried his full length in her bowels. His hand was ready to muffle her scream. Her musk rose fresh and sharp from his fingers to her nostrils.

He waited while she became accustomed to the novel sensations. The pain faded. He seemed to swell inside her, huge and hot. She fought the urge to expel him, trying to relax. He started to move, pulling partway out and then slamming his cock even deeper than before. He gripped her ass cheeks and held them apart, so that he could plunge his engorged, solid cock in, up to his very balls.

It was like nothing that she'd ever felt. Each stroke kindled a delicious burn that radiated from her pinioned ass to her extremities. When he filled her, the pressure rose to her chest, making her gasp. When he emptied her, tears filled her eyes at the yawning ache that swept over her.

Her cunt felt all the emptier, with his flesh stretching her behind. She desperately wished that he had two cocks, that he could penetrate her front and rear at once. She wanted him to take all of her.

As if he could hear her thoughts, he slipped a hand into her cunt, gathering her juices. The next thing she knew, he was sliding something hard and smooth into her pussy, raking it across her clit on the way in.

It might have been the new stimulation. It could have been her foggy realization that he'd just plunged a dildo into her cunt. Her muscles clenched down on the enormous bulk invading her. Her cunt convulsed, vibrations speeding through her, pleasure peaking and then climbing off the scale.

Then, just as the first climax subsided, the plane hit a pocket of bad air. It bucked and rocked, slamming her back against the rod of flesh embedded in her ass, then forward onto the dildo. She came again, a delicious shattering that left her hanging limp on the two poles that impaled her.

The 747 continued to shake. He grabbed her hips and fucked her hard, using her body to bring himself off. The plane dipped suddenly, leaving a hole in her gut. What a way to die, she thought, delirious with pleasure. With one cock in my ass and one in my cunt.

With a grunt, he slammed into her one last time. She felt the heat of his come in her bowels, even through the latex. Every sensation seemed to be heightened after her dual crisis. When his cock slipped out of her, she reveled in the feel of his half-hard penis slithering over her cheeks. When he reached to remove the toy, she ground her clit against it, and exploded a third time.

The plane still tossed like a feather on the transcontinental currents. She heard a ding; a red light came on near the ceiling.

"Ladies and gentlemen, we're experiencing some severe turbulence. Please return to your seats immediately and fasten your seatbelts."

She turned, seeing his face for the first time since he'd entered. He looked more serious than she would have expected, without his usual teasing grin.

"You'd better get back to your seat. If one of the other stewardesses notices that you're missing..."

He stopped her with a kiss, grabbing her shoulders, smearing KY all over her blouse. His mouth was as forceful as his cock. His tongue was brazen, taking her over. She relaxed into his embrace, floating on a pink cloud of happily ever afters. He devoured her as though she was his last meal.

The plane shook itself like a dog after swimming. The force of it pulled them apart.

He gazed at her, his dark eyes brimming with emotion. "Alison—thank you."

"Anytime, sir." Sure of herself, surer of him now than ever, she risked a bit of cheek. "You know that I'd do anything for you. Just let me know what you'd like for the next time."

He stroked her tousled blond hair. "I'm afraid that there won't be a next time."

Her heart skipped a beat, then another. She grabbed his shirt. "What? What do you mean?"

"My wife. She's been snooping around. Asking about all these trips to the east coast. Next time, she says, she wants to come with me. Visit the shops on Fifth Avenue. See a show."

"So? Take her some time when I'm not on call. Convince her there's nothing going on." She stood on tiptoe and tried to kiss him. He did not respond.

"I'm sorry..."

"Look, we can cool things off for a month or so. I can wait, if I have to, if that's the only way..."

"But I can't wait." He gently unclasped her hands where they gripped his clothing. "Between times—when we're apart—I can hardly stand it. I think of you all the time. I'm constantly tempted to write you, to tell you all the kinky things that I want to do to you..."

She snuggled against him. "So why don't you?"

"Don't you understand? I can't! I can't afford to be obsessed with you! It would ruin me. When I'm with you, I'm risking everything— my life, my fortune, my job, my reputation."

"And what about me? All I ever dreamed of as a kid was being a stewardess, but if we were caught—no airline would ever hire me again." She pulled herself to her full 5'4", just barely regulation height for air crew. "But I'd do anything for you. I love you."

He couldn't meet her eyes. "I know. I'm close to loving you too. You're the most perfect partner. It's like you can read my mind..."

A hint of triumph laced through her pain. He felt it too. It wasn't just her romantic imagination. "I know. I understand." She took his hands in hers. "Please, Carl. Give us a chance. What we have is something precious. It's once in a lifetime. Don't throw it away."

Anguish twisted his handsome face. "Alison, I don't have a choice." The bell dinged again, and the seatbelt light switched off. He backed out of the cubicle, closing it behind him. Not even saying goodbye.

She sank down onto the toilet, burying her face in her hands. Her whole body shook, but her tears were silent, spilling over her fingers and soaking her crumpled skirt. *Please*, she thought, her mind whirling desperately. *Let the plane crash. Let the world end.*

She cried and cried, until her throat rasped and her eyes burned. Finally, exhausted, she leaned back against the wall. There was something there, pressing against her buttocks. She reached behind and brought out the dildo.

It was hard rubber, bright purple, and shaped like a rabbit. It was so ridiculous that in the depths of her despair, she almost laughed. She ran her hand along its sticky length, remembering the glorious places he had taken her. She sniffed at it. The oceany reek of her cunt woke echoes of her climax. She suddenly felt how stretched she was, behind, the legacy of his cock plowing her. It burned a bit, but the sensation was pleasant, stirring further shadows of past lust.

She felt the plane nose downward, just as the PA came on. "Ladies and gentlemen, we're starting our descent to JFK. Please fasten your seatbelts, lock your tray tables and bring your seats to an upright position." She stood up resolutely and tried to brush the wrinkles from her uniform.

Let him go. If he left, then she must have been wrong. He was not the one for her, the one she'd been searching for all her life. That man was still out there, waiting for her, somewhere. And now she knew a lot more about how to recognize him, and how to make him happy.

She splashed some hot water on her face, and then peered at her reflection. Her eyes were bloodshot from all her crying, but otherwise, she looked pretty good. She pinned up her hair again, and reapplied her lipstick. After a moment's thought, she unfastened the top button on her blouse.

Lots of men had fantasies about stewardesses. She could take advantage of that. She smiled at the sexy young woman in the mirror, savoring the growing buzz between her thighs.

"Good evening, sir," she pouted. "Welcome aboard."

THE BACKUP SINGER
REBECCA KYLE

*"Don't feel my leg, don't feel my thigh
'Cause you wanna go up high."*

Don't You Make Me High – Merline Johnson (1939)

I GOT my start singing in the church choir. The choir director told Mama I had a four-octave range. Mama was delighted to scrimp for private lessons, since she believed I'd use my talent to praise the Lord. I might have become a soloist instead of a backup singer had my teacher and I remained vertical.

When my church-going Mama found out I was expecting, she went to the pastor who promised the choir director would be fired. When my backsliding Daddy heard, he used his shotgun and settled the matter permanently.

Daddy got life. The state disliked Black men taking the law into their own hands. Mama died after his sentencing, the church ladies whispered shame was what caused her early passing.

I ended up in a church-sponsored home for unwed mothers where I delivered my baby and finished my education. My little girl came on the first day of spring, but it felt like cold winter in my heart.

I knew an uneducated, unwed girl couldn't give that baby the kind of home she needed. I wish I could have held her in my arms just once before they took her to her new parents. I wasn't the only girl who cried herself to sleep at night in that place. We formed a kind of sisterhood in our grief and shame.

I rushed through my GED so I could leave at eighteen. I rode the dog as far West as my money would take me. That Greyhound got me to Nashville.

I started singing commercial jingles for politicians, dog food, and hygiene products. Five years later, I've worked from studio vocalist to backup singer with a rock band. You know the one, blonde haired, white lead singer who is pure sex in leather pants, integrated band, with a three-woman soul chorus.

I was elated when they told us we were going to do a nationwide tour. My hometown was near the last city scheduled. My heart pounded like a bass drum every time I thought about performing for that crowd. Who knows? My little girl could be there in the audience. That thought kept me going every lonely mile.

I believed I'd see the country. Instead, I'm looking at the inside of cheap hotels, the back of another band member's head on fetid tour busses, and raggedy-ass backstages. I'm up on stage every night, singing and hoping the folks in my hometown will see me and know the little girl who shamed her family is now a star.

I promised on Mama's grave that I wouldn't be with any man again until I married. Even when I was working my way up, I knew I didn't have time or money to mess around. The first few weeks of the tour, I managed to stay away from the nightly sex, drugs, and parties. Further from home I got, the more lonesome I became.

I contemplated seeing if I could hook up with one of the band members. A couple of stable pairings gave me hope. Being with someone beat playing soloist in my lonely bed every night.

I never planned on doing the nasty with the star—and I wouldn't suggest doing so to any girl unless she wanted bragging rights. But one day I ended up with him.

Backstage was crowded. You were constantly dodging roadies, musicians, press, and people with passes who wanted some of the star's luster.

I was edging along the back wall of the dark hallway in my heels and tight sequined dress, trying to get to the one bathroom when I had to scoot over for a rolling cart. My back pushed against the crash bar on an exit door. Before I realized, I'm falling out into the alley.

I screeched. The door closed before I could grab the edge. I teetered with one high heel caught on the first stair, arms flailing. I tumbled downward, screaming at the top of my lungs.

Strong arms wrapped around me and kept me from falling backwards onto the paved lot where we'd parked the bus. My tight sequined skirt was up around my thighs, my butt pressed up against a man's erect penis, and my bare back connected with someone else's warm skin. It felt like I'd stuck my finger in an electric plug. Beneath my wig, my Afro stood on end. I saw flashes and heard clicks and applause when I managed to teeter to my feet. Those arms released me after I was steady on the fuck-me heels the set designers dressed me in.

"Thank you," I turned to see the lead singer. We'd met when I auditioned. Although we'd occasionally exchange words during rehearsals, we weren't in the same class. I rode the bus with the band while he flew to the locales for concerts.

"You okay, Roxannah?" The singer had the most amazing eyes: blue as a clear spring morning and soft as a warm blanket. His speaking voice was just as sexy as he sang. I had no idea he knew my name.

My heart pounded eight-to-the-bar, now it was skipping beats. I was still wobbling on my heels and doe-eyed like his teenaged fans. He made my name sound like a song.

He helped me down the rest of the stairs to the parking lot. I struggled to get my sequined skirt where it was supposed to be, but I was certain everyone knew the color of my panties. Worse, the paparazzi got photographs.

My luck, my media debut would be with my skirt up around my waist. I could hear the hometown folks now.

"Kill those shots," the singer read my mind. He squeezed my hand and smiled down at me. "If you're going to show her falling, let's show our best sides."

I felt like my face was going to catch fire. I could barely breathe with his hand in mine. The problem got worse when he seemed genuinely concerned.

"Come on, give us something," one of the men holding a camera pleaded.

Half a dozen of the press following the tour surrounded us, expressions ranging from mild concern to amusement. Too many memories of the folks whispering behind my back about what I'd done to my family still haunted me.

"You mind?" the singer asked. I nodded. He wrapped his other arm around my shoulders and turned my body at an angle like I'd fallen. Hell yes, my shocked expression wasn't faked. The press totally ate it up.

"This is Roxannah, one of the backup singers, the little girl with the great big voice," the singer explained. "Our PR manager can provide more."

To one of the bodyguards, he added. "Take her to my trailer and let her rest."

"Will do, Boss."

"Be sure to drink some hot tea with honey," the singer told me as he released my hand and started to the theatre. He turned on the steps and delivered one last line to me in a conspiratorial whisper with a wink.

"Screaming's not good for your magnificent voice---unless, of course, you are enjoying yourself."

Magnificent!! From *him*. I floated to the big RV that followed behind our tour bus. Growing up, compliments were as scarce as new dresses and pretty shoes. I'd forgotten that was how the choir director had gotten into my pants.

Oh myyyy...the RV's interior was uptown as we'd all figured, glaring at it from the back of the stinky, overcrowded bus. I took a quick trip to the restroom. Then kicked off my shoes, slid out of my hose, and ran my bare toes through the luxuriant carpeting. I could live in a place like this full time and never feel crowded.

It took a bit for me to figure out how to work the fancy stainless steel flattop stove, but I had hot water for tea steaming in a pretty red teapot before the singer arrived. I tried to find the tea bags, but all I could come up with was cookies and some very interesting looking baggies full of what I figured was wacky dust.

The door opened and I saw the singer framed with daylight behind him. My mouth watered like I'd been in summer's heat for hours.

"You want some?" I asked, meaning more than the baggie I was too scared to open.

Eyes widened, he moved towards me, his sensuous mouth opening. He took the bag from me and sniffed the white powder like a hound. I was in his arms with my mouth sealing his lips. Our clothes went flying in that tiny kitchenette.

He picked me up and carried me to a red leather couch and laid me down, putting one leg on the floor and the other on the high back of the couch. I melted. That couch was softer than anything I'd felt against my bare skin.

My companion was on top of me and inside before I could draw a breath. My body shook with too-long suppressed desire. He moved fast, moaning loudly, spreading me even further with his hands 'til I knew I'd walk bowlegged the rest of my life.

"Give it to me," he demanded. "C'mon, C'mon, C'mon."

"Yes, yes, yes," I crooned back to him. My back arched hard against him.

We moved together, groaning like animals, our bodies slick with sweat, and our breaths coming faster with each red-hot thrust.

"Oh yeah!" He shouted when he came, shuddering hard against me.

"That was great," he panted as he slid off me and went for the baggie for another snort. "Wasn't I amazing?"

My bliss just flew away. He was chanting the chorus from one of his hits—and a come-on line he used for the audience while he was onstage shaking his pelvis like Elvis.

"Oh yeah, that was amazing." I needn't have lied, he was so immersed in his own post drug and sex high. Belatedly, I saw a mirror positioned near the front door of the RV that gave the star a perfect view—of himself.

"Hurry up and get dressed!" The star told me brusquely. "We're on in less than half an hour."

It hardly seemed possible. I was lonelier after the intimacy. I slid into my clothes fast and got out of there.

You'd think I'd avoid him after that. Whenever he twitched his finger, I was there for a booty call until I showed up to discover much of the band with a dozen teenaged groupies in a tangle of nude bodies. My eyes bugged out as they writhed in positions I'd never even thought possible. The stench of sex, weed, and alcohol hung heavy.

I backed away from the sight, knowing I'd never be able to meet my daughter's eyes if I participated.

THAT NIGHT and several after, I lay awake in my tangled sheets wondering how I could achieve what I'd dreamed of musically and shame myself with my behavior. I still did not regret the decision to give up my daughter, but I hoped someday I could meet her and have her be proud of me.

I knew better. I just couldn't do better. Having someone's hands on me, their meat pounding inside of me, more addictive than cigarettes or chocolate. Soon, I was zooming the lead guitarist, across the stage from me.

He was the tallest man I'd ever met and he increased his height with an old school Afro. Some said he'd be the next Hendrix.

The way that man cradled his guitar in his arms and those long dark fingers strumming the strings, I could almost hear sighs from the wood and wire even with the audience clapping and screaming beyond the stage lights. And, damn, if the old wives' tale about the length of a man's thumb telling about what he had below stood the test, I could see him making some fine ten-inch records with me.

Seems he'd been looking at me too, because one day I heard his voice behind me just as I was leaving the theatre for lunch after rehearsal.

"Foxy Roxie," he growled in a bass low enough to make the floorboards shiver. "Where you going?"

"I was feeling hungry," I purred back at him. "I think I saw a hot dog man around the corner and I could use some hot, juicy meat."

"I'll make you want thirds," he said. We hurried back to his hotel. His room was a twin to mine, save he'd stowed at least half a dozen guitars around the periphery. They leaned against each other like women whispering gossip.

We'd scarcely gotten the door closed before we were kissing. When I started to remove my clothes, the guitar man shook his head. He poured me a drink of some whiskey that burned like hellfire all the way down and made my body tingle like I'd bathed in soda pop.

"We've got all day long, baby," he growled as he pulled off only his shirt to expose a muscular chest. I laid down on the bed, not quite certain what to expect, my body hot and trembling despite the cool air.

Being in a place with a bed and an afternoon to kill was a whole new experience to me. Encounters before this were on the fast and nasty side. Now, the guitar man, he liked to play. He lay beside me on one elbow, letting his hands move slow over my body, baring me one item at a time while he teased me with his fingers until he could almost play me like a stringed instrument.

"Oooh, mama, ever since you almost fell down those stairs, I've been wondering every time I see you what color panties you've got on."He chuckled as he ran his finger along the top of my pink satin bikini bottom. I wiggled, hoping he'd take the hint and remove them, but he meant it when he said he was in no hurry.

Finally, he pulled off those panties and dipped his finger in my sweet honey hole. I squeaked, my body quaking with delight.

"Now, watch out girl, you're going to break that flatscreen TV." The next thing I know, he's kissing where his finger's just been.

I can't describe the sounds I was making. His tongue worked around my sweet spot as his fingers delved in.

I hit that high E I'd been aiming at all my life. And, the note held while my whole body shook.

When I was certain I could take no more, he slid out of his jeans and moved in on top of me. I was so wet, he slid right in smooth as butter. We moved together to a sweet, slow groove. He sure as hell wasn't a minute man.

When he finally came, he still stayed on top of me until he heard me groan one more time. I let my fingers and lips do some walking, exploring the parts of a man I'd never had time to enjoy.

"You said you wanted some hot dog?" he asked when he'd swelled up again. I wasn't sure what to do, but he guided me—and oooh, that man tasted strong and salty. He wasn't big down there like the choir director, but his fingers made up for that.

From his jeans on the floor, I heard "The Wind Cries Mary." His cell phone.

"Ah shit, it's my wife. How's she know when Little Axe gets me in trouble?" The guitarist mumbled boozily.

Little Axe? I stared down at my partner. That name fit. So much for the Rule of Thumb as far as male endowment went.

"Hi, baby," he breathed sexily into the phone. "I sure was missing you..."

I lay there beside him wishing I had someone to genuinely mean those words he was saying. When he hung up, he rolled over to me, pressing rock hard flesh against my belly.

Before he could enter, I rolled him over like a log and slid him inside of me. I rode that man like he was a racehorse in the Kentucky Derby and I made damn sure he hit some notes that'd put his TV in danger.

"Damn baby, I didn't know you had that in you," his eyes were half-closed and his voice slurred.

I slid off his hot and sweaty body and said in parting, "Ever wonder if Mary's got some hot man up beside her while you're out on the road?"

I swaggered out of that room, feeling high and happy. I nearly ran into a skinny, nappy haired, pale-skinned guy carrying a backpack almost near big as him.

"Sorry," he said, shifting the backpack.

The Road Manager had to run to catch up to him. He made introductions. The guy had a multisyllabic last name I doubted I could remember let alone pronounce. Thankfully, his first name was Marc.

"Marc's our new drummer," he ended. "Meet Roxannah, one of the backup singers."

Marc was short: one of the few men I could see eye-to-eye. He had melting puppy dog eyes that made me smile.

I NEEDED people. In some ways, I wished I could just get my pleasure from one-nighters, but the truth was I needed a stable relationship. Hard truth was that I didn't know how to date or be with a man on a regular basis. I'd spent the time I should have been with boys my age with the choir director and the years following in a church-run home.

Knowing what a man could do with his mouth, I eyed the horn players. The saxophonist was around when music was invented. He was a gravel voiced, ebony-skinned man from "Nawlins" who'd talk incessantly about the Chittlin' Circuit. I figured his pencil didn't have lead anymore, and if it did, he couldn't write long without those blue pills.

Now the trumpet player could lay down some licks that'd get you out on the floor. Any man played that good had to be great with his lips. I was so hot one night, I dragged that man to the bathroom after a particularly good show. It was a nasty place, but we weren't going to be lying down.

"Show me how you can blow, sister." He dropped his pants and I went down on my knees. He may have blown a trumpet, but the man had a trombone down there—and I mean *bone*. I could barely fit him in my mouth, but I played him just like he played his horn.

I took the tip of him into my mouth and started licking with my tongue. My hands cupped his hot nuts and caressed. I kept that up, eating him like my last meal. He groaned low in his throat and came fast in my mouth.

"That was good, baby. I'll catch you on the flip-side," he said once he came in a hot rush in my mouth.

And he did, in the motel lobby right after the next show. He wanted an encore.

"No way. You got yours the last time. This is mine."

I had my skirt up and his zipper down as he locked the room door. We didn't even stop to hit the bed. I was backed up with my butt against that paneled room door. My breath caught as he lifted me up and pressed me hard against the wall. My leg wrapped around his waist as I struggled to keep one foot on the ground to balance.

I slid him in by centimeters, gasping as he filled me. I was wet near to my wrists as I guided him inside.

"Your pussy's tight as your mouth," he whispered. He kissed me then, working that fabulous tongue around the bowl of my mouth until I couldn't tell which end of me felt more pleasure.

I felt the rest of him move inside me.

I squeaked, scared he'd forced it too fast and would tear me in half. He chuckled, cupping my ass in his hands and moving sweet and slow.

We made that door rattle like a tambourine. He came in a hot rush, thrusting hard enough to make the lock bang. I followed, gasping as he released me and we tumbled onto the sandpaper-rough hotel carpeting.

I stayed the whole night with that horn player—the first night I'd spent with any man. I hurt so bad the next day, I had to beg Vicodin from one of the other singers to stand up through the whole show. I had a bad feeling if I did him one more time, I'd need to get stitched up.

A SMART GIRL would've just given up and bought one of those expensive, battery-operated boyfriends. I still like to think of myself as smart, but now I'd gotten my clock wound just right, I wasn't willing to let time pass me by.

I made a checklist. *Make sure they weren't married* was right on top. No more lying dog blues, this sister wasn't going to share anymore.

The one cat from the band I hadn't considered was Marc, the drummer. Nobody wanted to sit behind him on the bus because he was always pounding out a beat with something on the back of his seat. Hell, most of the crew had just gotten back from a party and were sleeping 'til the next stop.

I overslept one morning. I climbed onto the bus with enough coffee to wake the dead and a headache that made me wish I could join them. I glanced at the bus and realized the only place left was up front; the seat between the driver and Marc. I noted at least a dozen unfamiliar people with press badges attached to their clothing scattered about the interior talking to band members and road crew. This had to be the day we'd have guests.

Sure enough, the minute we got moving, Marc was pounding something exotic on the back of my seat.

"Hey!" I glanced between the seats at his puppy dog brown eyes. "Trade places with me."

"Come and sit with me."

You could hear a pin drop in the seats close to us. I knew about locker room talk, and I figured there was some tongue waggin' and braggin' going on about the way I was giving it away. I couldn't look at the guitar player as I passed him to claim my seat.

"Don't you have an off button?" I grumbled, thinking it was going to be like sitting next to a two-year-old. Instead, he showed me the designs for a drum box he called a "cajon."

Daddy was a carpenter so I found myself giving him advice on how to put the box together and thinking of woods that'd produce a rich sound. I was surprised when the bus stopped at our hotel.

"You want to grab some food?"

I looked at him and managed to nod.

Marc consulted his cell phone.

"I found a good Mongolian Barbeque place," he said. "Would you like to join me for dinner?"

For the first time, I actually went out into a city we were touring. The place had a beautiful riverfront and more trees in the downtown area than I'd seen in any urban area. Busses were free downtown, but we opted to walk instead.

The restaurant was a pleasant surprise with local salmon and lots of fresh vegetables. Marc mixed a sauce for me. Dinner was the best I'd had since Mama passed.

He walked me back to my hotel room, then said, "Goodnight."

Damn! I was just about to find out if that rhythm man's stamina was as good as his beats.

That repeated for the next two weeks. The other two backup singers were teasing me that I had a boyfriend. I knew he wasn't married. I was wondering if Marc wasn't interested—or worse, gay.

Every day ended the same. We'd have a wonderful time exploring our host city and he'd return me to my hotel room. At first, I felt lightheaded. Then I realized, with an odd joy, this was dating. This was what Mama would have wanted me to do.

I was pulling out all the stops like a church organist at a revival. I normally wear demure clothing offstage because I'm a buxom sister and I get tired of the whistles and remarks men make in passing. Mama taught me if I put myself on display, I should expect remarks and sometimes worse. I picked out clothes in the colors Marc liked: rich jewel tones and classic black. I felt like a candle every time he smiled and told me I was beautiful.

Marc was making me crazy. Every night, I was playing with my poodle, waking up with sticky fingers and needing an ice cold shower to start my day. No loving from him was worse than bad loving from the rest of the band.

What was on his mind other than being in my company? He had a kind spot for every beggar and street busker we passed. Did he just see me as another project, a fallen sister who needed someone to give her respect?

"Congratulations," the road manager greeted us on the bus in the morning after a particularly grueling show that ran three encores. "The album's just hit number one on Billboard!"

Marc and I were the only ones awake to cheer and we did it quietly. I was sucking on a cough drop since I barely had a voice left after singing my heart out.

"We should celebrate," Marc said, flipping out his cell phone and Googling the next city for restaurants. The road manager got off the bus and headed for the RV, where the bigwigs rode.

I had something else in mind. By the time we'd pulled in to our hotel, I was ready. I told Marc to meet me at my room in an hour and we'd party.

In the meantime, I took a long bubble bath, and then slid into a silky nightie I'd bought at a place where women had no secrets. I met him at the door.

"Forget the restaurant," I kissed him on the mouth and dragged him into my room by his shirt front. "We're eating in."

"Get dressed, Roxannah, we're going out," Marc guided me back into my room, handling me carefully to avoid intimacy.

I stared at him for a moment, then I slammed the door in his face. I was so angry and embarrassed I wanted to cry, but the part of me that learned to keep going out on stage nightly despite my shame picked myself up and got dressed. I put on my highest white necked blouse and a floor-length black skirt. That man wasn't getting a peek.

"Classy," Marc smiled when I met him out in the hall where he'd found a seat. If looks could kill, he'd have busted out in flames in front of him. But the truth was, I realized as we walked to a fine restaurant, I was angry at myself for acting like the 'ho the church ladies proclaimed me to be.

I'd never seen a place so beautiful as that restaurant. A chandelier near as tall as me graced the entry. The booths were mahogany, leather, and private. Our table was candlelit like all the rest with a single red rose in a silver vase sitting at my place.

"It's beautiful," my voice was thick with tears. He'd chosen all of this carefully for me, for us.

I practically floated back to the hotel room on his arm. When I kissed him in thanks, there was nothing but my heart in it.

But that one kiss led to another.

No, I'm not going to tell you what happened in that room. I'm taking the advice of the lovely Sippie Wallace and sealing my smiling lips.

We emerged from my room to see half the band applauding. I nearly went inside, but I knew the teasing was inevitable. We shared a drink with the crew who were still celebrating our hit.

The party continued as we loaded up. We'd toasted everyone, including the roadies and the bus driver. The guitarist stood with his glass raised for the final tribute:

God Bless our singer
He's such a rose
When he's not snorting
Our profits up his nose!

The road manager came onboard. His grim expression stopped us, our glasses hoisted in front of our faces, breath held.

"The singer partied a bit too hearty. We found him this morning

144 | TOO MUCH BOOGIE

hanging. The coroner believes it was an accident—called it 'erotic asphyxiation.' The tour's cancelled. The bus'll take you back to Nashville."

Dead? I gripped Marc's hand in sick horror. Behind me, I heard a high keening. The guitarist, who'd known him since grade school, threw up. We scarcely spoke on that long ride home.

Fame's fickle. The singer went down in history, dying like he did at the first blush of his celebrity. Most musical analysts believe that had he lived, he'd be just another name among the One Hit Wonders. The band went back to Nashville and the life of scrabbling for session work.

Marc and I landed on our feet. We got married and went back to the fancy music school where he'd been recruited. Seems the band was high on sex appeal, but short on rhythm and the PR folks brought a percussion genius in to fix the situation. I'd agree. Of all the musicians I know, the drummer is the heartbeat of the band and Marc sure stole my heart.

I've gotten an education and I'm teaching high school chorus now. I never went back home. Someday, my daughter will learn she's adopted and she can make a choice to find me. I can hold my head up when we meet. The rest of that congregation doesn't mean a thing.

HOLE
REMITTANCE GIRL

*"The highest mountain can't be raced
It's something you must slowly climb."*

One Hour Mama – Ida Cox (1930)

THE ROOM was chilly and beige. It smelled faintly of stale cigarette smoke and carpet shampoo. Beyond the open curtains the streetlamps splayed in the cold winter air. From her place in the nondescript beige armchair, Emma thought the man on the bed looked vulnerable. Lit by the gloom of the bedside lamps, Sean lay with his back propped against the padded headboard, lanky legs stretched out in front of him. His shoes and socks were off, and his jeans were unbuttoned, the fly splayed open to his purpose. His fist stroked the pale column of his erect cock.

"Is this all you want?" His words were hesitant, breath heavy.

A lie of a nod and a tight smile: of course it wasn't all she wanted. What she wanted was to dispense with her panties, climb onto the bed and sink down onto his cock. But that wasn't going to happen. That she wouldn't allow herself and she had told him so.

"Are you sure?" Sean's handmade slick sounds as it moved over his oiled erection.

Outside, evening traffic noise seeped through the closed windows. Somewhere in the distance someone was breaking glass.

"Yes. I'm sure. Just what we agreed on. Okay?"

He stopped, fingers cupping the engorged head. His thumb brushed the blunted tip. "I thought maybe you'd change your mind. You know, when you got here. Once we actually met."

She'd worried about the same thing. She'd watched many, many men do this, witnessed many couples fuck in settings just like this one, but never with a friend. Never someone she felt any affection for. Now, there in that purgatory of a room, she wondered if she'd made a mistake.

"Don't be hurt, Sean. I told you it would be like this. I can't help the way I am."

"I know. I just thought..."

She smiled again—it took more of an effort this time—and shook her head. "Please, just come for me. That's all."

His throat was dry as he swallowed. She heard the effort of it above the ambient noise of the room. He glanced down at his crotch and began to masturbate again, not with much enthusiasm.

"Talk to me, then. It feels sterile with you just sitting there."

Her mouth crooked. This time it was effortless. "But you're hard anyway, aren't you?"

"My dick is stupid. But I'm not. Talk to me. Please."

She knew what he wanted, the things that got him off. She'd typed them often enough. But saying it aloud—that was harder. Nonetheless, she owed him that much. Closing her eyes, she took a deep breath and then began.

"You're such a slut, Sean. Such a filthy, dirty slut. Stroking your cock in some shabby, anonymous hotel room for a woman you've never met in your life."

He let out a jagged whisper of a breath. It ended in a little whine. His hand began to move again, encircled thumb and fingers tightening, pulling up and down on the skin the shaft.

"You're hard. So fucking hard," she let her tone drop, "and you just can't help yourself, can you? So filthy."

A groan wormed up from somewhere deep in his throat, the slick sounds grew louder, faster.

"That's it. Just like that. You love it don't you? Showing me just what a piece of cunt toy you are? All you want to do is come. But don't you dare do it without my permission." She injected a level of menace into the last of her words. "Don't you dare."

"Please, don't!" he stammered.

His eyes slid closed as his fist worked harder.

She felt better now that his eyes were shut. She pushed herself out of the chair. "Don't? Don't what?" Her voice descended to an almost-whisper as she approached the bed. "Look at you. Degenerate. That's what you are. And you can't help yourself, can you?"

"No." The word was strangled by arousal.

The imagery didn't turn her on. She'd never been all that interested in dominating men. But his reaction to her words, the lust they invoked, tightened her chest, made her belly flutter.

"Fuck, I should tie you to the bed, pillows piled under your hips until your shameless ass is as high as I want it. And then fuck you till you scream."

Sean let out a choked groan. He was pumping furiously now. Pearls of pre-cum teared from the tip. The droplets landed, with each stroke, onto his bare white stomach, catching and glistening in the darker hairs that ran up to his navel.

When she reached the bed, she bent over, leaning on her hands as she brought her mouth closer to his ear. "I'd use you like a hole," she growled. "Like the slutty, wanton little cunt you are."

"God. Fuck me. Please."

There it was. Need, desire so strong it burst onto the stillness of the room, tainting the air with an ache. It hurt. It hurt deliciously to stand so close, to see the beads of sweat that birthed and glinted along the line of his sternum. To smell the faded scent of morning soap rise off his skin, and the sweetness of the oil he'd used on his cock, and the richer musk of his crotch. The tip of her tongue prickled with want. Her cunt felt swollen, sticky. Afterwards, alone, she'd take care of it.

"Fuck you? Are you mad? I wouldn't fucking touch you. I wouldn't sully my skin with you. I'd use a dildo."

"No," he whimpered. "No. Ride me. I want you on me, around me."

"Never. I don't fuck trash like you."

His eyes flew open and he turned his head towards her. "Then kiss me. Kiss me."

Something in his voice had changed. He'd broken the spell. He'd cheated. A scythe-like blade of ice pushed into her gut. She pulled back.

"No."

"Yes! Please!"

His hand shot out, fingers surrounding one of her wrists. It was the hand he'd used to stroke his cock, slick with oil and hot with friction. She tugged against the grip that held, then slipped, then held again, suddenly terrified.

"Stop it. Let go, Sean."

"Just a kiss. Just one." He was on his knees, free hand curling around the back of her neck to pull her towards him. A desperate uncontrolled urgency in the embrace.

"No. Don't...don't spoil this," she said more softly, making her voice gentle, tamping down her own panic. Her gaze held his and she furrowed her brow. "Don't ruin everything."

The hold on her neck eased and he freed her wrist, leaving the smear of oil and heat behind. "Jesus. I'm sorry."

She knew better than to draw away just then. Instead she sat down on the side of the bed, smoothing her skirt over her thighs. "I'm sorry, too. It's not your fault. I shouldn't have asked you to do this."

"No. I said I could do it. I said I wanted to. It's my fault."

The fingers, still resting lightly on her neck, moved. His thumb caressed the tendon there. The sensation, no matter how sweet, how well meaning, was too much. Too tender. Too intimate. It was breaking her heart.

She shook her head and smiled at the wall. Tears pricked at her eyes. "Don't apologize. It's fine." Carefully pulling his hand off her neck, she laid it on the bed and patted it. "I should go."

"Don't. I can do this. I said I could, and I can. Do you still want me to?"

"I'm not sure."

"Please. We'll start again."

It had already gone too far, too wrong. Part of her wanted to get out of that fucking hotel room as quick as she could and drink herself into enough of a stupor to fall asleep. But the other part—the better part, she thought—didn't want to hurt him.

"Alright." She gave him a quick smile and got to her feet.

"Can't you just sit here, a little closer? It helps."

She thought for a moment, feeling blindly for her limitations, and then sat back down. "Okay, but don't touch me. Can you do that?"

Sean cocked his head. "Yes. I guess. I don't understand why not. I wouldn't force you, you know. I'd never do that."

"I know. Just...please don't touch me. Touch yourself."

He worried his lip. "Okay. But look at me. Talk to me."

"What do you want me to say? Do you want me to talk the way we do online?"

Shifting back on the bed, settling back against the headboard, he exhaled. "No, just...just tell me what you want."

"I want to watch you feel pleasure."

A smile bent the edge of his mouth; his hand returned to his cock. It was semi-erect and gave a little bob as he touched it. "What else?"

"I want to listen as the arousal begins to take you over."

He began to stroke again, slowly, deliberately. It only took three or four to regain his erection. He glanced from her, down to his groin, and then back again. "What else?" he repeated.

"I want to see you come."

"Why?"

"Because it's proof. Proof of pleasure."

He was looking into her eyes now, fist moving faster. Little twitches tugged at the muscles of his jaw. "Know what I want?"

"Not really. Tell me."

"I want to know what you taste like. Whether it's like I imagined."

She smiled. "What else?"

"I want..." His breath came quicker now, lips parted between his words. "To feel your lips around my cock. The heat, the pressure of them."

"My mouth? Wet? Tight?"

"Yes. Sucking. With my fingers in your hair."

Her nipples stung as they stiffened. She fought not to break eye contact with him, but his gaze was starving her of oxygen. "What else?"

"Then to kiss you. And taste my cock on your mouth."

"Not come in it?"

"No," he rasped. "No...against you. On your skin."

The ache in her cunt turned to sharp needles as the muscles fluttered. A single hot surge of wetness soaked her panties. "Where?"

Sean squeezed his cock, pumping it steadily. "Your skin."

"But where?"

"Your breasts...belly...thighs...I'd paint you."

"Why?"

"Because..."

"Because why?"

"I'm close. Very close." His jaw trembled as he spoke. The sinews on his throat stood out against his skin.

"I know. Come for me."

Sean took one enormous breath and held it. His eyes turned sightless as the orgasm overloaded his synapses. She glanced down. A pale stream of come spattered his stomach, and then another, then another.

The familiar surge of sharp-edged elation swept over her body, setting her skin aflame, making her heart pound against her ribcage. Then, after a few moments, she looked up and smiled.

"Well, that worked," he muttered.

"Yes, it did. Thank you."

"Oh, no. Thank you." He gave a little chuckle. "So, would it kill you to kiss me now?"

She stood up. The chemicals made it impossible for her to stop smiling. They fizzled in her veins like soda, her pulse almost deafening in her ears. She picked up her purse, avoiding his gaze.

"Yes, it would."
She left the room, shutting the door quietly behind her.

ONCE YOU GO BLACK
AMANDA FOX

"Nobody can thrill me like my baby can. He's a special man.
He's my king size papa. Never was nothin' like him since the day the world began."

King Size Papa — Julia Lee (1948)

MY HUSBAND says he knows I like black men. Says he doesn't care if I do. Says he's secure enough in his own masculinity not to be bothered by it. Says besides, he's happy being white (like he could ever change that). Says that nothing or no one could ever break us apart. Says that sexual attraction is best kept a controlled feeling, that no matter what, people always have a choice about what they do or don't do anyway. Says I should know that love is something that comes from a commitment to share the bad things in life—the fights, the in-laws, the unfairness of it all, the crap—not from the sex. Not from sharing really great, filthy, dirty whips and anal probes, cry out for more, wanna spread your legs so far apart they just might snap off or jack up your cock until it hits the moon—kind of sex.

I say, "Yeah, right."

"So do you want to be with one?"

"One what? What are you talking about?"

"A black guy?"

"Where the hell did that come from?"

"Didn't you say the other day that you thought Denzel Washington was sexy, even with his belly?"

"So what? How does that translate into wanting to sleep with a black man?"

"Well, I know you like them."

"Says who? You?"

"I saw you dancing with Owen at the Christmas party last year. Lucky I was there, or you might've done the nasty on the dance floor."

"What's gotten into you? I don't even know what you're talking about."

"What about Will, the UPS guy? I know you like him. You make it so obvious the way you always bend forward to sign that little computer thingamajig of his."

"Just drop it, OK, Jeff?"

"Whatever you say, Joanne. Whatever you say."

THE DAY started out pretty much normal except for the pervert masturbating on the street corner. It was early one fall morning, orange and red leaves littered the gutters, and squirrels with half-chewed tails were busy foraging for a winter's meal. I'd just dropped the kids off at school and was heading uptown to work—stopped at a red light— when I heard shrieks coming from across the street. And that's when everyone started pointing, when everyone began freaking out, when my brain finally kicked into gear for the day (no thanks to the large double-double I'd already consumed), and when life as I knew it, took a turn for the better. I will briefly outline for you how this all came about:

1. I heard the screams and wondered what the hell was going on.
2. I then followed the direction of the emphatic points of some pedestrians...
3. To a man in a windbreaker and deck shoes with his pants down around his ankles, his swollen, pink penis sticking straight out toward a row of cedars like a giant finger giving directions.
4. I watched as a mob of mothers from the school community swarmed the man, pushed him to the ground, and threw things like jackets, blankets and other sorts of domestic paraphernalia on top of his exposed groin.
5. Dumbfounded, I sat in traffic (which was now at a complete standstill) and contemplated yanking my kids from school for the day, or for the rest of their lives, hoping to prevent them from ever coming into contact with such an unstable individual.
6. When forced up into a neighbor's driveway to let two cop cars and an ambulance pass, I silently applauded the efficiency of my fair city's ancillary services.
7. With the whole neighborhood now out on the street, I watched as the man was taken into custody—his belt buckle still hanging open and loose around his waist, his hat and sunglasses now

stripped from his head, for the purpose, I supposed, of revealing his identity to the masses.

8. Once the commotion had died down, I decided that the school area wasn't likely to be bombarded by any more sexual deviants that day, or even that week or month, and I drove onward to my destination.

9. Moving up Wilmington Avenue, I seriously wondered what sort of person would whack off in front of a bunch of third graders and their mothers, finally coming to the conclusion that sexual urges can make an individual do things that are completely and utterly insane.

10. And, acknowledging that some people do things that are a little more insane and socially unacceptable than others, in that moment, it occurred to me that I too was heading down a slippery slope of concupiscent ruination.

TYRONE was my first, and let me add, an unsolicited conquest. He was a big man with rough hands and a thick cock. Trucker or city worker or some shit like that. The main reason we hooked up was because he made it so easy. Arguably, I think if it'd been any harder, I probably wouldn't have done it. But he made it simple indeed—way too simple—and we did it, after which his sexual equipment and the fact that he was of the darker persuasion, kept me going back for more, both to him and others like him.

We met at the supermarket. Tyrone was picking up some steaks for a barbeque, and I was having a roast cut.

"Good meat here, huh?" I turned and his eyes shot straight to my chest. "Not bad, but I think D'Lorenzo's is better."

"Never been there. Is it close?"

"You have to go uptown a bit, but it's definitely worth the drive."

"Yeah, some things are worth the hassle, you know." He was eyeing my wedding band. "You married?"

"Yup."

"Happily?"

"Yup."

"Super happily?" Obviously, Tyrone was *not* an academic.

"I guess so." Wrong answer on my part, but too late—I'd opened the door to further questioning.

"What's your name?"

"Who's asking?"

"Tyrone."

"Is that you?"

He leaned in close enough for me to smell his sweet breath. "It's all me and then some."

My roast was ready, so I put it in the cart and started walking away. When I felt his gaze burning through my jeans from behind, I couldn't resist. "My name's Joanne," I said, turning to flutter a kittenish farewell.

"Hey, Joanne. I come here every Friday around this time, right after work."

"Maybe I'll see you later then...Tyrone."

NEXT came Steve and he was a quickie, only a blowjob but a good one. His penis wasn't that large but when it was hard, it was hard as a rock, and he had lots of cum to shoot—so much that it was actually like swallowing a freakin' protein smoothie.

I met him at the grocery store as well, but in the produce aisle, and like with Tyrone, it was Steve who initiated things. "Excuse me, miss." Steve was so polite. "Do you know the difference between parsley and cilantro? My girlfriend has sent me out to get something to make salsa, but I can't remember what she said and it all looks the same to me." At that point, I didn't think Steve would be into sex with a complete stranger. He seemed too nice, and besides, he'd made mention of a "girlfriend" already.

"Cilantro smells better. Probably what you want," I said, staring at his big brown eyes and perfect smile. He was so beautiful that I could've kissed him right there on the spot.

"What I want? Oh, I don't think you know what I want!" he whispered, definitely not the saint I'd pegged him to be.

And thanks to Tyrone, I knew how the game worked. "I'll bet I can guess."

His eyes swept over the contours of my mouth, and he pressed at his own lips with his thumb, like my words had created a flesh wound. "Go ahead." Was it really that easy?

"OK." I picked up a cucumber and slid it up and down in my hand, cupping over the end with my palm and plucking at the saran wrap covering with my fingers. "Would you like *that*?" I asked seductively.

Steve looked around to see if anyone was watching, and then nodded his head slowly, his eyes twinkling under the fluorescent lights of the store. "Meet me out front in five minutes."

"Do you have a car?"

"It's a black SUV. I'll pick you up."

It *was* that simple, and after Steve I speculated that I could get more black cock than one white woman could ever dream of having.

And I did—lots. But then I got tired: tired of tramping around, tired of getting fucked and left, tired of sucking guys off and going home to my husband without a clue as to where my next hit was coming from, particularly tired of not having one of these spectacular human specimens all to myself. And that's the day that I saw the pervert at the school, and also the day that my life took on a whole new focus.

SOULEY was shy and different from the rest. Still black of course, but different—I knew it the minute I saw him. For one thing, he didn't seem interested in me for the sex, nor did it seem like he even cared that I was a female. After everything I'd done, I counted that as a good thing. And wouldn't you know, we met at the library of all places—at the automated checkout machine. He was having trouble with the new technology and I saw him floundering. When I saw how very round and pliable his ass appeared in his jeans, I happily moved in to offer my assistance. Peering over his shoulder, I said, "You have to move the books slowly under the scanner or it won't recognize the barcode."

"Oh." He didn't even bother to look back. Then, when my suggestion worked, he sheepishly turned and smiled. "Thanks."

"No problem," I replied, happy to get a peek at his intensely dark eyes. When he'd finished and was packing up to leave, I made another attempt to connect. "I see that you have Dean Koontz's new book."

"Uh huh."

"Not as good as Michael Crichton, though. Have you read his stuff?" I knew he must've, but I was hoping the question would get him to say more than one word, get him to open up to me *and* to the advances I was sure to make. Undeniably, he was sexy as hell—a little disheveled, a little geeky, but sexy nonetheless.

And it worked. "Yes, the man was a genius. Too bad he died. *Rising Sun* is one of my favorites."

"Agreed. How about Dan Brown?"

"Of course. All of his."

"I'll bet you haven't read *Casanegra* by Blair Underwood." He didn't really look like the type to read raunchy, mystery novels. He couldn't even button his shirt properly or tie his shoes, let alone be interested in a good fuck, fiction or otherwise.

"Not bad, but a little full of itself—the book, I mean. Does that make any sense?"

"No. Yes. Well, I sort of get what you're saying. But I'm impressed. You must read a lot."

"Why, because I've read a book by Blair Underwood?"

"Yeah."

And just as he was starting to let his guard down, he said, "I guess I'd better get home. My puppy will be waiting for me." No mention of a woman. "It was nice talking to you," he mumbled, turning to walk away.

"Hey wait," I called after him. "Have you heard about the new book club that is starting up next month? Mystery novel's only, I hear."

"No, I haven't. Are you going?" His eyes lit up.

"Sure." I needed to see him again because, unlike lots of other men I'd met, he had both a penis *and* a brain. "Actually, I'm running it." It was a lie. In fact, there was no book club—the words had just come flying out.

"Sounds good. I'll watch for the flyers. See you later." With that, he was gone.

SO I MADE a flyer—one flyer—and looked for my man of mismatched clothing at the library as often as I could. Two weeks later, around the same time as our first encounter, I saw him in the video section scanning the racks.

"Hey," was all I managed to say. He appeared delicious in soft corduroy pants and an old, cable-knit sweater.

When he clued in to who I was, he replied, "Hi. Good to see you again. I've been asking about that book club you mentioned and no one seems to know anything about it."

"Oh." I had hoped he'd forgotten. "Yeah, well, that didn't really work out. I didn't have the time, so they cancelled it."

"Is that right? It's too bad because you had me excited."

"Did I?" Was it a sign?

"Yes. I like talking about books. Reading is one of the great joys in my life."

"And dogs."

"You remembered?"

"Sure," I murmured, remembering everything from the shape of his ears to the breadth of his shoulders.

"Do you have a dog?" he asked hopefully.

"Actually I do." And I did, thank god.

"Maybe we could go walking together sometime. We could share our thoughts on some of the books we've read."

"That would be nice."

So later that week, we met up; one single black man and his Terrier pup, and one married white woman and her ten-year-old

Labrador retriever. As planned, we walked in the park and talked about books. We also talked about politics, religion, and life in general. It seemed we had lots in common. Near the end of the trail, and so out of the blue, Souley stopped. "How would you like to go out to dinner tomorrow night?" When he then reached over and touched my hand, I was elated, if not shocked.

"I would love that."

Supper was superb, our conversation continuing late into the evening. When it was finally time to go home, Souley walked me to my car and pecked me softly on the cheek. "I had a good time," he said, bashfully scuffing his shoes into the pavement.

"Me too," I replied, hoping someday to get my hands under his clothing.

TWO MONTHS and a half dozen more meetings later, the moment was upon us to be intimate, and I have to say, it was a heart-stopping experience. Until then, we hadn't so much as made out and the idea of fucking him was driving me crazy.

We'd rented a movie—*Jurassic Park*—and were cuddled up on the couch at his place. "I need you to do something for me," I said, unable to hold back my lasciviousness any longer.

"What's that?"

"I think you should show me your penis."

"Wow." He leaned back. "That's awkward."

"Sorry," I said, embarrassed.

"Don't be sorry. It's just that I wasn't expecting you to say something like that."

"I know, but nothing is happening between us and I'm dying..."

"Dying? Hmmm...Well, I really like you Joanne and I was trying to be a gentleman, but if you're *that* hot for me," he said sarcastically, "we could kiss." Interestingly enough, as he spoke, he was easing me down into the cushions and unbuttoning my shirt.

"Kiss me, please." Boldly unzipping the fly on my jeans, he then yanked down the cups of my bra and began suckling at my breasts with the fervor of a starving man.

"I've been waiting so long for you to do that," I whimpered, itching to get naked.

"You're hard up, aren't you?" He smiled. "Here, let's see if I can help." Two seconds later, his cock was out—all purple and wet—and he'd yanked off my pants. "Now show me that pretty, pink pussy of yours." Dr. Jekyll had made his transformation at last and I was thrilled.

Sliding my panties over and exposing my slick folds to his heady gaze, I commanded, "Put it in." And that was all it took. Souley then thrust into me, heaving and bucking like a man possessed.

NOW, to spare you the details of our long, drawn-out courtship (if you could even call it that), I will sum it up by saying that Souley and I saw each other quite regularly after that night of carnal nirvana, getting to know each other better and better as time passed. It's funny, after meeting Souley, I didn't need to look for other men because my mind was fixated on only one person—him.

Does having a black man make a difference? For me it does, but I'm not sure why. If you were wondering, I did leave Jeff, though l felt awful about it. I couldn't help what I really wanted or how I felt though and he graciously accepted the dissolution of our marriage by stating, "Well, Joanne. I can't say that I'm surprised." I can't say that I was surprised either. You know what they say. Once you go black...

GOODBYE BLUES
THOMAS S. ROCHE

"Graveyard ain't nothin', Lord, but a great lonesome place
You can lay flat on your back, little woman, and let the sun shine in your face."

T.B. Blues — Willie Jackson (1928)

IF I HADN'T been keeping such a close watch, nothing worse woulda happened than a sunburn, probably. It's not like she could have got a concussion hitting her head on the tomato furrows. But that's not how you feel when she goes down; you feel it's the end of the world, and you *run*.

That's what I did, when, scrubbing plum sauce from white Ikea plates, I saw from the high kitchen window that that dumbass yellow sun had had disappeared. I made the back porch in about three seconds flat and was on her faster than shit on a scientist at the monkey-house.

She'd gone down easy, yellow sun hat fluttering to the ground and rolling maybe half a body-length away before coming to rest, face down, over fresh-turned earth. She'd gone down easy, her face in soft soil, one tattooed arm stretched out among the tomato plants, one garden-gloved hand limply clutching at a weed. She'd gone down easy, flouncy hippy skirt pulling up as she fell, blowing in the wind, and she wasn't wearing shit underneath; her hoo-hah saluted the sun, mounting brightly up behind Mount Tamalpais. I didn't pull it down; the neighbors could look; scoundrels. Fuck 'em.

I scooped her up, one arm under her limply-bent knees, the other in the small of her back, working up to her shoulders as I lifted her. I wasn't supposed to move her, probably, but fuck that; I'll be damned if I'd leave Claire sprawled out there in the sun while I called 911. It was probably just a fainting spell. She came awake as I carried her, looking up at my face, uncomprehending.

"Hi," I said.

"I fainted."

"No shit. You okay?"

"I don't know."

I brought her inside and laid her gently on the immaculate white couch.

"I think I'm all right," she said, propping herself up.

"Just lie still," I said. "I'll get you some water."

She blinked after me emptily, breathing shallow. I brought her the water, double-filtered, in a chipped cup that said Mexico and showed Speedy Gonzalez firing up a fat, phallic reefer.

I helped her sip.

"You probably shouldn't have been gardening."

She swallowed.

"Whatever," she said. "Fuck that." She drank more.

"The sun," I said.

"That wouldn't make me faint."

"All right. But you shouldn't have exerted yourself."

"Stop being my mom."

I looked at her viciously, furiously.

"Your mom's dead," I told her. "Of *this*."

She sat up, finished the water like a shot of tequila.

"You're a prick when you wanna be," she said.

"I'm just worried," I said.

"Yeah? Well, stop."

I nodded. "All right. How are you feeling?"

"Like resting."

"Can I hold you?"

"God, you are such a SNAGgy wuss."

I scowled. "You're *welcome*," I said.

She beamed brightly, held out her hands in an inviting Y. She looked grim, tired, gorgeous. Her yellow halter top didn't do much to shroud her breasts, particularly the parts that peaked with the morning cold. It was barely ten o'clock, Marin fog dreaming in from Tennessee Cove, smacking full-force into mist from Bolinas Bay. Her flesh had goosebumped. Her teeth started chattering.

"This isn't L.A.," I said. "You should wear more."

"I like the sun," she said. "I'll take it when I can."

I frowned.

"Well, that's not now."

She shivered all over. I grabbed her, pulled her close, laid on top of her. She chattered; she trembled; she shivered.

"You all right?" I asked her.

She answered with an impatient grunt; she let me hold her, her smell good and earthy in my nostrils.

"Sometimes I wish I'd just fucking die already."

"Please don't," I said. "Who would grow me tomatoes?"

"Early girls," she said, teeth chattering.

"Huh?" I asked.

"Early girls," she told me. "They're ready. I was gonna pick 'em."

"I'll go get them."

"Uh-uh," she said, teeth tap-dancing violently. "I want to pick them."

"Let me get you a quilt."

"I'm fine," she chattered, not letting go of me. "Just...here. Lay on top of me."

"You're bones," I said.

She snapped, "Quit worrying." She was chattering violently, trying to reposition herself and drag me onto the couch. "Fine, lay under me."

"That defeats the purpose," I protested, but it felt too fucking good. She half-dragged, half-guided, all-seduced me onto the couch, my big broad body stretched out under her. She lay atop me, cuddling up and shivering.

"Here," I said. I reached up high with a big monkey arm and yanked my black leather jacket off the hat tree near the couch. I pulled it over her shoulders. She shivered and drew a deep breath.

"It smells like you," she said.

"Yeah?" I asked patronizingly.

"Why does it smell like you?"

I cocked my head.

"Seems obvious," I answered.

"No," she said. "I mean, why can I smell it? My sense of smell is all fucked up, usually. But I can smell your jacket."

"Well," I said. "It's probably time for a trip to the dry cleaners."

"Uh-uh." She grabbed my jacket and pulled it close around her shoulders, dipping her nose down to huff it deep. "Not a chance. It smells—" She huffed and huffed and huffed, and smiled and cuddled up against my chest, leather wrapped around her bare shoulders. "It smells like you."

"And that's good?"

"It's fucking incredible."

She started kissing my neck. Her hand grazed down my front.

"You okay to do this?" I asked.

"Shhhh," she purred in my ear. "I just fainted. No big deal." She started working at my belt buckle with one hand, undoing her halter with the other. She got her teacup-breasts free and the zipper of my jeans down at about the same moment. She reached in and groped after me, kissing her way down my chest, across the sweat-damp black fabric and Lou Reed's cracked bootleg iron-on mullet, circa *Magic and Loss*: older, yeah, and far from wiser if his hair was any indication. She pulled my shirt up.

"Hey," I told her. "Don't forget what they said."

"About what?"

"*Radiation*," I reminded her.

She sighed.

"Oh. That." She pouted. "Well...want a radioactive handjob?"

She took my cock out. I tipped my head back and closed my eyes. I was soft. So very soft. I breathed deep, thought of happier times: Amanda cocked jauntily on a Girl Bike 500, sheathed in leather, pulling a wheelie. I popped a boner. She started stroking.

"You're sure you want to do this?"

"Christ," she growled. "Are you a girl, or what?"

"All right," I said. "It feels good."

"It better," she said. "It's all the doctor will allow."

"Except with condoms."

She made a disgusted noise.

"Yeah, right," she said. "Shut up and spooge, you pervert."

"I guess chemotherapy doesn't improve your pillow talk?"

She bit my nipple, jerked my cock, breathed softly.

Thinking about the first time we kissed, I stayed hard; twenty-three. A girl's twenty-three, you ask her out, you don't think you're going to watch her croak, or do you? Maybe sometimes. Maybe never. I stayed hard by remembering how she'd looked to me that first time she'd wriggled on top of me, Dickies shirt at half-mast, ample tits spilling out. She had a half a C-cup left.

I kept my boner till I heard her snoring softly. She cuddled tight against my body. Her hand had gone limp. I went soft.

"Did you come?" she asked me, maybe ten minutes later.

I kissed her hair; I smelled the sharp hint of chemicals.

"Yeah," I said. "I blew my load everywhere. It was great."

She murmured happily and went back to sleep.

I WAS too hopped up to sleep, so after a half-hour, maybe less, I extricated myself. I zipped up and buckled and tied her halter back on her, no easy task to perform on a sleeping girl. I covered her with a quilt. I reached under and felt the flesh of her belly: still goosebumping. I put on another quilt. Under her skirt she wasn't wearing much— actually nothing, even her hair there had fallen out— so I added a third one. I looked at her sleeping face for a while, watching her breathe, wondering how many more times such a thing would exist to be seen. She stirred under quilts.

"What is this," she asked without opening her eyes. "*The Premature Burial*?"

"How do you feel?" I asked her.

"Tired," she said, again without opening her eyes.

"You want anything?"

"Jacket," she said petulantly, eyes still closed.

"My jacket?"

She nodded.

"All right." I took it back off the hat tree and draped it over her chest. She clutched it to her, never opening her eyes, and huffed.

"Anything else?" I asked.

"Music," she whined, juvenile-voiced, distant, speech slurred.

"What kind?" I asked.

She snored.

I found her MP3 player. It had been paused on a playlist: Bessie Smith, John Lee Hooker, Blue Lu Barker, Howlin' Wolf, Sonny Boy Williamson, Big Mama Thornton.

I plugged the output into the stereo and played it just loud enough to wake her. It didn't.

I fixed up a Scotch. I sat across from the couch, watching her sleep, and drank it neat, sip by sip.

Amanda snored softly.

IT WAS maybe two hours later that my cell phone buzzed against my thigh. I'm not sure if I was dozing or just sitting there with half-shut eyes listening to Bessie Smith. But I had my hand in my pocket and the cell phone out and was awake and said, "Hello" before the doc said my name, so I must have been at least half-awake.

"Sorry to call you here. I tried your home number, but I didn't get anyone."

"Oh," I said. "Yeah," I said. "I turn it off when she's sleeping. I forgot to turn it back on this morning."

"Is she sleeping now?"

"Yes," I said. "Should I wake her?"

"Well, I think you're gonna need to. We got the test results back."

"All right," I said. "And?"

"It's not great news. Amanda should probably come in as soon as possible."

"All right," I said.

"What is it, twelve-thirty? I have a three o'clock. Would that work for you?"

I looked at Amanda, sleeping with my leather jacket half-covering her face.

"That'd be fine," I said. "This is pretty bad news."

"Yeah. It's not great," said the doc. "I'm really sorry."

"See you at three."

I rang off.

AMANDA STIRRED.

"Who was that?"

"Dr. Samara," I told her. "She says you should come in today."

"Oh, for fuck's sake," grumbled Amanda. Her eyes opened; she yawned.

"I made a three o'clock appointment."

"Good," she said. She stretched under my jacket, arched her back. She threw my jacket on the floor. "You go."

I knelt down next to her and sighed. Behind me, Howlin' Wolf barked and blew. She reached out, grabbed me. She pulled me half on top of her, grabbed my hand and put it under the covers. Her flesh was hot; she was burning up.

"Why am I horny?" she asked playfully.

"The usual reasons," I said.

"No, I mean it. I'm dying. Why am I *horny*?"

"You're not dying," I said.

"How stupid do you think I am?" she asked. "Don't patronize me. Christ, why am I horny?" She groped after me, pulled me down, sniffed my face. "It's you, you son of a bitch! You've been drinking Scotch. What is it, nine in the morning?"

"Twelve-thirty."

"Still. You know what that does to me." She breathed deep, sighing softly. "It's all fucked up. I couldn't smell anything this time today. Now everything I smell turns me on."

"Don't look at me," I said.

She snapped her fingers. "Fucking Celexa."

"What?"

"I quit Celexa, remember? The chemo and the liver toxicity. Anti-depressants kill my sex drive. That's why I'm horny. It's my sex drive coming back." She pulled me down and started kissing me. "Ironic, isn't it?"

"Not at all," I said.

With a strong grasp, she molded my hand to her breast. Her nipple was erect.

"Will you fuck me?"

I sighed. "Amanda, I'm not sure that's a good idea."

All of a sudden she had the playful look of a sixteen-year-old slut trying to talk her Mormon boyfriend into giving it up. She pulled hard on me.

"Come on. Please? If I have to go back, at least...fuck me first, will you?"

"I don't know if I can," I said. My voice trembled a little.

Her lips grazed my ear. "Oh...you can," she purred. "I'll *make* you." She pressed her hand flat against my crotch. I started getting hard.

"Right here?"

"No, douchebag. In bed. What kind of girl do you think I am?"

"All right," I said. I tucked my arm under her knees and her back and lifted her, quilts and all, into the air with only moderate difficulty. She was down to maybe ninety-five. It scared me.

Her arms went around my neck. She mewled softly against my ear, her breath cool and her words slightly slurred.

"You gonna carry me back to your cave? That's fucking hot." She crooned, "Promise you'll fuck me *good*, studmuffin?"

She was asleep before I set her down on the bed.

I PILED more quilts on her and fetched another Scotch, switched the music to the bedside speakers. It was on Albert King. She'd apparently added the whole of *Blues at Sunrise* to the playlist. Albert wailed on as I sat there on the edge of the bed watching Amanda sleep.

"You promised," I think she murmured, then, whether in sleep or half-sleep I couldn't quite tell.

I did, I guessed. It wouldn't do to disappoint her.

WORKING as gently as I possibly could, I edged her over to one side of the bed and peeled the covers back. The sheets were clean; she liked them crisp, so I changed them every morning, since it encouraged her to nap. I untied her halter at her neck and eased my hand beneath her back and unfastened it there. I took the halter away. She weighed almost nothing. Without letting her come out from beneath the quilts, I slid her thin cotton skirt down her legs. She stretched, naked and beautiful, underneath her Danish great-grandmother's handiwork, her genitals shorn by chemotherapy. I touched them gently. She was swollen but dry.

Albert crooned "For the Love of a Woman."

Moving very slowly so as not to wake her, I worked her over onto the fresh, clean white sheets, tucked her slim naked legs under the flap. I covered her over and repositioned the quilts. I worked with meticulous, tortured grace.

Then I undressed.

My body was cool beneath the quilts and sheets, against her body. I thought for sure she'd startle awake as I embraced her. But, no; she slumbered on, snoring softly. "Blues at Sunrise" played as I stretched out on top of her.

I nuzzled her sleeping lips open with my own, and kissed her deeply.

At first her tongue was limp against mine. Her mouth was dry and tasted sour. She lay there, dead but for shallow breathing, limbs motionless beneath my weight. I touched her nipples, thumbed them. They stiffened, under the stimulation or the cold I'll never know. I tipped her head to the side and kissed her throat, biting gently, gnawing. I turned her shoulders to the side so I could nibble at the back of her neck and breathe on her ear. She fucking *loved* that. Not much response. I returned her to her back and let my weight bear her down.

"I'll Play the Blues for You."

I went under the covers, turned my body, planted my knees wide on either side of her head.

I brought my mouth to her sex.

This, of course, was strictly forbidden; radiation, you understand. Toxicity. All sorts of shit. Amanda was twice-distilled death, a beaker full of Dr. Doom's experiments, waiting to be gulped to turn me into a fucking superhero, supervillain—either or both depending on how you reckoned such things.

I pressed my mouth to her cunt. My tongue invaded her, feeling the snug, dry tightness of a sex untended. I planted my lips on her clit and suckled gently. It's always a trick in that position, because with Amanda, as with many, the up-stroke's the thing; a little suction goes a long way, and pressing up with the rough of the tongue goes a whole lot longer. But with practice, one can master it.

I guess I'd mastered it; she came alive.

My cock was stiff and in her mouth before her hips began to work. She whimpered loudly, writhing under me, moaning. For the weeks she'd languished, weak and weary, this was payback. She grasped my cock and took it deep. She didn't deep-throat, of course. I wouldn't have wanted her to. Can you imagine what that'd do to a stomach assaulted by chemo? But it didn't matter. She didn't care. I didn't care. Her mouth on my cock was all I wanted, that and my mouth on her cunt, slurping nuclear cunt-juice between long rhythmic tweaks on her irradiated clit. Guitar music wailed. Albert howled. Amanda started shuddering. She arched her back, worked her hips, pushed her cunt against me. Her spindly legs flailed, light as down, crossing and uncrossing and crisscrossing over me, her motions— uncoordinated. She kicked me repeatedly in the back of the head. She let go of my cock and reached down insistently, having to stretch something fierce to put her fingers, splayed, on the back of my head, and *push* by way of encouragement. Then she grabbed on for dear life and *rode* me. She begged, "Don't stop, don't stop, don't stop," her voice weak with chemo and reedy with doom. She threw her head back and seized my cock and gripped it so hard it fucking hurt, but I didn't care. I knew the sounds, the signs. She was coming.

I almost wept as she kissed my cock wetly, tongue all over, sighing.

"You taste good," she sighed happily, and fell asleep.

I extricated myself from her legs and stretched myself alongside her, listening to her even breathing. In her sleep, or maybe half-sleep, she cuddled up against me, holding me. The music had ended.

"Did you come?" she asked.

"Yeah," I told her. "I blew my load all over you."

"Liar," she breathed. "When's the doctor?"

"Three," I said.

"Early Girls," she slurred vaguely.

"Beg your pardon?"

"My tomatoes. Get my Early Girls."

"Later," I said.

"Don't forget."

She began snoring softly.

Her lips and cheeks and chin and nose were glazed with spittle and pre-come. My arm was tucked beneath her head. I didn't want to move it. I found her skirt just barely within reach. I used it to wipe her face dry. I was drizzling by then, cool and gloppy pre-come on my thigh, so I dabbed my soft cock as well.

I put my arms more tightly against her and looked at the clock: one-fifteen.

It always took a while to get Amanda ready nowadays; we should get started. God forbid we should be late to her funeral.

"Just another fifteen minutes," I said softly.

"What?"

"Twenty," I said. "Maybe twenty."

"What?"

"Twenty minutes," I said.

"Okay," she said happily. "Twenty minutes. Then we'll go."

An empty hiss issued from the bedside speakers.

Amanda snored softly.

EFFECTS OF MOONSHINE
DORLA MOOREHOUSE

"Keep on churnin', til the butter comes
Keep on pumpin', make the butter flow
Wipe off the paddle and churn some more."

Keep On Churnin' (Till the Butter Comes)
— Wynonie Harris (1952)

MY DANCE TEACHER, Ted, keeps bugging me to come out to Moonshine, the bar that proudly proclaims the biggest dance floor in town. "They have live blues bands on Fridays, and all of the best dancers show up. You should come out and join us, enjoy the music, explore some of the dances people do outside of the studio."

"I'm not interested in blues dance," I insist, every time he suggests I show up. "I dance tango, and only tango."

"It doesn't matter that you're not familiar with the dance itself to have a good time. You're a good follower, and will be able to pick up anything a leader throws at you. I can make sure to be your first partner, show you the ropes so you won't feel self-conscious. You'll have a great time."

"I don't think so. It's just not for me. Talk to me when a tango bar opens up, then we'll see."

But Ted remains undeterred. Every week, he tells me I should come out to the bar, and every week, I brush him off. I have better things to do than gyrate around the floor, some horny slob leading with his cock rather than his frame. And to add insult to injury, people dance to blues while wearing sneakers instead of heels. I dance in stilettos, with real technique and footwork. I'm a competitor and performer, not someone looking to gyrate drunkenly with strangers.

But one Friday, I don't have anything better to do. Somehow, I'm the only member of my social circle not included in anybody else's plans. I loathe the prospect of a Friday night in, so I check the movie listings—nothing I'm willing to pay for. I hate eating out by myself; I always feel pitiful and lonely if I'm not sharing a meal with someone. So I decide to head to the one place I know I'll have company: Moonshine. At least Ted will be there. I remind myself that I don't even have to dance if I don't feel like it. I'll be a newcomer in a big crowd. If I hang back, I can just sit there watching without anybody really noticing me.

The dance floor is packed when I arrive, even though it's still early. Ted wasn't lying; this is a big deal. And I can hear why: the band is amazing. Guitar, piano, trumpet, saxophone, drums, and a vocalist wailing out sorrow and syncopation better than anyone I've ever heard in my life. I grab a spot at the bar, order a vodka tonic, and scan the room for Ted's face. At first, all I can see is a mass of arms and legs, warm and glistening bodies spinning, hopping, slithering in time to the music. Finally, I see him sliding along the floor with someone else from the studio. We make eye contact, and I can tell by the way he twists his lips into a half-smile that he's trying to suppress a laugh.

Suddenly, I'm nervous. I down my drink as I watch Ted and his partner dance. They don't look bad at all. Now that I'm seeing it up close, by people who know what they're doing, I can't help but admit that blues dancing is sexy. Loose bodies, thrusting hips, freeform footwork, improvisation—the leaders need to be confident and the followers flexible to make it work well. Ted makes it look as classy, artistic, and sensual as any tango—and he makes himself look good too. Although I've been his student for a year, I've yet to watch him dance aside from classroom demonstrations. And while I've always known he's a talented dancer, he's soft-spoken, a little shy, and a little geeky. I hadn't imagined that watching him would be so arousing. But the way his hips thrust against his partner, the way his shoulders guide her flowing form across the floor, the way his moves are effortless...I've never seen anyone dance so artfully, and I've never imagined him so suave. I'm desperate to feel his hands on me, to have him lead me across the floor, even if I don't know what I'm doing and every move I make is awkward. I'll try blues dancing and risk looking foolish, just for one chance to be in his arms. Although I haven't moved beyond my bar stool, my skin starts to heat up at the thought of his hands on me, his pelvis directing me into spins and dips amidst a crowd of sweating, writhing bodies.

But I have to wait. I've arrived just in time for the band to take a break. The dance floor clears, and suddenly the bar is getting too crowded for comfort. I hurry to order another drink, and as I turn to escape the strange, dripping bodies, I bump into Ted, splashing both of us.

"Oh! I'm sorry!" I gasp.

"Don't worry about it. A little vodka never hurt anyone."

"Certainly not a little."

He grins. "I'm going to order myself a drink. There's a table in the back with my jacket on it. Why don't you meet me there?"

"Okay," I say with a smile, though I'm starting to lose my cool. I remind myself that Ted is my dance instructor. We're the same age, but he's still my teacher. And here I am, suddenly hot and bothered by seeing him shimmy around to twelve-bar blues. So hot that I can't imagine sitting at a table and making small talk while waiting for the band to finish their break. But I don't want to be rude, and if I reject his invitation, I doubt I'll have a chance to dance with him when the musicians come back for their next set.

I find the table with Ted's jacket and sit down. Trying to look cool, I keep lifting my eyes to the bar to see if he's headed towards me yet, and then quickly averting them so he won't be able to tell that I'm watching him. The burning below the surface of my skin starts to work its way deeper into my body, shaking up my stomach, my heart, my cunt. Finally, I see Ted in my peripheral vision, and dare to meet his gaze as he sits down.

"I never thought I'd get you to come out here," he says with a smirk. "I was just about to give up and quit asking. What made you change your mind?

"Don't be so smug. I just couldn't think of anything else to do tonight." The second the words escape my mouth I feel guilty. I'm nervous and uncomfortable, but there's no need for me to hurt his feelings. But Ted grins, and doesn't seem to mind my snarky tone.

"Trust me, this is the best thing to do in town on a Friday night."

We sit awkwardly with our drinks, and I curse myself for not being able to come up with something to say. In the studio, as a student, I'm always at ease, joking around. But here, out of my element, hot for teacher, I'm at a loss. I can't help but steal glances at his angular jaw, his messy hair, the sweat at his temples and behind his ears. I want to be pressed up against his body, lean into his neck and inhale his musk, salt and pheromones blended with alcohol and the bodies of his partners. I want to run my fingertips along his forearm, feel the heat of the dance floor rising off of his body. But then he catches me staring, raises his eyebrows, and I drop my gaze, trying to hold back a blush. I stay focused on my rapidly diminishing drink, and not until it's gone do I finally have the courage to look up again. I'm sure he's checking me out, but I banish the thought from my mind. He's my teacher, he's an amazing dancer, and there's no way he'd ever actually want me.

Finally, the band starts up again. A smooth, slow beat pours out of the instruments and Ted stands up, offering me his hand.

"Care to dance?"

"I won't know what I'm doing."

"Just follow."

Ted takes me in a loose frame, starts shifting his weight in time with the smoky, bourbon-infused tune. As the trumpet lets out a mournful wail rivaling the one pouring from the singer's lips, Ted starts sliding us around the floor. He keeps the steps simple, allowing me to get a feel for the rhythm and musical accents. Then suddenly he's spinning me, which isn't too much of a challenge. But it's the sudden drop at the end of the turn that throws me off. I nearly lose my footing, but Ted keeps me stable, grinning as he pulls me back up. Undeterred by my near spill, he eases me back along the floor, growing bolder, thrusting his pelvis up against me as he leads me into shimmies and hip twists. By the end of the song, a think I detect the beginnings of an erection in his pants, but I can't be sure. My own body is starting to heat up, and not just from the dancing. I can't even pinpoint where the feeling originated, because the sensation is radiating from every point. It's in the palms of my hands, my shoulder blades, my hips, my cunt, my nipples, my lips. As Ted releases his hold on me, I want to cling to him, absorb his sweat and energy, take his body into my own.

"Now don't ever let me hear you say that you don't know how to dance to blues music," Ted says as he leads me off the floor. "You were amazing out there. You're a natural. Everything you did out there was completely sexy."

I sit back down at the table while Ted walks off to find another dance partner. His words flatter me, but I'm still not confident enough in my own abilities to ask someone else to dance. So I saunter over to the bar, get myself another vodka tonic, and then take my seat again to watch the sights, feeling my clit pulse in time with the smoldering saxophone whine. I keep my eye on Ted, seeing his grace, the sexiness emanating from every step he takes. The pulsing in my clit increases, and it's as though I have no power over my body; without even thinking, my hand slides down between my legs, traces a finger up the seam of my jeans in time with a languid guitar lick. My better judgment tells me to pull my hand away, but I can't stop myself. I just keep stroking along to the 5/8 time, feeling myself getting wetter, the fabric getting warmer, a little worried that I might soak through completely before the song is over, but I don't really care. I just keep rubbing myself gently, only stopping when the music ends.

Ted comes back and grabs me for another dance; I follow all too willingly. As he takes me into frame, he pauses, then lifts my fingers to his nose, inhales, and smirks knowingly. My cunt scent is all over it. But he never says a word, just guides me along the floor, grinding himself against me, aggressive this time, thighs slipping between mine, chest pressed directly against me, my nipples getting harder as they rub up against him. The music is loud, frantic, pulsing, and while intellectually, I know that Ted is making his movement choices based on what he hears, it feels like the musicians are composing as they go, matching their rhythm and energy to the forcefulness that he's exerting on the floor. Ted pushes me into deep dips and backbends, hoists me up into the air. I drag a foot up his leg all the way to his hip, and I swear the trombone improvisation was inspired by my movement. This time, by the end of the number, I feel a definite hard-on beneath Ted's jeans.

"I promised my friend Alyssa I'd save a dance for her," he says when the song is done. "So I'm going to leave you for the next tune. But after that, what do you say to the idea of the two of us getting out of here?"

"Yes," I whisper, unable to believe my luck.

"One more thing. I want you to keep fingering yourself the entire time I'm dancing. You won't dance with anyone who asks and you won't invite anyone else onto the floor. You will just sit there, watch me, and touch your cunt." He saunters off into the crowd without giving me time to respond.

Sitting down at the table again, I avoid eye contact with any potential partners and let the beat take over me. I take my other hand to my pussy this time, wanting to soak all of my fingers in my scent. My hand dances between my legs, following the piano notes and cymbal brushes. By the time the introduction is over, there is a definitive wet spot on my jeans. Feeling a little bolder, I rub press harder, move my fingers a bit faster, really work my clit through the denim. The buzz in my cunt is increasing frequency, and suddenly I'm on the verge of orgasm. At first, I pull my hand away, certain Ted would not approve of me coming. He only asked for me to finger myself, not to get off. But I realize that if I want to keep myself from coming, I have to disobey orders and stop the touching. And Ted never specifically told me not to have an orgasm. So I have no choice. Bringing my hand back to my soaked jeans, I rub with increased fury.

As the music swells, so does my clit, and as the trumpet hits a high note, so do I. I doubt anyone can hear my moan as sparks go off in my body, but even if they can, I don't care right now. My knees shake a little as my body recovers, and I'm so sensitive that I have to brush my thighs with the lightest of strokes if I don't want to be over stimulated by the end of the song.

I stand up as Ted approaches the table. He takes my hand, inhales deeply, and closes his eyes as the aroma washes over him. Then, we head out of the bar into the night.

"Your place or mine?" I ask.

"I live five blocks away."

"Your place it is."

We hurry through the cool darkness, clamor up the stairs to his apartment, burst through the door and start kissing as though we've been waiting all our lives. Ted breaks away, fumbles around until he finds a remote control, hits a button, and suddenly the apartment is filled with sounds akin to what we heard in the club: throbbing beats, low tones, racy lyrics. Then his lips are back on mine, and between kisses he mouths along to the words he knows so well, his tongue gliding across my mouth as he forms the words, his mouth silent but filling every inch of my body with even more heat and tension. Breaking away from my lips, he turns to my earlobe, teeth caressing the skin. Pushing me into the couch, he starts to kiss again, deep and wet, his hands pinning my shoulders against the overstuffed furniture. Not one to sit quietly, I lunge back, sinking my teeth into his neck, feeling the flesh yield and his cock grow bigger beneath his clothes.

A bright jazz arpeggio blasting from the speakers inspires me; I want to dance, but not with Ted. I want to perform for him. Closing my eyes and letting the music seep into me, I stand up and begin to strip, letting the whines of the horns dictate when I rip off my shirt, how slowly I unzip my fly, how long I take before finally stepping out of my panties. When I'm done, Ted bursts into a tease of his own, unbuttoning his shirt to the beat, making it slide down his shoulders on the half-notes. His ass sways as he eases out of his pants, boxers sliding slowly off his lithe frame in response to the singer's growling voice.

Once he's naked, he takes me in his arms, brings my fingers up to inhale my scent, and starts to lead another dance, his hard cock pressing firm against my pelvis. Ted places deep kisses on my lips and neck, making my legs feel weak and struggling to stay balanced as we move. As we spin across the carpet, he moves his hands out of dance frame and onto my ass, still skillfully guiding me around the room until I'm pushed against the wall. No room left to dance, I writhe to the downbeat against his ready cock, and in return he pinches my nipples, watching me squirm as pleasure and pain build in my breasts.

I bring one hand up to grab his ass, the other to thrust up and down his cock. He rolls his head back and moans along with the music, and then grabs my arms and holds them against the wall, slides his cock into me, biting my collarbone as our bodies make a complete connection. Ted begins to thrust slowly, and as he does he releases one of my hands, licking every finger, tasting the scent that still remains. When he's done, he slaps my palm against his ass and moves on to the other hand, sucking and nibbling until he's satisfied. That hand he brings to his chest, and I pinch the nipple. He gasps, stops for a moment, and then begins to thrust again in time with the music, still dancing in his own way as he moves within me. As the music builds I let go, let my arms bang against the wall as I come, pleasure flowing out of my cunt and into the rest of my body, my voice rising with the trumpets on the stereo.

Just as I finish, Ted presses me even harder against the wall, freezes all movement, and reaches his own apex, his voice mirroring the bass line. He falls against me, and after a moment of trembling breathlessly, he regains control of his body, takes me over to the couch, where we curl up together, letting the undulating rhythm surround us.

"I told you that Moonshine is the best place to come on a Friday night."

"You know, I didn't actually come there."

"Guess you'll just have to show up next week so I can make that happen."

IT' S TIGHT LIKE THAT
COLE RILEY

"I felt a funny feeling from my head to my feet,
Well, she was lovin' so boogie-woogishly,
Aw, everybody wants her, 'cause she loves so peculiar."

She Loves So Good — Tampa Red (1935)

CHICAGO - SUMMER 1926

IT WAS after three in the morning when the show was over. We
packed up our instruments, content that we had done our best,
earned our bread. The owner of the Club Nutty, a speakeasy on the
city's swanky shore, invited us back to his penthouse place
overlooking the ships and the glittering lake. We knew better than to
refuse his offer. Flanked by his gunmen, he told us that he had some
people over there, and that we could pick up some more cash if we
stuck around.

One of Mr. Danton's bodyguards, with his gun in plain view, slung
the girl into our sedan, a female with the color of a dark plum. She
smiled at me and started going through her purse. The hood shoved
two more girls on top of us, cursed at them and slammed the door.

It was hot as hell. The kind of heat that made your skin stick to
your clothes. I was burning up. I kept coughing, coughing, coughing.
Everybody looked at me like I had TB, like I was going to cough up a
lung.

"You awight?" the purple girl asked. She had a bowl haircut,
almost mannish, but it fit her looks.

"No, I'm okay, smoke too damn much," I answered her.

The other girls were not convinced, casting me strange glances. All
of the dames wore the customary chorus girl outfits, tight in all the

right places, but the purple girl had slipped into a man's suit, pinstriped, starched white collar, and black crook's shoes. She toyed around with a thick, stinky cigar. Puffed on it like a burly dockworker.

Her man worked for Capone. The thin man with a beak nose was involved in every felonious activity imaginable: gun smuggling, bootlegging liquor, gambling, whores, and speakeasies. After the 1923 election of the reform mayor Bill Dever, everything changed. Capone and his boys moved into Cicero, making it their turf and doing battle with local gangster Myles O' Donnell. The skirmish cost over 200 lives.

"Bitch has too much rouge on," Mr. Danton said of his girl. He didn't make anything of her dressing in guy's clothes. He liked it. I replied yes. I didn't like the mobster but I knew better to get on his bad side.

Mr. Danton, like Capone, had other things on his mind. Their rivals, the gang from the North Side was trying to muscle into their turf. Bugs Moran and Hymie Weiss. They shot up the restaurant at the Lexington Hotel, where Capone and his boys hung out. A gang of cars, with hoods using Thompson sub-machine guns and shotguns, attacked the hotel and the restaurant. Many people were hurt. Following that ruckus, Capone ordered several armored Cadillacs with bullet-proof windows, for his favored men. Mr. Danton had one and used it to go between nightspots.

"How about going over to Inky's spot?" the mobster asked. "How about it, girls?" His voice didn't go with his body. It was shrill, high-pitched, and utterly feminine. Pug ugly bastard too.

The girls nodded submissively. Only the purple one sneered and folded her arms. The mobster noticed the gesture and slapped her viciously. She sure could take it.

"You come too, Viv," Mr. Danton growled, trembling with rage. His eyes narrowed into curious slits. He liked seeing the girl in her man's suit, possibly wearing his drawers, looking like a ripe fruit.

She made a bored face and rolled her eyes. Puffing the stinky stoogie.

"I own you body and soul," he seethed at her.

Later, when we got to Inky's place, I got her alone. Her hands were shaky. She told me she was scared of them, especially him. We shared a drink and a reefer stick, before she went in a back room.

"Look at me, I'm a real sinner," she chuckled. "Me, me, me the daughter of a fire-and-brimstone preacher. I'm sleepin' with evil."

"You got to sort it out," I said. "Your life is totally confused." I knew she was a good girl, deep underneath the surface.

"I'm scared of mens, all mens," Viv said as she made her exit after she changed hurriedly into her vixen garb. "Do you know what I mean?"

I shrugged.

"He makes me do things," she whispered as if he could hear her all the way across town. "He makes me lick his wife and her sister. Then they sat up and drink cocktails and watch him fuck me. That's they damn entertainment."

"Damn," I muttered.

"I feel safe with you." She grinned.

"You shouldn't," I retorted. "Like you said, I'm just like all the rest. Remember I am a man too. I will disappoint you."

"I need you," she moaned, shivered. Dragged on the reefer quickly.

I held her. Her slender arms went about me tightly, her body pressing against me, and I felt her crying. I kissed her tenderly, stroking her hair.

She stuck her thumb in her mouth. She always had to have something between her lips, something to comfort her. A thumb or a stiff pee-wee.

Just a once-innocent country girl corrupted by the Big City. Out of her depth.

AT THE REHEARSALS while Lil, Satchmo's wife, was suffering from a bad chest cold, he let me sat in and play her parts. The boys who he was going to make the record were all here: Kid Ory on trombone, Johnny Dodds on clarinet, Johnny St. Cyr on banjo, and myself on the ivories.

We did some of what the trumpet man planned for us to do, a little bit of "Dippermouth Blues," "Just Gone," "Mabel's Dream," and a good deal of "Canal Street Blues." I had trouble following these guys on that hopping Canal Street number, they chased me up and down the song until I got tired. Satchmo laughed and laughed.

Between numbers, Satchmo grinned. "I love to eat. Do you like chitlin'?"

I shook my head.

"What about smoky short ribs and rice," he asked. "Fried okra, turned out shrimps, cornbread, collard greens, and sweet potatoes?"

"You sound like a big timer." He tinkered with a few light notes.

"Yessuh, that's McKinney Cotton Pickers kind of grub."

He called me The Professor, maybe 'cause I had bright skin. Kinda light color. Yella. He didn't usually favor light complexion folks, but with me, he made a difference. He made an exception with me. He always stressed doing the right things.

Satchmo fingered the keys. "Professor, your mind can play tricks on you," he said with that growl of his. "It can lie to you. It can betray you. Your mind will tell you are a failure. That you're no good. Play no 'tention to it."

I let my fingers walk across the key in a mocking tone. He knew I was scared of failure. I knew failure was tough. It'll knock you on your ass.

"Failure is important to success," Satchmo suggested. "You got to fall down before you get back up. Or something like that."

My father, a house painter by trade and cornet player by night, told me I was a failure. A loser. His people came down a piece from Tutwiler, Mississippi. He said I was a big failure who didn't want to roll up my sleeves and tackle life.

He slurred a low bottom line. "Lemme tell you, Professor. Getting knocked down means you can look at the real man. All of his parts. When that happens, don't lie to yourself. Don't pretend you're something you're not."

Kid Ory cut me a new butt hole for playing the same solo note for note. He called me last. No juice. None of that cakewalk music or ragtime, he shouted. Satchmo nodded because he was right. See, ole Satchelmouth could remember phrases from songs and ditties back from the old days. King Oliver said about him.

"Don't forget the hambones," he snickered. "Or crawfish."

Suddenly, he brought the horn to his lips and took flight. The notes hung in the soft air above the crowd like blue jays riding the currents of wind. We were stunned, but then nobody had ever heard a trumpet played like that. This was new. He toyed with the valves, producing a sound like the blood red moon, the high hips of a warm chippie, the cold lines of sad tears. Slur, smear, triplet. Arpeggios, grace notes, slow or rocking. Always full of feeling.

"You dig, Professor?" he rasped.

I nodded.

There was a tradition of folks who played this music. Hippolyte Charles, Sam Morgan, Kid Rena, Punch Miller, Willie Coke, Leslie Dimes, Walter Blue. Like me, they had played all over: riverboats, circuses, vaudeville shows, roadhouses, juke joints, even funerals. I wasn't a big fan of dying. Rather than work a funeral one time, I went to work on a cane harvest.

"Take it on the downbeat," Kid said, holding his licorice stick.

"Easy Papa," Satchmo said.

I used to dream about coming to Chicago or New York. With Satchmo, this was possible. He was a first class showman. A teacher and father to us all. He doesn't remind white folk that his life was not that easy when he was a kid. And sometimes he would clown and do that darkie jive. But all of us knew what he was doing. Jim Crow was still on the throne. My great-aunt used to call Satchmo's routine: playing the fool.

He was a whole man, not a jester or a clown. He told me that a peckerwood asked him about if the blues reminded him of dying and death. The Great Man said everybody think about dying some time but the blues ain't about that. The blues was about getting the thorns, the pain and suffering of life. He explained nobody gone live forever and the white man shot back that nobody had come back from the other side.

Satchmo roared into laughter and said you just live as long as you can. Love life and let life love you.

The blues were here in this country before we was born.

LIKE SATCHMO, I was partial to brown and chocolate womens. He teased me because I had a purple gal. Skin color was important in the South. And Viv's skin had that purple sheen to it, the color of ripe plums, a deep dark hue. He didn't trust Viv but he didn't tell me why.

Viv would always say: "I got a battalion of mens falling all over themselves to get me, falling on they knees, bringing diamonds and flowers, proposing and asking me for my hand with they dicks out."

Sometimes I stalked her. Followed her around. I once watched her quietly in her room, without her knowing it. She was talking dirty to the mobster with the bare light bulb with a red scarf on it. Her middle fingers, wet and glistening, were jammed deep in her sex, her sweating face lolled back in sheer ecstasy. Her pussy scent hung thick in the air like candle smoke. She must have been stoking her cat for a long time before the mobster straddled her and brought her pouting lips to his hard bone. I was finished with her at that moment.

WE FINISHED the gig over at The Tulip and went over to The Hot Clam Club, which was much more swankier and high class. Tuxs and top hats. You could hear our echo walking through the long corridors of the place. Four servants, burly white guys, costumed like overdressed clowns stood guard. The customers and gamblers were milling around the premises, looking from room to room, seeing the crazy sights. Freak show.

One or two of the girls walked between rooms, jumping into action, adding a little spice. They wore silk robes as they switched their asses through the hallways. Everybody looked at them. I was wondering where was Viv in all of this hell?

I was carrying a set of drum sticks. The last thing some of these whites would accept a colored man wandering around in the club, big as you please, so I recalled the old trick used by my elders. Musicians are harmless. Maybe I should have taken up the banjo.

The gal with the big titties walked through the white crowd, twitching like a female in heat. Everything was jiggling and bouncing. Especially her round, wide ass. She was humming something.

"Ah stay nice brown all year around," she sang aloud. "'Member that."

I waded through them. The girls, now in greater number, moved like the undead, like zombies, floating like feathers through the mens as if they were sleepwalking. Shadowy figures. Often the girls screamed and giggled like silly schoolgirls and the mobsters felt them up, slipping into another room.

There was a crowd gathered at the doorway of one room. All of the mens were talking, drinking, laughing. It was a free and easy mood. I peeked inside and there was a woman, alone, dressing on top of a table, with her breasts out and a short black skirt showing off flashes of her sex and butt cheeks. She flirted with the men who pounded on the long table in a wild native rhythm, squeezing her breasts, wiggling until the music builds and takes over her flesh. All of the eyes were on her every twists and bump.

They were yelling and hollering like something crazy. She grinded her hips, her hands running up and down her thighs and long legs. Hot blood coursed through her Creole veins. It was like a drum beat beating an African rhythm. These mens came to see her, they were her friends. Her lovers. The men could see everything under the skirt and yelled rudely. Each man looked eyes on her and when she did a low bow where her business could be advertised, I grabbed her by the arm and dragged her off the table and we ran and ran. Her customers were mad at me.

"Will you do me a favor?" Viv said. "Don't worry about me anymore. I'm a big girl."

I shook my head. "Somebody needs to worry about you." I recalled the time when I felt the red welts striped on her high purple ass. One of the crooks caned her and she liked it.

"Nobody worries about Viv, nobody," she said. "When I was thirteen, I was raped by a man who roomed with my folks. He held a knife to my throat. He pulled me off in the woods where there was another man. They kept the knife at my neck as they took turns on me."

"Oh damn."

"One of them wanted to cut me," she said sadly. "He sliced the knife 'cross the soft part of my upper thigh. The tender part. The cut was very deep and made a bad scar."

"I felt it when we loved," I replied.

"How did you like the free show?" the purple girl asked. "I had them under control. They was eating out of my hand."

"That's crazy." I frowned.

"Are you afraid of crooks?"

"No, I don't like them using you like that. Like a toy. Like a cheap whore. You deserve better than that. You know that."

"Don't you turn out to be like a creep like the others?" there was a warning in her look. "These mens often confuse lust and love in a way gals don't. They can't separate sex and love like gals do. Most of these boys have some good sex with a woman, he will fall in love with her."

He grimaced. "Don't you trust me?"

"You're pathetic, just like the others," she laughed sweetly and walked toward the Maid's room. She closed the door gently behind her. I followed inside and no sooner than I get in before she dropped to her knees and unzip my pants. I felt the warmth of her mouth on me.

She sucked both balls into her mouth, cupped them, and licked me between my legs.

She laughed that special laugh of hers, that girlish giggle. Whispering sweetly in her ear, I opened her up with my fingers and slid down to kiss her belly, and then to run my moist tongue along the crease to her button. She whimpered and put both of her hands to crush my mouth against her pussy. I sucked and lapped at her juicy sex. She gasped as my tongue snaked inside her, in and out slowly, tongue fucking her until her legs trembled. Her pelvis grinded against my mouth, hotly and savagely, while I licked her deeper.

I could see she was close. My fingers were up in her, curling, fondling her thick lips of her sex. Now her button was between my teeth, swollen to its peak, and my tongue darted across it again and again and again. Her back arched as she screamed, cumming in my mouth and I swallowed.

SATCHMO sat in over at the Tulip, his trumpet under his arm, and the folks were happy to have him in the place. We rocked the club, the mobsters laughing and patting the chorus girls on their backsides, and the horn man would do his King Oliver thing by winking and grinning: "Hotter than a forty five."

When we joked around during the show, the owners liked it

because everything was free and easy. The customers loved it and ordered more drinks. They liked having Satchmo around; his smile and his gravel voice making the people happy. He was a whole man, not a jester or a clown.

I was playing behind him, with his greatness in full display, that brass tone bold and swaggering and manly. It was a tone which warmed and penetrated the spirit. We would listen to him, his mastery of ideas, turning and twisting the melody. He would really have his way with a song. Every night was a blowing session with everybody getting a chance to solo.

He knew what the customers wanted, he let you make mistakes because he knew that was the only way you could grow; he would talk to you when you needed his counsel.

Some of the white players sneaked in the place and started writing down the solos and stealing solos. He didn't care. Satchmo smiled at me and joked about them getting a good education from "dese cullud boys."

The trombonist did a two-step, snapping fingers. "Do it, boy!"

The gut-bucket blues. The Sportin' Girl Gone Bad blues. The Zulu blues. The Sharecropper blues. It all reminded me when the time when the Navy closed Storyville down because of the womens and hot sex. They emptied out the cribs, the baby dolls, the pimps, the strong-arm cullud boys, and they brought on themselves and kept robbing and killing the sailors. Gone was old Lulu White's place.

"You's a mess, Professor," Satchmo said. "You worried about that sporting gal. She gone git you killed."

"I loves her," I mumbled. "I know she ain't no good."

In a flash, I thought how hot she was. Over at Toy's place after our Easter show, she called me a sheik, a sweet hole jockey. I was laying back on the sofa while she was facing him on top of me, riding me. So tight, so sweet. She came so hard riding my dick, cream covering my pole, and I went at it forever before I pulled out.

Satchmo roared. "You got it real bad. I had a yen for one of them gals, a Creole gal, Daisy Parker. Oh baby, I would have done anything to get with that gal. She had my nose open real bad. I guess you got it like I had it for Daisy."

With the last song, he leaned back and reached those blazing, otherworldly high notes. When the clapping quieted, he bent over and aimed the horn at the floor. After it was over, he led me back to the dressing room, shoved a bunch of jack into my hand and pushed me out of the door. Outside, the dark was thick in the alley. And soon the headlights of a car momentarily blinded me as it pulled to a stop.

The car door opened, I could see fear in her eyes as she wiggled around on the seat, with two suitcases at her feet. There were tears in her eyes. We were going nowhere in particular but any place away from here. I scooted in next to her. We will disappear, vanish. Into shadow.

This was Satchmo's gift to me. A Storyville valentine.

THE PRINCIPAL OF THE THING
SAVANNAH STEPHENS SMITH

"Now the old folks like it, the young folks too
The old folks showing the young folks how to do
I'm getting sick and tired, of telling you to shake that
thing."

Shake That Thing – Papa Charlie Jackson (1925)

THE HALLWAY WAS SILENT, as quiet as the world outside the classroom windows, muffled by falling snow. In the stillness, Brian heard the distinctive tap-tap-tap of a woman's high-heeled shoes, striding purposefully. The steps approached his classroom, and slowed. He read student papers, slogging through juvenile arguments and laughable malapropisms, and waited, mildly curious, for them to continue. It wasn't unusual for a teacher to still be at school long after the hoards of students departed. It was probably a teacher, not a student; the footfalls just had a sound of authority to them.

"Brian."

Neither student nor teacher. The voice was firm, feminine, and still had the power, after two years, to unnerve him slightly. It was his high school principal, Mrs. Brunswick.

"Hi," Brian said. Should he stand up from the desk? Respect was always a good idea, especially with a woman who had a slightly old-fashioned sense of protocol to her. Brian stood.

Mrs. Brunswick came into his home room, closing the door behind her. She didn't speak, but glanced around with a neutral, almost expressionless, face. He guessed she was assessing everything—from the posters on the wall, the notes still up on the chalkboard, even the general level of tidiness. Brian waited. He'd only been teaching for two years. This was his first job, and he thought he was doing well so far. He'd made it through the first year with no major riots (on the students' part) or breakdowns (on his part). This second year had been easier.

"I wanted to speak with you."

That was never good. Brian felt like sitting down again. Why did school principals—even now—have that authoritative way about them? They made you feel like you were in trouble, even when you weren't. And he probably wasn't. He couldn't think of any issues recently that would concern Mrs. Brunswick. No disgruntled parents, no floundering students, no scandal in the lesson plans.

The principal nodded in measured approval at the state of his classroom, the empty seats facing them like so many possibilities. Beyond the rows of desks and the bookshelves beneath the windows, the day had turned black. In January, evening arrived early. He could see their reflections beneath the fluorescents. They were diminished and small, slightly blurred. One of the lights on the sport field below was on, and in its upside-down triangle of light, snow drifted down, illuminated like dust motes in August. He sat, feeling slightly more confident behind his desk. He was a teacher, after all. Not one of the kids.

Mrs. Brunswick turned on one heel, and perched herself on the corner of his desk, looking down at him, hands clasped in her lap. Her face now wore an expression of considered pleasantness. She was wearing a severe black suit, a skirt and jacket as tightly buttoned as the lady herself. The suit's austerity was broken only by a white blouse, still crisp at 4:47 p.m., which put him in mind of a nun's habit, stark and sexless. And a scarf. If there had been any chance of cleavage showing with the blouse, the scarf would cover that up. The scarf was a silky splash of colour and the only feminine thing about his principal. Well, the scarf and maybe her legs. They were pretty good. And the heels. So the scarf, the heels and the legs in black hose. And the lipstick? A soft pink shade that picked up the colours in the scarf and the—

The touch of colour in her cheeks. Mrs. Brunswick? Wearing blush? Perhaps she'd been outside in the cold, touring the grounds, making sure there was nothing going on that shouldn't: vandalism, a few tokes behind the dumpsters or a furtive make-out session in the cold. The woman kept a sharp eye on all things that went on at St. Andrew's High School, both inside and out.

Brian picked up his red pen, put it down, and then picked it up again. He felt better with something in his hand. He waited to hear what she had to say to him, but didn't know why she was perched on his desk like a crow.

"Melissa Whitmore."

Oh, shit. Melissa Whitmore. The clock on the wall above him seemed to tick too loudly, like a countdown on a bomb. Because Brian couldn't want Melissa one whit more than he already did. Wanted, and wanted very badly.

Melissa Whitmore was hot. Melissa was seventeen going on twenty-seven, and she was achingly perfect, at least physically. She had honey-blonde hair and smooth skin that seemed to hold summer's kiss, even in January. She had great bone structure and startlingly blue eyes. That was from the neck up. From the neck down, it only got better. Long legs, flat belly, hips and ass curved like an architect's wet dream, and best of all, a set of high, firm, young, full breasts. Christ. Melissa Whitmore had played a starring role in many sessions in Brian's apartment between the ten o'clock news and the six o'clock alarm. Melissa Whitmore and he had done some amazing, wonderful, dirty, and probably illegal things. Two or a dozen times over. Melissa Whitmore had warmed many a cold night for Brian.

And there was one more thing: Brian guessed that he could have a shot at really doing all the things that he fantasized about doing to Melissa Whitmore. Things he imagined while closing his eyes and stroking his aching, rigid cock. He could probably have her in real life.

Melissa Whitmore had a boyfriend—of course—but she also had a crush on him. She'd as much told him so, more than once. Each smiling, flirtatious revelation that he was her "absolutely, honestly, favourite teacher, you know?" only served to bring Brian to another shuddering climax. On one notable occasion it had been in the staff men's room during the Christmas dance, only three weeks ago. He was supposed to be chaperoning.

"Melissa?" Brian said.

"Melissa Whitmore. You do have her in one of your classes, don't you?"

"Two," Brian admitted. "English and history."

Mrs. Brunswick's gaze held his as if she were accessing every dirty thought he'd ever had about Melissa—sweet Melissa—and even retrieving and rating the occasional fantasy that involved Melissa's closest friend, Ashley Woodburn. Ashley was a brunette, with about fifteen more pounds than Melissa. But they were in all the right places. Oops—he thought the principal had pulled up the rare daydream that involved Melissa Whitmore and Ashley Woodburn at the same time. Talk about making his wood burn.

"She has a crush on you."

"Oh—well—er. I don't know. Maybe. Just a little one."

Mrs. Brunswick was still sitting on the corner of his desk, looming there like a black eagle, he decided, more weighty than a crow. She drilled into his soul with her eyes, stern as a judge. "Don't give into temptation, Brian." Her voice was crisp and flat like the virtuous whole grain crackers she nibbled when she sometimes joined the teachers in the lounge.

"Of course not! I wouldn't."

"Although you may want to. I understand. The girl is certainly attractive, very attractive. And she knows it. Flaunts it. Prettiest girl in school?"

The silence was broken only by the clock ticking on the wall, its sound unnaturally loud again in the stillness of the after-hours classroom. Brian finally realised the question wasn't rhetorical. "Uh...one of them. Very pretty. Yes."

"Confident too. In her looks."

"That she is."

"Doing well in your class?"

"Okay. She's not as academically inclined as some of the kids." Kids, he reminded himself. They walk like women, talk like women, probably fuck their boyfriends like women, but they're only girls. The kind of girls who didn't pay any attention to you when you were seventeen.

"Maybe she thinks she doesn't have to work in your classes. Because you'll let her skate through. Because you want her—and she knows it."

"No," Brian protested. "I've never."

"Responded to her flirtations?" One brow went up, sceptical as an atheist at a revival. Not aloud, never giving the girl any reason to believe he felt nothing but a teacher's interest in her. In her schoolwork. But physically? Oh, yes, Brian had responded to Melissa Whitmore's flirtations. She probably would be elated to know that she could more than unnerve him—she could give him a hard-on. Was she a cock-tease?

The lecture was continuing. *Pay attention*, Brian thought. He kept his eyes on Mrs. Brunswick, but it was hard not to think of Melissa. "Don't let it," the principal was saying. "Don't give into temptation. Nubile young women like Melissa have their wiles. And their ways. It's flattering, isn't it? The way she looks up at you? The way she tilts her head, smiles, flashes you a bit of breast. Or thigh. Of course, we don't see those tiny little skirts now that the cold weather's here, but the tight jeans she wears show just as much, don't they? Hugging every inch of her. Those jeans make love to her ass."

Brian realised his mouth was agape. The principal continued to speak softly. "Who wouldn't want to as well?"

"I...I don't know what to say here, Mrs. Brunswick." *I'm trapped*, he almost said.

Trapped, and slightly aroused—against his will. And his principal wasn't finished. "Call me Juliana, please. You need to be careful, Brian. Of young women with a lot of nonsensical hormones running through their bodies. Their lush, young bodies."

Mrs. Brunswick shifted on Brian's desk, crossing her left leg over her right. Her black skirt rode up, but she didn't seem to notice. Brian found it hard not to look at his principal's thigh. It was easier than looking up into her eyes. He clutched his red marking pen tighter. Black hose—and they were shapely thighs too. Who knew that under the plain suits there were such lines and curves? "We may be tempted, Brian, but it would be a very big mistake to give into that temptation. You may want to fuck her—"

Brian's throat was dry and he felt slightly sick. He'd never imagined his principal speaking so...frankly. Her mouth so easily slipped the word "fuck" into the conversation. Or was it a lecture? It was more like a lecture. A warning. She'd seen right through him, knew every nasty fantasy he'd had while he stood at the front of the classroom, his eyes roaming up and down the rows of desks, head cocked to one side, listening to students discover *The Great Gatsby* and groan at the length of *Fifth Business*.

"...and I can't say I blame you. It's only natural that a man should look at a woman that way. Especially a young, healthy man like yourself. But remember this—she's not a woman. She's a girl. I don't know what's going on—" Mrs. Brunswick shrugged, loosening her scarf. She plucked it away from her throat. "Something in the air, the chemicals in our food, or maybe it's just watching all that television, and being exposed to what in my day we'd simply call pornography. But their bodies mature much faster than they used to. But their minds, Brian, don't. She's a young girl who has a typical schoolgirl crush on you."

The principal smiled. "Not that I blame her, of course. You are an attractive young man. Good-looking. Pleasant. Nicely built—yes, I've seen you out running—and compared to so many of my staff here, so young. Approachable. The kids all like you, don't they?"

Brian didn't speak; he hadn't prepared for this...conversation—and maybe that was all it was, a very unexpectedly frank, heart-to-heart talk from an older, wiser professional. A mentor, of sorts.

A mentor who was sliding off her scarf, looking down at it. She was twisting it gently in her hands, running its flimsy silk through her fingers. Fingers that were tipped by nails polished in a dark red shade.

Red for danger.

The scarf was off, and Brian noticed that Mrs. Brunswick's blouse was actually unbuttoned at the top. Unbuttoned an inch or three more than he'd ever expected it to be, opened to the lace edge of Mrs. Brunswick's brassiere. Lace? Mrs. Brunswick? The two didn't go together.

And yet, suddenly, they did.

"Mrs. Brunswick," he said. "I—"

"Juliana, please. The kids all like you. I think you're a very promising teacher. But I'd hate to see your career end before it's even begun. The stories that have come out with distressing regularity— and they're all over the Internet, where these incidents are mocked and sometimes even lauded...That can't happen here. And it won't."

Juliana Brunswick was smiling at him, belying the warning in her words. She ran her hand along her throat where the scarf used to be. And then she began to unbutton her blouse as he watched, unable to move. He opened his mouth to speak, but nothing emerged. She unbuttoned it easily, casually, as if she were undoing her winter coat at the front doors. "If a young man such as yourself is stirred by the enticements surrounding him, I understand, I really do. But Brian, stay well away from the girls. You need a woman."

The red pen escaped from his sweaty hand, skittered across the desk and clattered to the floor. He couldn't look away from the sight as Mrs. Brunswick's breasts emerged, cupped by a lacy, too-flimsy-to-be-practical bra. It was a bra he could see through. It was a piece of women's lingerie that whispered of secrets in the dark, not administration of the school. It was a bra that begged to be unfastened by fingers that may have trembled just a little bit.

Wasn't she chilly, doing that? Her nipples were hard, raising enticing bumps against the sheer fabric. Brian's cock, already woken by the context of the conversation and the reminders of his lustful fantasies, uncoiled and twitched against his will. He could see her nipples through the bra, dark pink circles, perfect targets for a mouth. Mrs. Brunswick's nipples. He could feel himself harden further, just as susceptible to arousal as the boys in his classes.

"But maybe it's not the teenaged girls," she was saying, as her fingertips left her throat, and drifted down to the sweet swell of her breast, lingering over a nipple. "That you have to watch out for. They just gush and dream, and their flirtations are clumsy and obvious for the most part. They linger too long, hang around your home room. They just happen to be where you are, stalking you through the halls.

Surely you've noticed?"

Mrs. Brunswick stayed perched on the desk, the long fingers that had caressed her scarf now touching the blouse, the blouse she'd unbuttoned to show the lace of her bra. She seemed to be longing to touch. Brian couldn't help but notice that Juliana had a good-looking pair of breasts. It was difficult not to notice, with the scarf off, jacket open, and blouse unbuttoned.

He was halfway to hard, but also halfway to bolting out the door and into the snow.

Even after two years teaching, Brian wasn't quite used to thinking of the principal as anything but an authority figure, someone to be deferred to, though most kids these days didn't respect any adult. And it still felt like he was new to this grown-up stuff, himself. It was only five years ago, after all, that it was Brian sitting on the other side of the desk in the classroom. A quiet kid, saved from being a nerd by his natural gift for sport. Girls, on the other hand, eluded—or evaded—him. They remained mysterious. By the time he acquired his first girlfriend, it was someone much like him: fond of books and not prone to unruliness, there was barely time to lose their virginity and part ways, bound for universities on different sides of the country. And at university, Brian had buckled down and bucked most of the partying, knowing that his scholarships depended on his grades, his grades depended on working hard, and the rest of his expenses depended on working. Staying in school meant working, not only on the books, but in the book store. He scored well in university, but not so much with the girls.

But he did all right. He was, as Juliana had pointed out, a reasonably good-looking young man. And now, in the insular world of a small high school, he'd taken on an aura he'd never achieved otherwise. It was heady. And the principal was right: he'd been tempted.

Juliana shifted on his desk, and her skirt slid higher. She tugged the blouse from the waistband, and toyed with the front clasp of her bra. Brian couldn't look away. She raised her skirt as if checking for runs in her hose. She was wearing thigh-high black stockings with a wide band of lace at the top.

Then she was off the desk and leaning into him. She turned his chair around, with a protesting squeak as it swivelled, so that he faced her. A smile played on her lips. She stroked his thigh as if appraising him. She eyed the bulge in his trousers, and her hand moved ever upward with each caress. Brian said nothing as her exploration continued. Then she was touching him right there, where his erection poked against his trousers, making him groan. As she bent forward to touch his crotch, his hard-on was impossible to deny, not with her fingers in a vee, moving up and down it. Brian swallowed. All he knew was the sight of her breasts in the scant brassiere and the touch of her hand on his erection.

All he knew was desire. He leaned forward, and his lips brushed exposed skin of her décolletage, and found the swell of her breast. Juliana unbuckled his belt without hesitation, and unfastened his trousers. The sound of his zipper descending was clearly audible, and he inhaled sharply as she expertly pulled out his penis, now stiff. Hands that typed officious memos and school policy now stroked his silky, taut skin, the ball of her thumb sliding over the swollen head of his cock.

She sank down in front of him, and popped the brassiere open, exposing the glory of her breasts. They were fine: heavy, full, not yet fallen with age. Her nipples, which had teased him when veiled by the sheer bra, now stood out proudly. Her breasts were a good size, and while they didn't sit as high, round, and perky as the oft-imagined (and with some of the tops she wore, there wasn't much left to imagine) Melissa Whitmore's, they were full and inviting. She shrugged her black jacket off, and placed it on Brian's desk blotter. She took hold of his cock again, and bent to him.

Mrs. Brunswick's mouth slid lightly over his erection, her touch making him groan with desire. Then she took him into her mouth, hot and tight, moving up and down, relentless and slow. She squeezed his cock at the base, until the swollen head seeped with need. Then her tongue lashed over and around the crown, and lingered to tease him in that spot, that one spot on the underside...Brian groaned. How did she know about that spot? She circled around and around until he thought he would explode, and then slowly moved down, taking more of him into her mouth than he ever imagined would fit. She sucked his cock nothing like a school principal, taking her time, teasing him. She tasted him, tugging open his shorts, finding his balls, Jesus, finding them with her tongue. She sucked until he was begging for release.

"Please," he whimpered.

She wouldn't let him come. She grasped his cock, laughing, as he sat there, sprawled out on his chair, harder than he'd ever been in a midnight fantasy, throbbing and helpless. He was ragingly tumescent. Juliana's hair had come loose, and she looked... young. Pretty. Her face was flushed again, and her lips swollen. Maybe he should kiss her. Did she want to be kissed? He could do that. He wouldn't mind.

Before he could, her mouth went down on his cock again, and Brian groaned. He watched, in the unforgiving fluorescent lights overhead, the skin of his cock, taut and glistening against the soft warmth of his principal's lips, emerging and disappearing. She was fucking him with her mouth.

Juliana finally eased off his prick, and stood. She was breathing hard, and her eyes had a glitter to them that brooked no refusal. Her breasts, with generous nipples, were too tempting for Brian. He pulled the principal onto his lap with a low growl, his face against the soft flesh. When he sucked at the hard nubs of her erect nipples, Juliana moaned. He sucked, the principal arching her back, her fingers in his hair, guiding him to one, then the other. Brian sucked harder, and her hand wiggled into his lap again, slowly jacking his cock. He wasn't thinking about Melissa Whitmore at all.

He stroked Juliana's back, met her skirt at the waistband, and went over it to cup the globes of her ass. His mouth came off one nipple with an audible pop. "You're not wearing any panties," Brian said, shocked.

The principal chuckled, a low, throaty sound that he found he liked, and Juliana wriggled on him. She straddled him, and he could feel her pussy against his cock. She was wet. And as he sucked, teasing her as she'd done to him, he could feel her getting wetter. He sucked until she began to thrash, grinding her hips against him.

Juliana, with athletic grace, moved up over his prick. She parted her thighs and stroked his cock with the swollen lips of her pussy. There was heat and slippery wetness, inviting him. He had her hips, and tried to get his cock into her, but she evaded him. The skirt bunched in his fist, he pulled her to him. She rose, and the chair rolled a few precarious inches, coming to a halt against the chalkboard. Brian cried out, the principal gasped, and then laughed, giddy. He steadied her, still kneeling over him. It didn't seem real: Juliana, wet, her bra dangling open like a parted curtain. Juliana, with a thatch of dark pubic hair that was both primal and exciting. She had a lush bush, and Brian was slightly surprised by it. He thought of all women as being neatly trimmed and edged, as formal and tamed as hedges in an English garden. Not his principal. She had a wild tangle of damp curls, with a hint of musk that sent a shock through his body, from his nose as he bent, unable to help himself, and inhaled, the scent in his nose shooting down to make his cock twitch again, iron hard.

He wanted to taste, but before he could bend deeper and taste the swollen folds of her sex, she was off the chair and leaning over Brian's desk, pushing papers, his planner, his coffee mug aside, and raising her ass to him.

He never imagined this: she was bent over his desk, scattering

English compositions and yellow pencils. A sheet of paper fluttered to the floor, and both ignored it. Her ass was delectable: full, round buttocks, pale, framed by the stocking bands on her thighs and the black skirt, rudely shoved up to her waist. It looked like a gift coming out of tissue paper. He caught the scent of her excitement, and grunted. His cock twitched, throbbing. Juliana parted her thighs wider, and over her shoulder, hissed an urgent command: "Fuck me."

Brian was more than willing to comply.

He pushed his trousers down, his cock rampantly erect, teased without mercy, aching to bury it someplace warm and tight. He clasped it, squeezed, and guided his prick to her moist folds. She made a sound when he touched the swollen head to her lips. He took a moment, using his prick to open her up, sliding up and down her sex, slick heat greeting him. Then he pushed inside the principal with a grunt of pleasure and grabbed her hips. He thrust in, slowly, savouring every inch of contact. In a moment, Brian was buried inside her up to his balls.

Fucking was easy. He stood at his desk, feet apart, the principal raising her ass up, clutching the edges of his desk. She wriggled and pushed back at him as his cock moved in and out of her. She began to make soft sounds, distress or enjoyment. He figured it was the latter. Brian began to stroke the principal harder.

He looked up and saw them again, two figures at the front of the classroom. This was a lesson he'd never planned on learning. He groaned, and thrust even faster. There was no going back now.

Orgasm came quickly. In just a few moments, the pleasure was unbearable and he could feel it building. Beneath him, she thrust back, mewling. He could feel it when she came. She pushed back at him, keeping him buried inside her, and cried out, shuddering. He'd made Juliana Brunswick come. He'd fucked her.

Brian exploded.

He stood there, still inside her, heart pounding, his grateful cock still twitching.

Then she moved impatiently, and he stepped away, still hard as he pulled out of her. Brian stumbled against the chair, knocking it a foot to the right. He felt behind him, found the chair again and collapsed into it. The ordinary smell of the classroom: chalk, pencil shavings, orange peel, the lingering pine of disinfectant was eclipsed by the unmistakable aroma of sex. He closed his eyes.

"Ah, much better," Mrs. Brunswick said. The bra was fastened again. She was straightening her skirt, and the blouse buttoned up beneath her nimble fingers, her skin disappearing under the pristine white. The generous flesh he'd explored was hidden by the stark black and white clothes, reminiscent of a memo to the staff in black print and white paper, or of an exam he'd failed.

Or passed. "I hope we can do this again soon," she said. "Now, don't stay too late. All work and no play."

She picked up the scarf from the floor where it had fallen, brushed off the desk in the midst of their frantic coupling.

"I will be keeping a close eye on your career. You can always come—" with an ever-so-slight pause, "to me, you know. The principal's door should always be open to those in need. Don't be afraid to ask for—guidance, when you think you want it."

Then she was leaving, her heels tap-tap-tapping away, fading down the hall to the principal's office. Brian sat there a while, watching the snow falling outside, idly stacking the essays he'd never finished marking. Life was full of lessons. And surprises.

P.K.
ART NIXON

For Adilifu and Bjorn

"Yes, if you make it to your house
Knock on the front door, run around to the back
You'll catch him just before he go."

Evil Going On — Howling Wolf (1952)

TREASURE NILES, M.D. snapped out of a dead man's sleep and reached for the ringing iPhone inside the faux headboard of his brand new Ethan Allen RL edition platform bed. The phone continued to ring while he felt for the recessed control button.

"Doctor Niles," he mumbled with his eyes closed.

A female's voice began to snap off a description of urgency that, to the untrained ear, sounding like big words with lots of Greek and Latin in them. The voice resembled static or, at its worse, like it was coming from a mental clinic.

"Give me forty minutes," he said, now halfway across the bedroom, butt naked, and glancing at the red dot pulsing on the video camera indicating it was still recording. He takes a quick peek through the camera's monitor. There they are: two thirty-something females, also naked except for the matching leather harnesses and studded dog collars. They've closed the gap, blissfully unaware that the "middle spoon" is no longer there. But, oh what a fun time they had the night before!

DR. TREASURE NILES was always grateful for how the proverbial dice fell in his life.

Looking back on it, he grew up with so many in his hood that certainly had the dice loaded against them. Over the years, however, a low grade sense of guilt or anger or whatever-the-hell-it-was seemed to throw him off kilter at the strangest times. Luckily, it didn't last long. Luckily, his was the last car to arrive at his own surprise birthday party. *And the last shall be first.* The words seemed to come from nowhere, as he backed his pristine 1957 Buick Road Master out of his oval driveway. *And the last shall be first.* From time to time, bits and pieces of scripture would briefly emerge from nowhere, even though he hadn't been to church in decades. Mostly, he accepted it as a harmless echo or a side effect of having had a photographic memory when he was a child. Even without it, his memory capacity was still more than adequate. After all, he was a top shelf M.D., wasn't he?

Still, some parts of his life didn't make sense to him. Like the scene with the two naked women in his bed. A lot of things were happening to him like that. Crazy things.

Normally, he' should be more than teed off at being paged to come in on his short but long overdue vacation. But he wasn't. In fact, he was relieved. The Nguyen triplets were coming a whole month earlier than expected and he would feel better if he was there to monitor and provide backup. They specified that only he oversee their development through to the delivery, and not his partner, who had a tendency to resolve most complications by cesarean.

Without taking his eyes off the road, he flipped open the armrest, counted down to the eighth CD and selected Steely Dan's *Babylon Sisters*. He was only thirty minutes away from the hospital at this point, but he needed some travelling music, something with a bluesy bottom but hip.

Usually, the 405 freeway is a parking lot during the week, but the road belonged to him on this sparkling summer morning. He was driving through a passage of foothills on either side of the freeway. Then he began to feel the deep pangs that something was missing. Impulsively, he turned the music off. He was on to something.

Time was catching up with him. He'd just hit the big six-O. Yet this Sunday morning riding in his head-turning classic on a gorgeous Sunday made him feel particularly incomplete. *Relax, man*, he told himself. *Just...relax.* If a memory had a rope attached to it, then he had just enough grip on it to delicately, yet intensely, finesse it—hand over hand—into the present where he could finally dissect it. Now forty-seven years later, he was ready to do a biopsy.

JULY 4th was a Saturday. The temperature was almost 100 degrees in

Cleveland and it was his thirteenth birthday. His father, Reverend Niles, had recently been laid off from the foundry at U.S. Steel, so he agreed to let him go to Cedar Point Amusement Park as a birthday present with Reverend Webber and his six kids who lived a couple of streets over. This was certainly not a casual gesture on Reverend Niles' part. His father had righteous contempt for most folks in their neighborhood, referring to them as a bunch of "heathens and Ethiopians." Secretly, Reverend Niles didn't like Reverend Webber either. But they were the only family Treasure and his younger sister was allowed to visit.

Reverend Webber's kids watched American Bandstand. The Niles' didn't own a TV. Reverend Webber's kids had a hi-fi stereo player. Although the Webber kids weren't allowed to dance, they did know all the words to "The Duke of Earl, "Sherrie," "Stagolee" and a whole bunch of other good songs, and they were kind enough to let Treasure learn the lyrics off their 45's. The Webbers allowed Wolfman Jack, the raspy-voiced disc jockey, in their house, but the Niles' didn't own a radio—they did, but the dial could not be moved from the very end of the dial, where a small colored-owned station only broadcast static and devotional music a couple of times a month.

His family had no record player, but they did have several gospel records their mother Ruth bought at Goodwill. Reverend Niles promised to buy the family a hi-fi and a television set as soon as he was selected the new pastor of New Tabernacle of The Second Coming. Reverend Webber had his own church. Reverend Niles didn't. The Honorable E.L.C. Bishop, who founded the church forty-five years ago, was to retire. He would name the new pastor on Sunday, the 5th of July. Reverend Niles, according to the congregation, was the overwhelmingly best preacher. He had the fire and then some, but the young Ezell Robinson was Reverend Bishop's nephew.

Even so, everyone was expecting their new shepherd would be Treasure's father. But now there were rumors that this might not be. No pastorship meant no television, no high fidelity stereo or radio that Treasure and his sister could play. No life worth living, really. So lately it didn't look like he would have his own church unless a miracle literally prevailed.

Treasure stopped at the small grocery store in the middle of the block on the way to the Webber's. Inside, he pulled out the dollar his father had given him to have something to munch on during the long trip to the amusement park. "Give me one Hostess cupcake and a Hostess Twinkie," he told Miss Lola, the old white lady who lived above the store and was too old to move out of the neighborhood with the rest of the white people years ago. There was a jingle that signaled another customer had entered. Treasure looked up and recognized her as Prettyman's mom. Everyone, including Prettyman, called her Red.

"Hey there, P.K. What you up to this early?" She slid Treasure's dollar back across the counter at him and replaced it with one from her white patent leather purse.

"I'm on my way to Cedar Point. It's my birthday." Red gave Treasure a twenty dollar bill, "Happy birthday, handsome."

Treasure looked surprised, then incredulous. Red took it all in.

It's O.K.—it's yours."

"Thank you very much, Miss Boudreaux," he said, and then looked away embarrassed.

Miss Lola sized up Red with a look that signified that there was a pile of something disgusting standing in the middle of her squalid little store. Red ignored the old white woman's contemptuous gaze as if it was the most natural thing in the world. But then, in a sense, it was natural for Red—all the women in the neighborhood regarded her about the same way right in front of her face. Whore. Tramp. Slut. She even seemed to get perverse joy from it.

Yes, granted, Red loved to have her fun. She loved men and what she could get from them. She descended from a supposed long line of New Orleans Creoles and red bones before moving to Cleveland after serving two years for killing the man who kicked her in the stomach while she carried Prettyman. As a parting shot, the man's razor left a scar that started above her left eyebrow, down her perfect cheekbones and jerked straight toward the corner of her mouth and through it. If she was in the mood, Red was not above smiling at the good women neighbors when they openly sneered at her.

It was as if Red telepathically whispered with her smile: "Yeah, heifers. You don't really want to know, do you self-righteous bitches?" That always forced the good ladies to suddenly lower their gaze.

Most women subjected to such withering looks would probably only venture out into the neighborhood when it was absolutely unavoidable. Red strode down the street wherever and whenever she felt like it. Proudly, she owned the huge three story Victorian-style house she lived in with her employees and the two smaller houses on each side of it. But today was The Fourth and it was unavoidable that she would be out and about, and she desperately needed help. She motioned to Treasure with her head to follow her out of the store.

"You going to Cedar Point...what time your daddy say you supposed to be back?" she asked, flicking a spent match with her thumb and middle finger with enough force that it landed in the

middle of the street. It was the same force that she uses to thump
Prettyman on the back of his head when he pretended he doesn't hear
anybody.

One time she even snuck up behind Treasure, Prettyman, and
Kenny Webber and thumped them all on the back of the head real
hard. Prettyman had cracked Little Mama's bedroom door just wide
enough to let Treasure and Kenny for the first time peep at a grown
woman in a black brassiere and matching silk panties.

"He didn't tell me...but...I guess when Reverend Webber brings us
back."

She took a thoughtful drag on her cigarette.

"You been to that park before?"

"No..."

Red glanced back through the grocery store window. There she
was, Miss Lola glaring at the both of them.

"Com'on, walk with me for a minute," she whispered. They headed
slowly away from the direction of the Webbers, and then stopped.

"I need you to run a bunch of errands for me today. All day I'm
going to need you. You know Prettyman ain't no help. This the biggest
party I throw every Fourth of July. Red's Special. This is when I make
most of my money for the year. I'll need you to put down fresh towels
for the rooms. Run and get cigarettes, rubbers, Massengils douche.
Whatever the girls need. The two girls I thought was supposed to be
let out by now got their hearing postponed for another month..." Her
voice trailed off.

"I'll be glad to pay you fifty dollars." There was a softness in her
face, even a bit of sadness in her voice. Treasure looked frightened.

"I—I don't know, Miss Boudreaux," he said, looking at the
sidewalk. Red looked at her watch.

Red looked him straight in the eyes. Her words came fast and
even, without the slightest emotion, as if she were ticking off an
itemized debt that Treasure had blatantly ignored.

"Now look, I know your daddy don't know nothing about you and
Reverend Webber's boy sneaking home with Prettyman and playing
with his nice baseball and gloves and games I buy him. Or trying on
all them nice hats he got. I'm sure he don't know nothing 'bout you
and Kenny looking all up under my girls' dresses and skirts when they
downstairs relax'n and watching their stories. Your mama know my
girls teach y'all The Pony? Twistin'? The Stroll, and The Dog, and all
that dancing and clowning I let y'all do in my living room? And you
the main one ask all them nosey questions 'bout men and women
your daddy should be telling you..."She put her hand gently on his
shoulder. She took another approach.

She quieted, measuring him silently. "Now...I heard your daddy ain't gone get that pastorship tomorrow. I don't know how true it is. I also heard that Reverend Bishop want to give it to your daddy, but your daddy came up short on the building fund," she said, pausing to gauge how much of what she was saying struck its point.

"We know that. We already know that, Miss Boudreaux." Treasure looked frightened, and then inexplicably he felt like he wanted to cry, which made him even more frightened.

Red mashed the cigarette out with her patent leather stiletto.

"Look, Treasure, you come on down to the house with me. Call Reverend Webber and tell him your daddy put you on punishment again and that you won't be going this time. But thank you, anyway. I will pay you two hundred dollars. That should cover the building fund your daddy owe," she studied the boy's face. Maybe she said too much.

She quickly added, "I mean, maybe it will...I really don't know nothing 'bout that kind of stuff..."

Treasure wasn't sure he heard her right. "Two hundred dollars...?"

"—Two hundred, doll heart."

Just up ahead Dr. Niles could see that the sparse early Sunday morning traffic was beginning to thicken. In fact it had already begun several miles back, but he was too deep in reverie to notice. Now, he may have a change of plans. That was the one thing about Los Angeles traffic or life in general, but ever so much more in L.A.: always expect an obstacle or two.

Maybe that's what made this coastal paradise so sinister, so dishonest and conniving. Ahead, it looked like the traffic was picking up a bit. Maybe the tow truck had removed the unseen accident. Maybe the spectacle of someone changing their tire on the shoulder of the 405 had finished. Then there was always the possibility of not making it to the delivery room at all. Everything was a gamble, you just try the best you can to load the odds as much in your favor as possible. That day in Cleveland on his thirteenth birthday was the last time he prayed for anything. From that day on he relied mostly on whatever daring, sheer will, or skill he had acquired or discovered at his disposal. He saw his chance and cut over one, two, four lanes and caught the Santa Monica 10 exchange going east. Now, heading into the California sun, he flipped down the sun visor and slipped on a pair of Oliver Peoples shades.

Treasure had no idea how much work was involved preparing for the "Red's Fourth of July Special." Right from the beginning, the girls made it very clear to him: Cut that shyness out, do it quickly, and never mind about what's going on inside his pants. His first task was to go to every girl's room and take her list of things to get from the drug store, but they were impressed because they didn't need to write anything. He carried it all in his head: bottles of vinegar, jars of alum, which some of the girls only knew as "nice-n-tight," Sheiks, Peacock, Trojans, Chesterfields, Winston's, Pall Malls, foams and applicators, hot water bottles, small tins of Anacin, and on and on. In no time, he was efficient at unhooking and fastening brassieres and handing them their panties and stockings and slips and shoes to try on, and then ran to another room and repeated something similar, and return in time to another room to fetch a new pair of items, rotating his way deftly through several rooms simultaneously.

By eleven o'clock, the sun felt like it was in full blaze. Red pinned a wide, thick, green rubber band to his belt loop that had all the keys he would need. He was beginning to feel a little tired already. The first key was to all the closets in the house and endless rooms. The second key was to Red's bedroom and the large liquor cabinet inside. The third key was to the drawer built into the underside of the long buffet table in the large kitchen. That's where Red kept a loaded .45 and cash from the guests' purchase of rib or fish dinners or the three-hundred dollar "Red's Special" pass that entitled the buyer to sample every room for a three hour period.

By late afternoon, the men were drinking good Scotch and dancing to slow blues tunes with loose women who didn't belong to Red's house, but trying to pry some of those dollars loose from those who couldn't wait their turn to go up stairs. Jimmy Reed's "Further On Down The Road" must have played a hundred times but nobody seemed to mind. Treasure and Prettyman seemed to have vanished. Red needed Treasure to get three pints of Wild Irish Rose to give to three neighborhood men who mostly spent their days drinking out of brown paper bags and sitting on discarded old couches in a field of weeds in the middle of the block. But today Red had them turning ribs over several metal tubs in her back yard. She suspected that Prettyman had lured Treasure into peeping at what it was that the girls actually did on the other side of the door because he knew Treasure had room keys.

She tried not to panic and found them on the second floor collecting and putting down new towels outside Loretta's door. Red hauled them down to the kitchen, suspecting they were up to no good. This was about the third or fourth time they were seen hanging around Loretta's door, when her only guest—a numbers runner and goofy playboy named Bobby Beck, who was extremely jealous and who Loretta detested—had bought up Loretta's whole day and the night.

Red laid down the law. "Look P.K.—your ass is here to work. Don't let Prettyman get you fired before you get that jack your daddy needs. Now, first thing. Don't let Prettyman out of your sight for one minute, you hear me? You the Big Boss. Prettyman—you the little boss."

Prettyman, who was a year older than Treasure but almost a foot shorter, suddenly bolted so quickly toward the backyard door that it made Treasure jump. He spun around and sprinted back. He did it again. And again, like he was waiting for Red to yell at him. When she didn't, he came to a complete stop just inches from Treasure's face and just grinned, making his eyes move silly from side to side.

Red only smiled gently and kissed him on the back of his frizzy process, and then said softly to Treasure, " You'd think it was his birthday…Keep an eye on him, will you P.K.?"

Prettyman followed closely behind Treasure toward the door, when Treasure turned around.

"Miss Boudreaux?"

"Yes, baby"

"Why do you call me that…what's P.K.?"

Red stopped taking paper plates from a cabinet and looked down from a step-ladder. "Preacher's kid. You're a Preacher's kid. Right?"

Treasure nodded slowly, as if he had to think about it. When they got to the room, Prettyman dove onto his mother's bed. They were suddenly in another world, so calm and soft in this room, its decor plush and excessive, its colors ranging from blood red to burgundy to pink to light, light pink. Treasure found the box full of the cheap wine beneath her bed.

"No way. Come on now…," Treasure said with little conviction as he tried to yank Pettyman to his feet. He sat down on the bed and playfully smacked Prettyman on the head. Prettyman yawned. Treasure found himself lying across the bed on his back. Sleep was about to overcome him when he noticed the pictures on the wall.

"Who is that?" Treasure asked, almost demanding.

"Wh-Who?" Prettyman seemed baffled.

"All those white women in old style clothes and stuff?"

"Th-they m-my grandmamas and aunties. They not white. They colored."

"And who is that?" Treasure asked, almost as irritated as he was shocked.

Prettyman seemed puzzled why Treasure didn't recognize the woman. "—That's Lorretta." Prettyman was irritated now, because it was obvious who she was, as she was one that taught Treasure and Kenny The Twist, and The Dog, and other funny dances. Treasure sat up now and looked closely at the picture.

"No...I mean the man in the shark skin suit and the nice wavy process."

"That's Red. Th-that's when they got married. But I was too little," he said proudly. Suddenly Treasure didn't feel sleepy. He pulled a pair of scissors out of Prettyman's hand and placed it back on the night stand, and then pulled him by the arm until he got him out of the room.

Downstairs, the house was really filling up with more men and women, but mostly men, well-to-do looking men, men who kept their process fresh, their nails glazed and buffed, and smelled of Aqua Velva and Old Spice. Treasure moved among them removing empty shot glasses off the stereo and coffee tables.

Somebody took "Further on Down the Road" off and replaced it with the deeper and raw-throated sound of Howlin' Wolf. This new song played repeatedly too, and it seemed to change the energy of the room. Even Treasure felt it.

In church, he knew when the Holy Spirit was present and had seen it many times moving among and into worshipers. But this was another kind of spirit, and just as real. This song had a primal, stalking gait of a rhythm and the men seemed to respond with a decidedly more direct and sexual intent. The women too. The liquor flowed. The men felt up any woman near them. Women who came with men as well as Red's girls pressed themselves against men standing in line for ribs and fish and repeated lines from the song close to the men's faces. Treasure liked what he saw and what he was feeling in the midst of it. The sweet-sour smell of the liquor really tantalized him, and knew he would take a sip if he could get away with it. If this was sinful, then he wanted more of it.

By now Treasure wasn't tired one bit and was in the flow of things. Occasionally he recognized a few men and older relatives of children in the neighborhood. For some reason, perhaps because of the unlikely possibility that a preacher's child would blend in so smoothly and be so helpful in knowing his way around the house, he was, in a sense, hiding in plain sight. A hoard of newcomers invaded the food and liquor table. Red made each one of them feel like a war hero returning to an adoring wife, as he stood beside her , handing her paper plates while she filled them heartily. He went to the back yard to bring in a new platter of ribs when he discovered it was dark already. His heart sank. A jolt of fear jarred him more than the Wild Irish Rose drunks setting off a cherry bomb near him and laughing.

"Miss Boudreaux, you said I could leave before it got dark," he said as politely as he could, placing the platter of ribs near her. Red ignored him and greeted another new arrival who was still wearing his work clothes, a greasy blue gas station uniform and matching cap. It was obvious that he was extremely uncomfortable, but Red fussed over him like he was royalty, piled his plate high, and gave him a free, ice-cold Schlitz.

"Miss Boudreaux," he started again. Red suddenly pulled him away from the crowded table, her graciousness gone like it was a light switch.

"Listen. I know what I told you," she whispered." She removed two hundred dollar bills from her bra and stuck it under his nose.

"*This* is yours. You can have the other half when things die down a bit," she said, then tore the two bills in half and stuffed the other half of the bills in his back pocket. She pulled out her rubber band key ring and unlocked the flat drawer built into the table, deposited the other half, and locked it.

"O.K, big boy?" She paused and just stared at him. Treasure thought that he saw a mist in her eyes.

"I intend this to be my *last* special, baby. I'm going back down South and open me a real nice beauty shop. Me and Loretta and Prettyman. Now go find his behind, will you please? Bring him here and I'll give you your money so you can go."

Knowing Prettyman and himself, Treasure went right up to the third floor because Red had instructed them not to, unless she gave them permission. And she certainly didn't. It was kind scary up there, the narrow hall was lit by dim light bulbs shaped like candles on each side. Prettyman had told him that the third floor had ghosts and that Ce-Ce liked it up there because she could have it all to herself. The floor even had its own private stairs and entrance that opened up directly into the oversized bedroom. She always had the rich men up there, because Ce-Ce was stuck up too, just like them.

Treasure heard some stirring in the room, and turned to go back down the stairs. The door swung open and Ce-Ce rushed out into the hallway naked and swaying off balance toward him.

"Why the hell it took you so damn long to bring up what I asked for?" she slurred.

"We done ran outta ice and my best friend in this world want a bottle of...a bottle of...?" She wet her lips and stared at the floor, having drawn a blank.

Words began to tumble out of the boy's mouth. "I-I-I have to let Red bring you what you need because—"

Ce-Ce grabbed him by the shoulders and marched him down to the room, stood him in the doorway and announced into the room: "Tell'm what you need big, pretty, baby doll daddy—any damn thing you want he gone get it, baby," she said, grabbing hold of Treasure to keep her balance.

"Daughter?...daughter...? Who—somebody up here?" The man had a sonorous, almost booming voice that still held its diction. "Lord Jesusss! *Lord* Jesus! Close that door—Close it!" The man's mountainous belly obscured his face, but there was an instant recognition of whose voice it was. He was lying on his back and snatching the red silk sheets up to his chin. Treasure felt dizzy. He didn't feel real. Then he felt as though he had experienced this very scene before.

"Daddy, ain't no cause for you to talk to me like that. I ain't gone have it now, and I sure ain't gone have after we tie the knot," she scolded, and then turned to Treasure. "What's your name, again? I know you Prettyman's little friend."

Treasure's voice barely worked, "Treasure..."

Ce-Ce raised her voice indignantly, "I *said* what is your name?...Speak up when grown folks ask you something." This time he said it with enough force, as though he needed to awake from a bad dream. "Well Treasure, you get down stairs and get Red up here right now 'cause we out of everything," she said. The man slowly struggled to sit up, took his thick wireframes specs from the night stand and put them on. He struggled out of the bed with the red silk sheet wrapped around him, hustled to the doorway, and looked Treasure square in the face.

"Lord sweet Jesusss," he bellowed out. He shoved Ce-Ce and Treasure out of the doorway with such force that they both bounced off the hallway wall. The soon-to-be-retired pastor of The Tabernacle of the Second Coming slammed the door with a thunderous bang and locked himself in the room. All that Treasure and Ce-Ce could hear was the deep bass rumble of moaning and the high pitch of regretful appeals to his Savior.

Treasure ran down the stairs. Outside, the fire crackers burst with insane ferocity. Some fool had evidently set off a cherry bomb in the house it sounded like. He reached the second floor but couldn't go much further because the girls were crowded into the hallway. Somebody was screaming. Then there were anguished cries calling on Jesus mixed with foul curses and pitiful pleas of mercy from God in heaven. Treasure tried to push his way through the crowded hallway, determined to drag Prettyman from whatever mess he might get into and deliver him to Red, but men seemed to sprint out of every room and hidden space, carrying shirts and pants and shoes and hats. They converged on Treasure at the landing, pushing him down, down the stairs like a discarded Popsicle stick floating down a stream of dirty rain water to the sewer.

At the bottom of the stairs, everyone scattered. Some ran with their clothes through the kitchen snatching bottles of good liquor off the food table. Others went straight into the front yard and onto the sidewalk and tried to put their clothes on there. This drew even more onlookers. They cracked jokes at the spectacle and swiped pants and shoes out of their hands and ran around in circles in the middle of the street with them.

Treasure ran to the kitchen but Red was nowhere to be seen. He remembered what Red had forgotten. He had his own keys to the drawer of the food and liquor table. He tugged at the handle. It was still locked. He felt for his rubber band key ring, but felt nothing. He looked at his belt loop. There were no keys; the loop had been cut.

Suddenly, he heard what sounded like a horse falling down the stairs and galloping across on the second floor. More curses, and then sirens. He joined another surge of folks flooding through the kitchen and out into the back yard. He climbed the fence and burst full speed down an alley and knew he could be on his front porch in twenty minutes because that was his routine after visiting Prettyman after school. He leaned into the corner and ran smack into a padded wall.

A huge, dark-skinned policeman helped him up off his back. "Are you alright, son?" He said, rubbing his own stomach and winching.

At the front door of Treasure's house, the policeman spoke very kindly to Reverend Niles and advised him to keep better tabs on his child. He told Reverend Niles that a kid about Treasure's age was shot to death no more than thirty minutes ago. He said the shooting happened in a whore house, and that the Reverend's son obviously shouldn't be around that kind of place.

Reverend Niles thanked the huge but kind policeman profusely, closed the door, and stared at Treasure. He began to move the dining room table and the chairs to make room for the killing floor. Treasure got the whipping of his life and cried until he vomited, but he didn't remember feeling the stings of the wide leather belt his father wore to hold up his foundry work pants. Until this day, he didn't remember the whipping until forty-seven years later. What he has always remembered is what happened to Prettyman. It pained him still, at times. His father did stop whipping him at one point.

In truth, his father stopped because he had gotten a call from Reverend Bishop. It was Reverend Bishop who told his father to never ask his son where he had been that day and what he knew about last night. If he agreed to that, then he would present him as the new pastor of the Tabernacle of The Second Coming tomorrow morning in front of the whole church. Reverend Niles agreed readily and went on to become an incredible shepherd of the church.

Treasure was left to worship his own holy trinity of science, girls, and television. He wasn't even required to attend church. In fact, it was Reverend Bishop who put aside a scholarship for him to go through college and medical school.

Now, years later, Dr. Niles got off the O/R elevator just in time to stop the gurney carrying Mrs. Nguyen to her cesarean. He made a slashing motion across his throat and pushed the gurney back on to the elevator to head back to the delivery room. Two hours later, he delivered the three infants, after having finessed their positions, ever so delicately, down the birth canal. There were cheers in the operating room. There were tears from nurses, Mrs. Nguyen, and her husband, but not from the older nurse with the clinically cold voice that called him early that morning.

The nurse ran her hand up the back of his sweat-soaked scrub shirt, which had risen up a bit on his back, and yanked it down. Dr. Niles, startled by the gesture, quickly turned to her. She discretely ran her hand up his back, pulled the studded leather harness and let it snap. It answered his question to his ongoing conflict between the flesh and the spirit. He felt guilt and relief from the muddled solutions he found in his youth. Something about all of this confusion felt strangely familiar. Pain mixed with pleasure. This woman, who knew his secrets, smiled wickedly. This woman, who knew his turbulent soul, stared with knowing eyes at him. He mouthed the words to her: "God bless you..."

WARMING UP
MAXIMILIAN LAGOS

"He's got a stick of candy jus' nine inch long
He sells it as fast as a hog eats his corn
His stick candy don't melt away
Jus' gets better, so the ladies say."

Candy Man Blues – Mississippi John Hurt (1927)

"AHHH, love...that feels so good," he cooed, English accent muffled by the pillow.

The redhead remained silent, working her tongue in, out and around his puckered opening. Joey was face down, moaning his pleasure into a cushion, pale white ass in the air. His clothes were strewn about the tiny room, having shed them as he entered.

There was a rap on the door. "Five minutes," said the voice of the band's manager. The sound of the rest of the band heading to the stage was muted by the locked dressing room door. Another bang on the door.

"Just hurry up and fuck. We got a gig now, in case you didn't remember," laughed Mike, the band's drummer.

Joey moaned again, either in reply or in lust. She had been working on his hole for what seemed like hours, making him moan and writhe with intense pleasure.

"Alright baby, enough of that," panted Joey as he turned to face the girl. "I need to cum." Roughly, he pushed her onto her back on the filthy backstage dressing room carpet. She was still fully clothed: Joey was far too consumed with his own lust to worry about hers.

"Fucking hell, love! You still got all your kit on. I gotta do everything my fuckin' self." Reaching over her prone body, Joey fumbled for his jeans. Snagging the black denim, he plunged his hand into a pocket, removing his well-used pocket knife.

The blade clicked as Joey opened it with one hand. He looked down at her for a reaction but her eyes remained vacant and her expression blank. "This doesn't scare you, does it baby?" he teased. "My little knife here? No? Well how about now?"

He lunged forward and straddled her stomach, pinning her to the floor. She rolled and fought but Joey was bigger and stronger, but not by much. He had the look and stature of someone who abused his body in every way possible. Feeling the sharp edge of the steel pressed against her smooth cheek, she stopped struggling.

Her eyes remained fixed on his, not betraying any emotion for him to see, to use against her. Through the tinny monitor speaker above the door, the sound of the band starting to warm up their instruments on stage flowed into the room.

"Fuckin' hell! I'm gonna miss the show," he joked. "And I'm really close to the stage too..."

The humor drained from his face as Joey pushed the girl down by the throat and quickly sliced open the redhead's tight black commemorative concert T-shirt, revealing smallish but perfectly beautiful tits. Like a starving man jumping on a steak, Joey attacked a hard, brown nipple with his teeth and tongue. A sharp intake of breath was the first indication to Joey that his playmate was still alive.

"Ahh, finally. You like that do you, baby? You like a bit of pain, don't you?" He traced the point of the knife over the roughness of her other nipple, making her shudder. He bit down and pulled on her nipple like a dog with a blanket, shaking his head back and forth. The redhead screamed at the pain and her chest flushed at the pleasure. Her scream earned her a hard slap on her exposed tit, unwillingly making her back arch upward.

"Shall I cut you, baby?" Joey whispered. "Make you bleed?" He ran the knife's tip across the swell of her breasts. The redhead started to wriggle and fight again at his words but another hard bite on the nipple quieted her instantly. The sound of the cheering crowd getting louder stopped the travel of the steel across her flesh before it could open her skin.

"Oh fuck this!" Joey exploded and spun around so his hard cock was hovering above her ruby red lips. "Suck me you fucking slag. Make me cum in your fucking mouth." He thrust his cock into her mouth, knocking her head against the hard floor.

The sensation of her lips and tongue on his hot shaft almost made him orgasm immediately. She moaned at the rough treatment, but feeling her tongue pressing flat against the top of his cock, rubbing the head on every stroke, Joey was ignorant to everything but the fire building in his body.

Bucking his hips up and down, he fucked the girl's mouth, hard and rough, not caring if he was hurting her. She reached up and grabbed him by the ass and pulled him more forcefully against and into her. The intensity took Joey by surprise. His head was resting on her thigh and the smell of her arousal was teasing his nose. He had to taste her.

The girl's thin yoga pants were no match for Joey's blade and met the same fate as her shirt. Her cunt was hairless and the sight of its wetness drove Joey to further heights of lust fueled madness.

He slammed his face against her mound with a growl and started licking ferociously. The attack slammed the redhead's thighs against Joey's head, rocking him back and forth as he ate her pussy. Her teeth clamped down firmly on his shaft and this time it was Joey's turn to moan into her.

Flinging his knife across the room, he brought his arms around her legs, prying his head loose. His fingers spread her pussy as wide as he could, searching for her clit. It was erect and almost looked like it was throbbing, begging to be licked and sucked. Pulling her tight against his face, Joey felt the girl moan against his dick, her tongue sliding all over the shaft, her hands teasing and penetrating his asshole.

"Oh yes you fucking slut...you like this rock star shit don't you? Like getting fucked backstage. You could get used to this, eh love?" Her juice covered his lips and chin and her hips were pressing upwards trying to find his mouth again.

Joey smashed his face against her again and took one of her pink lips into his mouth. His sucking and biting matched with both the tempo of the music coming from the stage and the rhythm of the redhead on his cock. Joey could feel the cum start to boil in his balls but he had to have this beautiful cunt around his cock.

"Right. Up on your knees you fucking slag." He pulled his rod out of her mouth and slapped her hard on her thigh, leaving a bright pink handprint. As she got to her knees and crawled over to bend over the sofa, Joey could hear the sound of the band's first hit from the stage, vamping, waiting for their lead singer.

Music is so like fucking, thought Joey. The first hit was his favorite so he started to sing quietly as he moved behind the redhead. "Oh yeah baby, you are the one I need..."

Joey rammed his dripping cock into her spread pussy, pushing a growling scream from the ruby lips. "I know you want me too, let's find someplace private..." he panted. The music was entrancing and Joey's thrusting matched the beat of the bass drum perfectly.

"Baby Baby, let me undress you...I need to feel your skin..." Every thrust brought him closer and closer to the edge as the song worked the crowd into frenzy. The redhead pushed back against his thrusts, struggling to build her own orgasm before Joey went off.

"Show me that you want me...That I am the best you ever had...The last you ever want..." The girl screamed when Joey's hand smacked the tight cheek of her ass. Again, he landed a blow, causing another scream. The mix of her pain and his lust pushed him over the edge.

"Oh fuck baby, I'm coming!" Joey pulled his throbbing cock out of her cunt with a slurping noise and sprayed his fluid all over her back and ass. Wailing with frustration, the redhead rolled and sat heavily against the couch. She flung her legs wide and attacked her clit with one hand while torturing her nipple with the other.

Joey smirked as she rubbed herself to a screaming climax, and then relaxed, twitching, against the couch.

"It's about time baby...I have been finished forever and there are five hundred thousand insane fans screaming for the music to start." He hoisted himself onto the ratty couch and laid on his side, cock dripping onto the fabric.

The redhead struggled to her feet and started cleaning herself up. Joey's eyes followed her across the room as she pulled extra clothes off the rack in the corner of the dressing room. With practiced speed, she put on her makeup and fixed her hair.

With one final check in the mirror, she caught Joey's stare in the reflection. "Fuck off Joey. Have a drink...have a shower...have whatever the fuck you want...but don't be here when I get off stage."

The sound of Holly's boots echoed from the hallway as the door to the dressing room closed behind her. Her band had been vamping forever but now that she was warmed up, she needed to perform.

MY STRONGEST WEAKNESS
C. DENNIS MOORE

"But they'll find a whiskey glass and a woman's ass
Will make a good man go bad
Well, each will leave you broke and hurt
And they'll take what you once had."

A Whiskey Glass and A Woman's Ass
– Chuck Roberson (1996)

I'VE NEVER had trouble getting women. I've had trouble turning them down, trouble getting rid of them, but never trouble getting them. That's not to say they necessarily throw themselves at me or that they're just on my doorstep when I walk outside. But they turn up here and there.

I was walking home from a buddy's house one night, a few too many beers in me—and when I'm drunk, I'm horny, you better believe that—and my buddy lived just off downtown, so I cut through this parking garage to get across the block, and there was a woman getting into her car. I said hi and she said hi and I noticed her shirt and I am a gentleman so I complimented the outfit.

She chuckled a nervous thank you and I stopped and collected myself so I didn't sound like a drunken idiot and I said I'm sorry, I didn't mean to make you nervous I'm harmless, just wanted to say I like the shirt.

She stopped chuckling and looked at me pretty straight and said thank you again, seriously this time, and I don't think it was thirty minutes later before we were in her back seat.

You ever meet someone and just know you can fuck them if you want? They're not desperate or ugly, it's just something between the two of you, and you know all you have to do is put forth the smallest amount of effort.

Her skin tasted like salt and I dug it against the bourbon, and when my hands went to her stomach, she was warm and getting warmer. A little bit of sweat had begun to break out between her breasts and I lifted her shirt higher and licked it off, and then unclipped the front of her bra—my favorite kind—and took each nipple in my mouth while one hand steadied me on the seat, and the other pulled her slacks down and moved her panties aside. No point in taking them off unless we had to, out here in the parking garage.

She was wet when I touched her and got even wetter when I slid one finger quickly inside her, then put in another. She squeezed down around my fingers and my cock was throbbing. I pulled out of her and got my pants open, took it out, and she reached down and touched it, grabbed it tight in her hand, and pulled me closer.

I slid inside her and felt heaven like never before. This girl was a knockout. Short red bob, plump lips, and skin like cream. Blue eyes looked up at me and her face brightened for a second when I hit bottom in her.

She moaned and the sound of her voice made my cock flex inside her, and that got her too.

We started moving together and our rhythm felt like we'd been doing it for years. It was insane how perfect it felt with this girl, how hot it was, how much I wished right then we had a room, a bed, hell, a mattress in the park, something to give us more room, I had the need to move this girl around, toss her about and fuck her till she loved me.

She was hardly my first one-night-stand, but I knew only a couple minutes in it would be a chore topping this woman.

Just the right combination of moans and panting, biting her lip and bracing herself against the back door. The passenger side back door was open and I was leaning in, across the back seat she was draped across, fucking her and keeping watch out the other window for anyone coming into the garage.

She begged, "More," and I thrust into her with all I had, rocking the car, and she said, "God yes!" so I kept on like that. My hips slammed against her. She pulled her legs up, opening them wider and using her arms for leverage against the closed door and push herself closer, fucking me back.

I leaned in and we kissed and at the feel of her tongue, my cock twitched again, got just a little harder. She moaned louder and I glanced around to make sure we were still alone.

A minute passed like that, we fucked like it was the last thing we'd ever do. She was just downright soaked clear through, and I was throbbing like it was about to burst, and then I felt my orgasm getting closer and that just made me even harder.

She noticed the change and she said, "Yes, yes, do it, please," and her urging me on helped immensely, and before I knew it, there was my orgasm, rushing full speed up my cock, and I came so hard I knew it was literally splashing inside her. She felt it and started pressing down harder against me, moving her hips forward, grinding her clit down against my shaft, and then her thighs started to twitch and she made a noise like she was crying before saying, "Holy fuck yes!" then letting out her breath in a long deep sigh before pushing me away and rolling over on her side to finish riding out her wave.

She had beautiful thighs when she was curled up on her side in the back seat like that, and I wished I hadn't just finished because I'd love to have another go at her.

"That was amazing," I said and she just smiled and nodded.

I almost asked her what she was doing tomorrow, but I didn't think Tess would care much for me leaving a second night in a row. Instead I just moved back and pulled my pants back up, gave her some room to collect herself and get out. She put her arms around me and we kissed and before she could say anything I told her, "I'm really sorry about being so forward like that, I wasn't trying to do that. I just liked your shirt, really."

"That's okay," she said. "It was so fucking good, I haven't come like that in a long time."

"Glad to help," I smiled.

"Fuck, any time," she offered.

"I just might take you up on that," but I knew I never would. "It's so late, though, I have to work tomorrow. I need to get to sleep."

"You can call me tomorrow if you like," she said, and I took her number. I deleted it before I ever got home, and never even saw her out on the street again after that. I did go through that garage again once or twice after a night's drinking with my buddies, but she was never there. Just as well. I don't have any trouble getting them, it's getting rid of them that's the hard part.

THERE was this other one once. We worked together, but she was nothing to write home about. She was nice, just not someone you'd ever make a big show of having been on. I saw her out at this bar my friends and I went to one night. I'd never seen her outside of work and I went over and said hey and we got to talking about work and trashing on everyone there. It was a good time, laughing and getting along. Then she said she had to be getting home and I said I'd walk her out cuz I'm a gentleman and all, so we got outside and I started walking her to her car saying something about this supervisor we had, a real skanky-ass broad, three hundred pounds if she's an ounce, wearing short shorts when she comes in on the weekends. Gross as shit and everyone made fun of her, and me and this work chick were cracking up when she veered off into this alley.

"You ain't gonna throw up, are you?" I asked, wondering why we were in this alley, and she said, "Nope," just that.

"Where we going?"

"Wanna show you something," she slurred. This chick was so wasted that night. But I have to admit, seeing her out like that in regular clothes...the T-shirt really hugged her tits and I'd been staring at them all night. I didn't have to ask what it was she wanted to show me; I thought I had a pretty good idea, and in the state I was in that night, I wanted to see it.

We fucked standing up against a brick wall. I got her from behind after I worked her jeans down over her ass. I've never been into the big ass thing, and this chick had a big one, but something about the way she carried it made it sexy. There wasn't any working up to it, making out, or anything, she just turned toward the wall, shoved her ass against my cock, and grabbed my hand, put it up under her shirt. She wasn't wearing a bra, which was awesome, and her tits were so big and full and smooth. I started rubbing 'em, cupping 'em and pressing myself against her.

She said something about how she'd wanted this forever but wasn't looking to get fired for it, but she had her chance now and didn't want to let it go. She unzipped her pants and started working them down and I said, "I'll get it."

I got 'em down, then her panties, and I was in her in seconds, her ass so hard and cool against my skin when I got all the way inside her.

She moaned low and smooth and it was sexy as shit, and when I started moving in and out of her, she responded by not waiting for me; she fucked me hard, all I had to do was stand there and this chick took care of the rest.

Her hair smelled like coconut, but her perfume was like a warm spring day and it turned me on even more.

I know I was drunk that night, but I remember pretty clearly that girl fucked me like there was no tomorrow, ramming herself backward with all she had. I held onto her tits, felt the nipples hard under my palms, and her breathing was fast but not too loud. She looked determined. That was hot. And she was so tight and soft inside, that was even hotter.

It didn't take long to feel the orgasm growing steadily deep down inside, and I hoped she was working toward hers, too, because I wasn't going to last long like this.

I grabbed her by the hips and said, "Let me," and then I started pounding the hell out of her, that big ass slapping against my hips. That did the trick and I could tell the way she leaned further against the wall, practically bent over to the ground, and let me work that she was about to get off.

I gave it to her as hard as I could, and my cock was like a metal piston working in and out at a hundred rpm's a minute and she was moaning now, "Oh my God oh my God oh my God." When she put her hands against the wall again and started moving her hips with me I knew she was about to go, so I doubled my efforts, the smell of that perfume driving me crazy and she was so damn tight this girl. I couldn't help it any longer and I finally gave that last killer shove inside her, trying to force her orgasm and mine at the same time, feeling those hot waves shooting through me as she squeezed me even tighter when she came too.

We stayed there, drunk as fuck, and locked together for another minute before my cock slid out of her and we both stumbled away from each other and pulled up our pants.

"Thanks," she said as she zipped her pants up and got her balance with a hand against the wall. "Couldn't do that at work."

"Unfortunately not," I said, and I meant it, because if this chick ever came onto me again, I knew I'd never be able to tell her no.

It never happened again, but not because I didn't want it to. I tried a few times, but I just never saw her out again, alone, and she was adamant about not risking it at work. Smart girl, but I admit my pride was hurt a little at that; I thought for sure I'd given it to her good enough that night she'd almost have to have it again, as soon as possible.

Then again, truth be told, it didn't much matter. I mean, I looked at her in a whole new light after that. Her shirts never seemed to hide her tits anymore, and I watched her walk by a million times and just wanted to get my mouth around them. And that ass was like a beacon shining in the night, luring me in from the storm and there were at least two times I was so moved by what she was wearing that day, I had to head to the bathroom and knock it out real quick before getting back to work. I told her once I'd done it, hoping it would trigger something and she'd want to meet up after work, but she just giggled and said, "That's pretty hot. I wish we could go somewhere right now."

Well, "right now" was no good, I'd just taken care of it. I kept trying to get her to agree to later, but no dice.

That's okay, though. Because little did I know, but I was already in deep shit with this girl. It's easy to hate yourself when you know every wrong thing that's ever happened to you is a direct result of your own bad choices. Easier still, knowing you'll make those same mistakes again. That no matter how good things get in your life, no matter how happy your home, how productive your job, how healthy your relationship, the seeds of destruction for everything you love and hold dear is inside you and sooner or later it will come out, those things will be destroyed, one day this happy life you're smiling through every day and night will be a memory, and when you look in the mirror, you'll be looking directly into the eyes of the man responsible.

Tess knew about her. I don't know how she found out, but she did, and she started right then on getting herself out.

She started moving stuff, a piece or two at a time, to her sister's, just little stuff I wouldn't notice, her stuff mostly. It was only two weeks after the late night alley fuck with the chick from work that I came home one evening and found Tess and our son in the living room, suitcases at the ready.

"What's all this?"

"What's it look like?"

I shrugged, confused, knowing right away, though, that she'd found out. I didn't know which one blabbed, but I knew one of those stupid whores had found out where I lived, shown up, and told my wife everything.

But that wasn't what happened. Like I said, I don't know how she found out, but the chick from work never said a thing.

I didn't even bother trying to lie my way out, she had me good. So I admitted it. Then told her it was just once, it was a drunken mistake, and it would never happen again. I wouldn't go out, I wouldn't drink, she'd see how much she meant to me.

Nothing I said worked. She grabbed the suitcases and took our son, who had just turned five, out to the car. She took the car. That fucking sneaky bitch, man, she waited till I got home and she took the car.

To say I hit a depression is putting it mildly.

My drinking wasn't confined to the weekends anymore, nor to the bars. I was drunk from the moment I got home from work, till the moment I passed out, usually too late to even bother going to sleep, before I had to get up again and go to work.

My job was on the line too. Everyone knew Tess had left me, and with no wife at home to take care of me, I tried to bang every woman within a ten mile radius. None took the pathetic, I'm–so–down–on–myself bait—so I guess I lied when I said I never had any trouble getting women, it's just that when I finally could get them, I couldn't get them because I was such a broken-down loser and it showed.

The final straw hit one morning when I was stumbling outside to go to work and my landlady, who lived next door, was outside walking her dog. I met her in the alley and she shook her head and said something about how sad it was to see me in this state.

Landlord in the technical sense; her husband owned my house and I paid rent to them every month, but this woman was no old bag with a hundred cats and a dumpy body. She had tits for days, for one. And while she wasn't a beauty queen, I'd always wanted to see them puppies, and, hopefully whatever else she was hiding. I'd been drinking whiskey all night, I reeked and could hardly see straight, was gonna just stumble into work, probably get fired, and go drink away the rest of what was in my pockets. But I saw this woman out there in the alley, with the early morning sun glaring down, and her tank top visible under her thin robe, which wasn't closed at all, and her tits were just begging for me right then.

"You really look like hell," she said, and chuckled.

"And you're one sexy, smoking ass, hot angel," I said. What the fuck? I'd lost everything else.

She just laughed.

"What's so funny?"

"Well," she said, "you are seriously one drunk dude."

"Not too drunk to know a hot chick when I see her. Seriously, I've thought you were so fucking hot since the day I moved in, but, you know, it's like feeling up your boss, you don't do it."

"Hmm, too bad for you, then," she smiled, and I couldn't tell at first if she was honestly interested, or just playing along.

She started to walk away and I said, "Where you going?"

"Don't you have to get to work?"

"Look at me. Do you really think they give a shit if I'm on time or not? They're probably hoping I'll call in."

"That's probably not a good idea. You're still my tenant, and the rent still needs paid."

Now, I'm not the smoothest cat in the alley, but I've done my share of bullshit-talking, and right then, I was so horny looking at this woman, I could have hit a home run with it. I fed her some more nonsense and eventually got her into the garage where my car was no longer parked. I showed her I was dead serious about wanting her and, funny enough, she was pretty open to what I was dishing out. She dropped her robe and was just wearing that tank and a pair of shorts and while she wouldn't have been hurting if she lost, say twenty pounds or so, what she had she wore with confidence, and it was killing me.

We danced around the issue for another minute, until finally, she said, "So you like these, huh?" and grabbed her tits, seeing how I hadn't taken my eyes off them in over a minute.

"I love 'em," I said.

"Too bad you don't get to touch 'em."

Well, that wasn't true at all, as I proved by taking a handful. They were so huge, and so firm. My cock twitched in my pants.

"My husband would kill you, you know."

"Good thing I didn't plan on telling him," and I pulled the shoulder strap of her tank down so I could get at her tits. It was like the Holy Grail, this thing. I sucked it, ran my tongue over the nipple, and she let out her breath real slow.

"You're gonna get me so damn wet doing that."

"Good," I said, then pulled down the other strap and had them both out.

"Hold on now," she said. "We don't even know what you've got for me. What are you working with that makes this worth the risk?"

I showed her and she seemed impressed enough. She didn't laugh. Took it in her hand and I think I coulda lost it right then. I wanted to be in her, between her legs, between her lips, I didn't care, hell bite the fucking thing, just do something. I was dying here.

She asked, "You want me?" and I nodded and made a noise in the affirmative. "Right here?" she asked. "In the garage?"

"Good enough for me," I said. It was hotter than hell out there and I was already sweating my ass off, but I honestly didn't expect this to take long, and anyway, I was sweating out mostly alcohol, which I seriously needed.

She got down in front of me and took it in her mouth, and I sucked in my breath and moaned, "Holy shit!" and that's when Tess walked in.

She had been saying something about picking up our son from kindergarten because she had a job interview today and when she walked in, this was the sight she found.

THERE is a darkness in my heart. It's not something I tended. I didn't cultivate it over the years in order to harden my heart or set my defenses against a cold and bitter world. I'm just weak. I know the things in life that will make me a better person, a more fulfilled man: the love of my wife and child, success and happiness in my job, a peaceful and calm home. And I had all of these things. But I threw them away, and I knew while I did it exactly what was happening.

And I did it anyway.

Why?

Just like I said: I'm weak. We've all got out weaknesses, of course. Drugs for some, power for others. They make us do ridiculous things in pursuit of them. My strongest weakness however is women. And if I've got a few drinks in me, and my body is telling me I need to be taken care of, any woman will do. Never mind my wife at home who's never told me no and who has never ever failed to turn me on.

My mind doesn't work like that. Wine, women, and song, minus the song, that's all I need sometimes.

Tess hadn't filed for divorce yet the day she walked in to find the landlady blowing me in the stifling hot garage, but she had by the end of the day. I lost my job that day, as I knew I was going to. And with no job, never mind the landlady having a sudden bout of conscience and telling me I needed to leave before she felt compelled to tell her husband, I lost my house, too.

I've got a few friends now who are kind enough to let me bounce around from couch to couch, and I'm thankful to have them. But on nights like tonight, a Wednesday, everyone's at home sleeping, preparing for work the next morning, I don't feel like reminding them how horribly I messed up my own life. So I leave early, start drinking before the sun even goes down. Yes, it's part of what got me in this mess, but it's easy, it's cheap, and I'm good at it. So I drink. A whiskey glass in front of me is a beautiful sight.

I stare at myself in the mirror behind the bar, wondering how I dig myself out of this mess. Put the glass down, for one. Stop banging anything that moves. I could do that, I tell myself. I know I could. And if there wasn't a hot, dark-haired mess behind me, eyeballing me in the mirror, I might even give it some serious thought. But this whiskey's taking its toll on me, and right now I think I gotta go talk to this girl.

HEAD GAMES
ROBERT BUCKLEY

"What kind of love is that you made
The world starts a-tremblin' and the buildings shake
Love me and hug me once again
Let the roof and the walls come tremblin' in."

Lipstick, Powder and Paint — Big Joe Turner (1956)

WHO IN HELL was hitting the door with a sledgehammer? All he wanted to do was sleep. Six straight 12-hour days had finally come to an end, and he had planned to sleep right through his three-day weekend.

The banging resumed. Someone was trying the break down the damned door. He groaned as he rolled out of bed and pulled a robe around his nakedness. He stumbled toward the front door mumbling, "The fucking place had better be on fire."

He yanked the door open to find..."Dave?"

"You slimy, fucking, sneaky, rat-shit, motherfucker, son-of-a-bitch bastard prick!"

"Huh?"

"Back-stabbing piece of shit...you fuck, you lousy bastard..."

He closed the door, counted off two seconds and opened it again."

"... Low-life scumbag ..."

"Dave...what the fuck are you going on about?"

"Yeah, right. Pretend you don't know."

"Dave, I'm so fucking tired I can't see. I'm not going to play puzzle games. What's your problem?"

"You! You're my fucking problem. Backstabber!"

"What the hell's the matter?"

"You fucked my wife."

He shook himself like a wet dog. "You're drunk, Dave. Or you're on something. Sniffing glue maybe. I don't know; I don't give a shit. I'm going back to bed."

"Is that where you fucked her? In that bed?"

"Where the hell did you get the idea I fucked Denise?"

"She told me, you shit!"

"Huh?"

"Yeah, she confessed. She was all broken up about it, said she never wanted it to happen, until you seduced her. My pal, my buddy...lousy prick."

"I'm closing the door, Dave. I'll talk to you later. I'm going back to bed."

"You ain't getting away with this, you—you..."

"Yeah...later."

He slammed the door, turned and shuffled back toward his bedroom. What the hell was that all about? Dave must have gone nuts. He'd think about it again when he woke up in a few more days, but not now. He craved sleep.

The phone rang. "Ah, shit," he whined.

"Hello?"

"Tommy?"

"Denise?"

"Is Dave there?"

"He just left."

"Oh, dear. I was hoping I'd reach you before he got there."

"Denise, I'm exhausted. What the hell is going on?"

"Oh, Tom. I did something awful. I feel so guilty."

"Uh-huh."

"You know, I love Dave more than anything. I wouldn't ever want to hurt him."

"Denise, please, I'm fading here."

"Well, the thing is, Tom...things haven't been real good between Dave and me in, you know...the bedroom..."

"Uhhhnnng..."

"Tommy? Are you still there?"

"Huh? Uh, yeah. Denise, please, come to the point."

"Tommy, I had sex with another man."

"Okay."

"Tommy?"

"I mean—you did?"

"Yes. My boss. Oh, Tommy, I didn't mean to. It's just...I guess when you've been married for thirteen years things get kinda stale. I mean, every night...well, not *every* night—not by a long shot—but, when we do it's just so routine, you know? I rub his dick and he rubs my tits and then..."

"Yeah, Denise, okay...routine."

"Yeah, well, my boss is younger than me and just full of life and snazzy...like Dave used to be. And Friday he took us all out for drinks after work because we landed a big account, and I had some drinks, and then the other girls left, and we were by ourselves, and then he said he'd give me a ride home, but when we got to the garage...Oh, Tommy, he fucked me in his car. In the garage. It was...glorious."

"Denise, why does Dave think I screwed you?"

"'Cause I told him you did."

"Uh-huh. Sweetie, I'm really, really, really tired. I can't think too much. So tell me straight out, okay? Why the fuck did you tell him that?"

"Well, when I came home he was up waiting for me, and he wanted to have some sex, and before I could clean myself up...Well, the thing is, James came in me about four times and, see, I was pretty sticky. Like, his cum was kinda oozing out of me. Well, Dave's not blind, you know."

"Denise? Hon? You still haven't told me—"

"Aw, Jesus, Tom. I'm so sorry, but Dave just demanded I tell him who fucked me and I...well, I just blurted out the first name that popped into my head...Yours."

"Oh."

"Tommy? Hello?"

"I'm going to sleep, Denise. I'll talk to you later."

"But, Tommy?"

He hung up the phone and walked with eyes half-closed to his bedroom. He let the robe fall off his shoulders and tumbled into the bed. As sleep enveloped him, one thought trailed off: *Fuck Denise? What, are they kidding?*

PINK remnants of sunset glowed off the walls as his eyelids broke the seal of sleep. He stretched and rolled out of bed. Standing, stretching again, he glanced at the clock. Enough sleep. Time to enjoy the weekend.

Under the shower he chuckled to himself. Funny what fatigue will do to your head. What a fucked-up dream.

As he emerged from the shower he heard soft knocking. He retrieved his robe, stopping to knot the cloth belt before opening the door. Dave and Denise nodded, but said nothing.

"Hey, guys, funny you should drop by. I had this screwy dream that—"

"We need to talk, Tom," Dave said.

"Huh?"

"About this morning, Tommy." Denise added.

"This morning?"

"I was pretty hot this morning," Dave continued. "I've calmed down now."

"Oh, shit. It wasn't a dream."

They stepped past him. He motioned for them to sit down.

Dave began, "Tom, I was wrong—"

"Oh, good, I—"

"Don't interrupt."

"Huh? Oh, sure. Sorry."

"Anyway," Dave continued, "I talked this out with Denise and I hadn't realized how... well...how our intimate life had deteriorated. It's mostly my fault."

"Oh, Dave, darling, no it isn't—"

"Now, Denise, please. I let things get to the point they are now. I've been negligent to your needs, there's no other word for it."

"I love you, Darling."

"I love you too, Denise." Dave smiled and looked at Tom. "And that's why I want to apologize to you, Tom."

"Oh, hey, think nothing more of it..."

"Tom, please, let me finish."

"Sorry."

"You see, I understand now. I haven't been attentive to Denise's needs. And, to be honest, I'm not sure I ever did...completely...satisfy her, you know, intimately?"

"Oh, Dave, Darling," Denise smiled. A tear rolled down her cheek.

Dave smiled back. "So, understanding my, uh, shortcomings, I also understand why Denise would seek affection from someone who has been our friend, well, from the beginning."

"Huh?"

"Tom, rather than curse you, I should be thanking you."

"For what?"

"For giving Denise what she needed, when she needed it. She went to a trusted friend, and like a friend you helped her."

"Now hold on a minute—"

"Tom, it's okay. I think it's wonderful what you did. Do you think I'd feel better if she turned to a total stranger?"

"But, I didn't—"

Denise stood quickly and stepped over to Tom. "Oh, Tommy, yes you did. You're the most wonderful friend a girl ever had. And now,

Dave understands that too." She gave Tom an exaggerated wink.

"Yes," Dave said. "You're a good friend, Tom. You've been a best friend for fifteen years, and you've continued to be our friend throughout our marriage. That's why, Denise and I have decided, we want you to become a part of our marriage."

"What?"

"Tom, I'm man enough to accept the fact that I don't satisfy all of Denise's needs. And I adore her so much; I would do all I could to see that she is completely happy. We decided that means opening our marriage bed to a third partner, and who better to open it to than the best friend any couple could want."

"Tommy?" Denise smiled. "Well, say something."

"Okay. You're both fucking crazy."

Denise giggled. "Dave, could you let me and Tommy be alone for a little bit?"

"Uh, sure, Babe. I'll wait out on the deck."

Denise waited for Dave to step outside. She kneeled in front of Tom and took his hands. "I'm sorry, Tommy. I don't blame you for being, well, confused."

"Confused? Jesus, Denise. Why didn't you tell him it was your boss?"

"Tom, you just heard what he said."

"Yeah, he thinks I fucked you."

"Okay. First of all, I can't tell him about James. I have to go away on a business trip with him for three days next week. If I told Dave, no trip, no job. We can't afford to lose my job."

Tom swiped a hand over his forehead. "Okay, I can *almost* see the logic in that. But what the hell is this about him inviting me into your bed? What the hell is he talking about?"

Denise's smile widened. "Isn't it great? It's just the most perfect thing that could happen."

"Perfect? Denise, either I'm crazy, or Dave just said it was okay for me to fuck you. Hell, not just fuck you, but fuck you in his bed. Christ, maybe fuck you in his bed while he's in bed too."

"I know. Isn't it amazing? I couldn't believe it when he suggested it. He's so wonderful."

"Denise! You can't be saying it's okay with you?"

"But, of course it is, Tommy."

"But—but, we've been friends since high school."

"I know, the best of friends. I knew you for years before I met Dave. I even came to you to ask you if you thought I should marry him, remember? And then you were best man at our wedding and—"

"Yes, so, that's what I mean...why?"

"Tom, didn't you ever think about me...sexually, I mean?"

"Huh? Denise, I...well...no, not really."

He wasn't prepared for the hurt look on her face. He hastened to add, "I mean, maybe, when we first met. But, then you became my best friend."

"Uh-huh," her smile returned. "And you used to tell me about your dates, and I'd tell you about mine. Sometimes, I got so jealous of those girls, but I thought, maybe, you got jealous a little bit too, of the boys I dated."

"Denise...Honey, you've always been my best friend. Jesus, fucking you would be like fucking my sister."

Dave knocked and let himself in. "You guys had your talk?"

"Yes," Denise said and stood. "Let's go."

"But—"

"Now, David."

Tom shrugged as his friends left.

IT WAS all crazy. What had gotten into his friends? These were people he'd known forever. Maybe if Denise had just confessed to him about the affair with her boss, it wouldn't seem so odd. Such things happened in the best of relationships. But this crazy through-the-looking-glass madness about him becoming a third partner in their marriage had pulled the rug out from under him.

His head hurt. He decided to go out.

Valeria was working behind the bar at the Pour House. She was a big-boned Russian beauty who was fond of low-rise shorts with crotch-high legs. She flirted carelessly with Tom, but his mind kept returning to the scene in his apartment.

Valeria cupped his chin and squeezed. "Hey, Joe!" She called every male "Joe."

"Huh," Tom reacted to her green-blue eyes as she held him firmly in her right hand.

"What's matter with you? I show you my ass all night. I lean over and let you see down my shirt. See, no bra. And you? You got as much life as Lenin. What, you drink so much you embalmed?"

"Ah, hell," Tom shook his head. "Sorry...I just...well, have you ever had a friend? I mean, a friend you had so long you thought you knew them like you knew yourself? And then, out of the blue, they do something that just...I dunno, makes you wonder if you know them at all."

"I think maybe you get new friend, then everything be okay. Big, beautiful Russian girl, with great tits, and long legs, and ass, like you say, 'to die for, Baby.' I get off at one."

"I hate myself already, but I wouldn't be much company tonight."

"Humph, I don't give many second chances, but for you I make exception. You better come by tomorrow night." Valeria winked and Tom answered with a smile.

Tom flipped the light switch as he entered his apartment and leaned against the door as he closed it behind him. After a long sigh, he shook his head and said, "What a fucking day."

The fatigue had caught up to him again. He didn't want to think any more about his friends or anything else, except a quick visit to the bathroom, and then sleep. He had just noted the time, 2:30 a.m., when the phone rang. He let the machine answer.

"Tom? Tom, are you there? C'mon, pick up." It was Dave.

Reluctantly he lifted the receiver. "What?"

"Jesus, what did you say to Denise?"

"What now?"

"She's been in her room all day since we got home. She's crying her eyes out. Damn it, Tom, I thought we had an understanding."

"What understanding? I don't understand any of this."

"So, you treat the best friend you ever had like a casual fuck? Get her out of your system? Is that it?"

"Man, I can't believe you're saying this. Aw, hell, listen, Dave: I did not fuck Denise. I don't care what she told you. It would never occur to me to fuck Denise—"

"That's cold, Tom. That's so unlike you."

"Mother of Jesus! What do I have to do to prove to you?"

"Tom, don't say another thing. I just want you to know that a very sweet girl is suffering right now. Frankly, I'm scared. I've never seen Denise so depressed. Look—you have to come over here. We can deal with everything else later, but, please, come over here and talk to Denise."

"Oh, god. Okay, I'll be there in fifteen minutes."

Tom parked in the driveway and made his way around back and past the pool. The sliding patio door was open and he slipped in. Dave sat in the living room with his head in his hands.

"Dave."

He looked up. "Thanks, Tom. Please, she's in the bedroom. Just go in and talk to her."

"I don't know what to say."

"Anything, anything will be fine."

Tom nodded and strode along the corridor to the bedroom door, knocked lightly and let himself in. Denise lay under the sheets on her side. Her face was buried in the plush pillows.

"Denise?"

"Tommy?" She turned her head to look at him out of one eye. "Know what? I've been lying here all day, soaked in my own girl juice, finger-fucking myself, wishing it was your cock inside me."

"What? I—but—"

Denise rolled into a sitting position. The sheets fell from her shoulders revealing her naked breasts. Tom stood like a mute, riveted at the sight of her hard, dusky red nipples. A sense of unreality enveloped him.

"It's true, Tommy. God, I want you to fuck me so badly."

"D-Den-Denise...Jesus, what's with you? Dave's just outside."

"Dave wants it too. He loves it when a real man's cock fills me up. He always has."

"But, Denise. God, what are you saying?"

She kicked the sheets off altogether and spread her thighs. Her pussy was bare, glistening, as she playfully fingered her plump labia.

"You see, Tommy. Dave isn't really—adequate. But, nothing turns him on, nothing gets him as excited as when another man is having me. I knew it before we were even married. It turned me on too."

She giggled. "Tommy, our honeymoon? I think I fucked the whole island of Jamaica. Room service, bartenders, guys at the pool. And Dave got to watch. He was so happy...well, he made himself sore jerking off."

Tom's head was spinning. He wondered if Denise was having some kind of breakdown.

"Denise..."

"Shhh, Baby. It's okay. We joined clubs. You have no idea how many couples are into the same thing." She laughed again. "You wanna know how many times I've been auctioned off to some guy for a weekend?"

"Jesus, Denise, I had no idea..."

"I know. You're sweet. You couldn't imagine your little Denise could be such a...slut."

"I—I have to go. I can't..."

She crept toward him, panther-like on all fours. "You want to fuck me, don't you, Tommy?"

"No. No, I don't—"

"That bulge in your crotch is telling me different. You *do* want to fuck me, don't you? Do you still think it would be like—how'd you put it—fucking your little sister?" She sniffed his crotch and giggled. "Actually, that would be kinda kinky too," she purred as she rubbed her nose against the bulging fabric.

Tom didn't answer, except in ragged breaths.

"Give me your cock," she ordered sharply.

"Denise, don't do this..."

Before he could finish, she deftly opened his pants, like she had had years of experience, and his cock sprung from its confines. He tried to speak, but her mouth closed over the head and her tongue slithered along the underside. Tom felt blood coursing through his head as white pinpoints of light exploded across his vision. Denise sucked him deeper into her mouth and he could feel the tip graze the back of her throat. A low groan escaped him.

Denise languidly withdrew her head until Tom's cock plopped out of her mouth. She spun around and lifted her ass to him. Her plump pussy lips beckoned. "Now, fuck me. Damn, I said, fuck me!"

Tom's pants dribbled down his thighs. Reason faded like a tiny voice down a long canyon. He gripped her hips and thrust his cock between those honey-glazed lips. He immediately fell into a brutal rhythm, slamming his pelvis into her pink, freckled buttocks.

"God, yes! Fuck me harder," she shrieked. "Damn, you're huge. Fuck me, fuck the slut...fuck..."

Tom was in a zone of utter carnal desire that her words stoked until he thought he would burst into flame.

Denise growled like a beast, thrashing her head, whipping the air with her red mane. Her exhortations shifted into third person, "Fuck her...fuck her cunt...yes, yes...her cunt."

Tom felt wild, brutal. Denise cried, "I'm a whore, a filthy whore...fuck me like a whore. God, fuck this filthy whore..."

Tom felt his scrotum tighten and the electrical charge begin at the base of his cock. He cried out as he launched, almost painfully, a stream of cream as her cunt clenched him in a wet, fleshy vice.

He tumbled onto the bed, but she rolled him over. "I want more from you," she said, and began to suck his cock back to rigidity. Tom winced, but his recovery amazed him. He was as rigid as a pole again. Denise glared with severe, glinty eyes.

"Fuck me in the ass," she ordered. She lay on her back and lifted her legs as if she would touch the ceiling with the soles of her feet. Tom kneeled and grasped her calves, pushing back until her anus beckoned him like a bull's-eye. He pushed his penis against the pucker, past the tight resistance, and then deep into her innards. Again he found a rapid, industrial rhythm and plowed her bowels as she groaned and mouthed unintelligible curses. He had only fucked her five minutes when she shuddered and cried like she was on fire. His release came seconds later as she whimpered the last of her orgasm.

Tom's eyes winked open. He lay on his back as his flaccid cock oozed the remnants of its last discharge. Denise nuzzled beside him. He felt like he had mislaid a section of time. But, hard reality settled in. He had fucked Denise; fucked her like he had never fucked any woman in his life. His body told him to savor the afterglow, but that tiny, insistent voice kept calling from far away. Something was wrong, it was all wrong.

Denise stirred and kissed his cheek. "I feel so good; so thoroughly fucked, and so good."

Tom sat up as her head slipped off his shoulder. In the dark, a tiny red light blinked at him. He caught another in the corner of his eye. 'What the fuck?'

He stood and hauled his pants up. Flicking on the light he investigated the shelves and dressers surrounding him. Three video cameras were recording. Tom flung open the door and stepped toward the living room. Dave sat directly in front of the TV, cock in hand as his wife's ass filled the screen and the back of her head bobbed up and down on Tom's cock.

"Jesus!" Tom blurted.

Dave froze the image and turned just as Denise stepped behind Tom. "See, Tommy. He likes it, don't you, Honey?"

Dave smiled sheepishly. "Yes, I love to watch men fuck my sweet, sexy wife."

"You—you arranged this," Tom said, his eyes searching their faces. "You played me like a cheap tune."

"Oh, Tommy," Denise grinned. "Really, I've known you forever. I wanted you. Strangers weren't much of a thrill any more, not even my boss."

"You mean...he knows about your boss?" Tom said, making a backhanded motion toward Dave.

"Tommy, James has been up here before. He fucked me right on the floor here while Dave took pictures for his little collection."

"You mean all this was about getting me to fuck you too?"

"Like I said, Tommy, I know you...and I wanted you."

"Damn it, Denise. I don't know you at all."

"I figured you'd have some problems with this, Tommy. That's why I wouldn't just come right out and ask. You're feeling a little uncomfortable now, but soon you'll get over it. It'll be wonderful, Tommy. I've already made plans for us to go away for a weekend, while wimpy-dick here can sit home alone and let his imagination run wild about what you're doing to me."

"I keep thinking I'm going to wake up," Tom said flatly.

"It's no dream, Baby."

"You're right. It's a nightmare. I don't want any part of this—this thing."

"Oh, Sweetie, you'll come around."

Tom glared at the woman he once knew, turned and stepped through the door. Driving home as dawn broke, his only thought was to get into the shower, scrub himself down, get clean again. Guilt and outrage percolated through him. He wondered if he would ever get over it.

SUNDAY MORNING
DEAN JEAN-PIERRE

"Wild about jelly, 'bout sweet jelly roll
If you taste good jelly, satisfy yo' weary soul."

New Jelly Blues – Peg Leg Howell (1927)

HEADS TURNED to watch the hypnotic sway of Sunday Morning's curvaceous figure under her white form-fitting dress as she glided by on her way to The Dive after attending church. Women walking with their husbands from churches of different faiths held onto their men a little closer; but the closer you hold a man is the further he sometimes wants to get away from you. Sunday Morning smiled at all the couples as they hurried past her—the men with their Bibles in their left hand, wives on their right arm, and an unholy erection rising quicker than a sinner lying to God that he deserved one more chance at redemption. The men stared at Sunday Morning as if they were bearing witness to beauty giving birth at the dawn of creation.

It was as if the sun had risen in her smile and the joy of the day ahead was there to be found in the secrets that lay hidden under her dress and waiting to be kissed from the sensuality of her lips. Her body still tingled from making love earlier that morning and, as she prayed in church for a better world, the images and sounds of making love made her smile.

It was the smile of a woman whose man had taken her to heaven even before she had come to church. There was nothing that a priest could tell her about heaven that she didn't already know after calling God's name multiple times. Calling his name would instantly trigger the great floods and dry land would not be seen for hours.

The secrets of Sunday's pleasure were known to only one man in Chicago and he was the envy of every other man in town. He was a known womanizer with a trail of broken hearts from New York to

Chicago that could fill the top ten charts with tales of the blues, and yet, Sunday Morning had fallen harder for Sax Sampson than any man who had ever had the pleasure of indulging in her sweetness. Rumor was that Sunday Morning's black pearl was so sweet that just a sample of it was enough to give a man a cavity so painful that there wasn't any cure—his only option was to keep coming back for more until she grew tired of him.

"Good afternoon, Ms. Morning. May I say you are looking as lovely as ever," Marty said as he poured Sunday her favorite drink, French champagne.

"You can say it, Mr. Robinson but only if you call me Sunday."

"Okay, Sunday but only if you call me Marty."

It was their own private joke that Sunday and Marty Robinson, The Dive's bartender, retold every time she came into the club.

They both nodded their heads as Sunday took a sip of her champagne. She couldn't sing unless she had a drink. It calmed her nerves down because, even after many years of singing and performing, she still got nervous whenever she stepped on the stage.

Marty took a quick glance around the still-empty club and nervously cast his eyes upstairs in the direction of the dressing room where Sax was enjoying the company of one of his many female admirers. Sunday wasn't expected to be in the club this early and Sax was known to have one or two young girls in his dressing room before she arrived. Like Sunday, he needed something to relax him before a big show. Sax would always brag to anyone who would listen that he could make any woman sound like any instrument of his choosing when she came. From the sounds coming from his dressing room earlier, he was either playing the piano with the passion of Little Richard or banging hard on the drum.

For the life of him, Marty couldn't understand why beautiful and smart women like Sunday Morning fell for scoundrels like Sax Sampson. Marty could still remember the first day she walked into The Dive five years ago while both he and Sax sat at the bar. Some women come with more than just their beauty when they enter your consciousness, and Marty knew even before she had said a word that Sunday Morning, or Ann-Marie Planter as she was known back then, would somehow break his heart. She breezed into the bar wearing a yellow sun dress under a thin black coat which was wide open in the middle of a harsh Chicago winter, but you could never tell by the smile on her face and strut in her steps that she was freezing.

Both men had rushed to her assistance that day to help her with her coat and one suitcase. Marty had tried valiantly to be a gentleman that day, but the weakness of desire and lust swept through his body, and his thoughts as his eyes quietly undressed and made love to the shy Ann-Marie. Though there was nothing shy about her body.

It said seductive things to men that she didn't yet have the experience or moxie at twenty-two to tell them, but both men knew that, in time, when she found her voice and confidence, that they would be as expendable to her as the next dime-a-dozen jazz or blues singer in Chicago who thought she was the next Lena Horne or Bessie Smith. They all wanted to be Lena and Bessie but talent doesn't come with just the arbitrary luck of being born beautiful. If it did, then every beautiful smile and beautiful body who knew the secrets to a man's heart would be crowned the next blues legend.

That cold day in November, when Sunday Morning first stepped into The Dive, her nipples announced her arrival before she had even said a word. They were supposed to be her back-up singers but instead they were competing to be the headline act. Both Marty and Sax made assumptions about her virtue but they assumed incorrectly when they thought that they could bed her before her body turned warm. Her brown eyes and soft smile invited them to imagine her naked but it was pleasure without the fulfillment of release or hearing her moaning their names as her body thrashed about in the throes of passion's heated swell. She was 5'8", which was not too tall or too short, with her long legs giving her the appearance of being taller. Hers was a natural beauty not processed with makeup or wigs to accentuate what did not need to be improved. She was regarded as a beautiful thick woman before the label of being "thick" was used as a dirty word to qualify how beautiful a woman was, as if "being thick" was one step beneath being beautiful. An aura of decadent sexuality lived in the way she had walked towards them—sunlight streamed through the front door and framed her beauty as rays of light framed her wavy brown hair.

It's the kind of imagery that men recall on their deathbed even as their wives hold their hands and pray to God to spare them the agony of becoming a widow. There was softness to her beauty that was inviting—wide hips that spoke silently of the pleasures that whispered and moaned between her inner thighs and breasts that could act as a soft pillow for a man to rest his weary head.

It was love at first sight for Marty but, as with all stories, the bartender never gets the girl. They just watch from the sidelines or behind the bar while the no good scoundrel steals the girl away.

It tore Marty up every time he watched Sunday Morning sing on stage. Sax had given her that stage name because he said that, whenever she smiled, he knew that God lived in her smile like a beautiful Sunday morning sunrise. Marty could see the chemistry they shared on stage growing more intense and he knew the music was their sexual foreplay, an appetizer for the main course after the performance. Decked out in his customary black pinstriped suit and black fedora, Sax strutted around the stage playing the saxophone as Sunday matched him note for note. Each note from his instrument penetrated Sunday's soft skin and her brown, round face would light up in ecstasy as if Sax was making love to her with each note, with each stroke. She would dramatically toss aside her red feather boa and the men in the audience, dressed like gentlemen in their three-piece suits, would crane their necks forward to get a closer look at Sunday Morning dressed in one of her tight strapless dresses that made sweet love to every curve on her body.

The plunge of her cleavage was so deep that the stares of her captive audience could get lost in her bosoms and never find their way out. Sunday Morning continued swaying to the seduction of her own voice and moved in tandem to Sax as he gyrated around the stage.

The smoke from men puffing on their cigars hung thick in the air and conversation from around the tables died down as Sunday Morning's voice soared over the clouds of smoke, caressing the notes blowing from Sax's horn and filled The Dive with her seductive vocals. Her voice was like sunshine breaking through the clouds illuminating what was once dark with the music emanating from deep within her soul.

Long after the history of blues will be written, the old-timers from the Southside of Chicago will debate whether Sunday Morning had the chops to go voice-to-voice with the greatest ladies of blues from Billie Holiday, Ma Rainey to Clara Smith. Patrons of The Dive claimed her as their own and blamed the scoundrel Sax Johnson for eventually breaking her heart and making her lose her passion for the gift she was given. A gift that is squandered is like a slap in the face to God—that you did not care enough about yourself and Him to treasure what He gave to you. But that would be years away from now, and the men listened enthralled as Sunday Morning broke into a heart wrenching rendition of "Nobody Knows You When You're Down and Out" by Bessie Smith.

When she was done, grown men could be seen looking around teary-eyed, explaining to their companions that it was all the smoke in the air making their eyes water. Such was the power of Sunday Morning's voice.

"Where is that sweet-talking man of mines?" Sunday Morning asked Marty as she finished off the last of her champagne.

From behind the bar, Marty looked at the woman he loved and still saw the same innocence he saw in her when she first walked into The Dive. Women like her who are looking for love always end up with a broken heart. Looking for love is like looking for trouble. You always get more than what you bargained for.

"He must be somewhere around here working on a new song. You know how you musician folks are," Marty said with a chuckle as he took another quick glance upstairs.

"If I was a jealous woman, I might think he loves playing his saxophone more than he enjoys making love to all of this," Sunday said playfully as she turned around to give Marty a view of what he craved for everyday. "Every man has his vices," Sunday said without a hint of irony in her voice.

There was a discernable tremor in Marty's voice as he tightly grasped the bar counter to stop himself from just jumping over it and taking Sunday Morning in his arms and proclaim his love. The curves of her body were wrapped tightly in a sexy, white spaghetti strapped dress, secretly taunting him to come closer and find out if what he imagined in his mind was true. If her body was dying, there would be no room for air to pass through that dress to save it from a lack of oxygen.

This was Marty's chance to expose Sax for the womanizer that he was. He knew that all he had to do was to send her upstairs to find her man enjoying the sweet flesh of another woman that would break Sunday Morning's heart. She would be hurt, but women always seem to get over pain because they know that at some point a man is going to hurt them in some way. The knowledge of that impending pain still hurts even when it's expected but the effect is tempered when you see the truth without the mask of denial. Marty's love for her was so powerful that he always thought that he would do anything to have her and, now that the opportunity was there for him to take, he could not let her be hurt by a scumbag like Sax Johnson. He had to protect her because he knew it is the right thing to do when you love someone.

"Have another drink on the house while I go fetch your man."

"Tell him don't keep me waiting. It's bad luck to keep Sunday Morning waiting on a Sunday," she winked.

It's even worse luck to catch your man in the act of blessing another woman and giving her holy communion in all her orifices, Marty thought to himself as climbed the stairs, taking two steps at a time.

The office, which doubled as a studio, was all the way to the back of the second floor's long corridor. It sounded like an entire band was back there rehearsing but it was only Sax who was fine tuning every part of some young woman's body. He was the maestro and was deep in the midst of an inspired performance.

The girl's skin was so dark that her sweat looked like black rain as Sax's hands and fingers played her body like the black keys on a piano being caressed by a pair of knowing hands. She wasn't much to look at but she was wild and the studio was her jungle as she grinded her round, firm behind into Sax's manhood. They didn't hear the door open or see Marty staring at them with sheer disgust etched in his face and murder in his eyes because of the hurt this would do to Sunday. Watching the violent thrashing they did to each other's bodies was like watching a car accident—Marty could not turn away from the beauty of their sexual expression as moans of ecstasy sounded like the heart wrenching sounds of a guitar. Each stroke of Sax's black manhood into the fevered moistness of her black pearl from behind looked like he was beating relentlessly on a drum. *Thump! Thump! Thump!* Her body let him know, as she thrust back hard onto his thick shaft, that she could take more than what he was giving out. She was auditioning for the part of his current "pretty young thing," and the competition of other available legs to spread open was stiffer than his erection pulsating inside of warmth.

Marty cleared his throat to get Sax's attention and Sax turned around smiling as if he didn't have a care in the world. One hand grasped her ass and the other sliced through the air as if he were conducting an orchestra. An evil grin crept across Sax's face as he stared at Marty and simultaneously punched hard through the air with his invisible wand and penetrated his lady friend with the real one. He continued this showmanship routine and seemed to gain strength with every scream, yelp, and moans of pleasure that she could not contain. Worried that Sunday would hear the commotion and come upstairs, Marty closed the door behind him.

"You have company downstairs."

"Tell them I'm busy so come back later."

"Yeah, tell them Sax is busy with his new woman," the young lady smirked as she stared at Marty, buck naked with sweat dripping down her body and not a hint of embarrassment on her face. She was still bent over the chair as if waiting another penal inspection.

"Hold up with all that *new woman* talk before I send your ass out of here and cut you off," Sax said angrily as their bodies separated.

"Sorry, baby," she sheepishly replied as Sax turned his back to her.

"The sun is rising," Marty hinted.

"Can you get it to set somewhere else?" Sax casually asked Marty as if he were ordering his favorite rum and Coke drink.

"You're the boss—if that's what you want then that's what I will do."

Sax mistook Marty's deference as a sign of loyalty and respect for him but, if he looked closer, he would see contempt behind Marty's eyes that went so deep that it was a miracle that Marty hadn't already beaten him to a pulp. It's never too late to give a man a beating that he deserves—a just beating can be administered even years later—and Marty promised himself that Sax would one day get exactly what was coming to him.

"That's what I want."

"Okay."

Marty abruptly turned around to walk away as if he were turning a corner or as part of a military formation.

When Marty went downstairs, he saw that there was no one at the bar.

Sunday Morning had disappeared.

Marty called out to her but the only sound in the bar was coming from the jukebox blaring the voice of Clarence Williams singing, "You Rascal, You." The lyrics were appropriate for the love that Sunday Morning had placed in Sax though he was nothing more than a rascal who deserved to die.

She wouldn't have left the club without telling Marty goodbye. A sudden feeling of anxiety came over Marty as he looked upstairs and realized that she may have gone to the ladies' room and then went upstairs to surprise Sax in his office. Marty was a hefty man, but he sprinted back up the stairs as if he were Jesse Owens on his way to gold with the entire German team chasing him. By the time he ran down the long corridor and got to Sax's office, Marty was sweating profusely. The scene in front of him was straight out of a movie and, if it were a movie, the audience would be holding their breath, watching and waiting for something violent to happen.

Sax hurriedly tried to put back on his suit as he tried to explain to Sunday Morning that what she saw was merely a mirage. He sang the familiar refrain of "it's not what you think," that song so familiar to women that they knew the chords by heart.

Sax's naked "new woman" defiantly stared at Sunday Morning and did a few twirls to show her exactly what Sax had been enjoying for the last few weeks. Out of respect for Sunday Morning, Marty stared off to the side without making eye contact with her enemy's naked body.

There is always calm before a storm but, surprisingly, the storm never came as Sunday Morning, dressed like the star and lady she was, remained ladylike.

"This is what you've been sneaking around to taste?" She

addressed Sax without looking at his trollop. "You have a star, a woman who is in love with you, and you traded it all in for a woman who probably has more miles on her pussy than all the cars in Chicago."

Both men visibly winced at Sunday Morning's last comment, and Sax's trollop opened her mouth to defend herself. It's hard to defend yourself against a charge like that when you're butt naked and engaged in sex with another woman's man.

"She doesn't mean anything to me, baby," he countered.

"Then I must mean less to you to make you treat me this way."

Sunday Morning turned around and left the studio as the same woman she came in as, with her pride and dignity on full display. She briskly walked up East Hubbard Street with a serene expression on her face which wasn't exactly a smile or a frown. People said hello to her and she nodded without breaking stride. It wasn't until she opened her apartment door that Sunday Morning took of her mask and gave in to the pain of heartbreak overflowing in heart. Tears streamed down her face. She felt naked, vulnerable and stupid that she had allowed Sax to use her for so many years. She tore at the dress she wore that Sax had bought her because it felt filthy, and stood in the middle of her apartment in a matching pair of black bra, panties, garter and stockings, which soon found the same fate.

Worried that Sunday Morning might do something irrational, Marty quickly left the bar and followed her to her apartment. The door was slightly ajar and after knocking several times without a response, he stepped into her apartment for the first time. He found strewn across the hardwood floor the dress she wore earlier and a few feet away were her bra and panties. He picked up each one as if they were something precious that should never be sullied on a dirty floor.

Marty called Sunday's name several times as he slowly walked through the apartment until he finally found her standing naked in her bedroom with the windows open and a breeze stiffer than a convict's erection blowing through the room, slapping her naked body with the weight of its frustration.

"What the hell are you doing?" Marty barked at her as he rushed to her side.

He quickly shut the windows and guided her shivering body to her bed and under her sheets and blanket.

Marty wouldn't be a man if he hadn't noticed the special blessing of a body that he had dreamed of every night staring right back at him. It was as if God had taken time out of his busy schedule, even worked overtime, to make sure that Sunday Morning received a flawless body. The deepened dark circles around her nipples were so perfect that only a true artist could have painted something so exquisite. The cold air had awakened her thick nipples and, for a brief moment, Marty wanted to take them between his lips to warm them up as if his lips were a hot toddy warming the body. He refused to look at the dark, curly patch of softness cradled between her brown thighs. It was a place that he thought should remain private until she offered him the many gifts of its pleasures.

"What did I do to deserve this, Marty?"

"Nothing. It's just Sax being Sax. He thinks that just because he's a musician that the world should bow at his feet."

Sunday Morning curled up into a ball under the quilted blanket that her grandmother had given her when she left home and sobbed uncontrollably. Her body heaved up and down under the blanket and Marty stood there, unsure of how to comfort her. He did the only thing he could think of and crawled into bed with her.

Under the blanket, the coldness of her skin had been quickly replaced with the heat that lives inside the body of women. Marty felt as if he was caught in a burning bed of fire—he had no desire to escape. He eased his body against hers and wrapped one hand around her waist and eased the other under her head. Her wet, tear-stained face touched his and it felt as if he had been electrocuted. He struggled to not become aroused with her naked body pressed warmly against his. The warmth of her moist black pearl radiated a special heat that carried the heat of the sun, of a woman scorned and passion so angry that it ached for release.

"This hurts too much," she sobbed again as her naked body pressed deeper into Marty.

"You should get some rest and you will feel better," Marty offered as he tried to ease out from the bed but Sunday Morning's grip on him became tighter.

"You're a good man, Marty, and Sax is worthless. Why didn't I end up with you instead of him?"

Her eyes pleaded for an answer from him, expecting him to somehow magically make her pain disappear. He knew the answer but knew it wasn't the right time to tell her. Women like her never went for the ordinary, hardworking guys like him. They craved the excitement of love and passion and, like men, judged the physical before finding out what else a man had to offer. Only in retrospect, with the pain of heartbreak throbbing in their bones and aching in their hearts, do they question their judgment.

"Kiss me, Marty," Sunday's voice pleaded and begged.

A woman like her didn't have to beg a man for anything.

"You're in pain. You're not thinking straight."

"Don't father me, Marty. Just give me what I need right now."

Her lips touched his and Marty felt her heart in her kiss with a mixture of pain, passion, and tears. He wanted to kiss her back, to caress her ass in his big hands and whisper in her ears as he entered the warm depths of passion that he would never hurt her. The words lived on his lips and breathed in his soul like a mantra he gave life to everyday. *What would be the harm in giving her what she asked for*, he thought to himself. He wasn't really taking advantage of her, but deep down he knew the truth. The truth lives within us, walks in our every step, even when we try to deny its existence.

"This is wrong. This isn't you."

Her right hand slid up his crotch and found the bulge in his pants that wanted to kiss the heat of her black pearl. Marty shuddered as Sunday sensually stroked his manhood. The feeling reminded him of how he felt every time she took to the stage, when the first note kissed its way through her lips and left her mouth. He became inebriated without having taken a drink. He was intoxicated by her.

Marty looked down into the pain that had set in her eyes like an anchor, wiped away her tears and did something that he never thought he would ever do in his life. He removed the hand of Sunday Morning from the throbbing ache in his pants.

"Don't let Sax take away your dignity. Don't let him change the woman that you are. You are better than him. Someone will appreciate the classy, beautiful woman that you are and will not take your love for granted. Not all men are like Sax."

"How do you know that?"

"I just know," Marty said as he closed his eyes so that Sunday Morning could not see the love he had for her that was evident in his eyes. If she hadn't been in so much pain, she would have seen that Marty Robinson was in love with her. She would have seen in his eyes love so deep that he would do anything to protect her. He had seen her first that cold day in November, but she had looked right past him and had fallen almost instantaneously for Sax.

Two men.

The wrong one was chosen.

If we could go back and change the path of our choices, would we? Or would we just try and be better, try harder for the sake of another person to get them to love us deeper? The cruelty of Love sometimes is that even when we innately know the outcome, we still walk into her arms, hoping that, maybe this time, she will be good to us.

Sunday Morning closed her eyes and began to sing, the sound of her sultry voice soothed her pain into a restless sleep filled with images of her singing, making love to Sax and killing him in every imaginable and unimaginable way.

As she drifted off, Marty held her tightly in his arms using his arms as a force field against the pain and, with every breath that she exhaled, felt her body heat was increasing. Maybe one day she would love him like he loved her but, for now, he would give her what she needed from a man, which was simply to be held. He refused to take advantage of her. His love and respect for her was deeper than the ache that was filling his erection.

He kissed her forehead, hummed an obscure blues tune that his daddy used to sing while working on his land back home in Mississippi, and fell asleep with her in his arms.

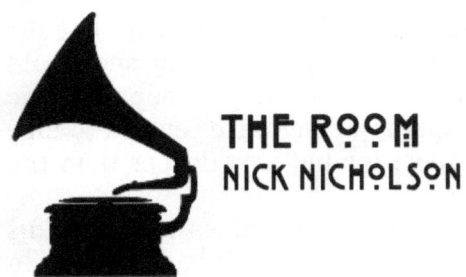

THE ROOM
NICK NICHOLSON

"Bright lights, big city, gone to my baby's head
I'd tried to tell the woman, but she don't believe a word I
said."

Bright Lights, Big City – Jimmy Reed (1961)

THERE IS A ROOM. A square room. There is a bed in the middle of the room. A square table. A chair. There are no windows, no doors. There is a single fluorescent tube, on the ceiling, washing the room with a bleached light. And in the middle of the wall facing the foot of the bed there is a television. There is static on the screen, a chaos of frequencies, the television trapped between channels.

You see all this when you wake up. You lie still on the bed, your head on the pillow, your gaze shifting erratically from one object to another. The sound of your breath scrapes against the silence. Your body is covered by a sheet. You are conscious of being naked under the sheet. You decide to move your hands and touch your face, your stomach, your penis, your legs, to assure yourself that you are intact.

It's a dream. You think it's a dream.

You sit up, put your feet on the floor, look down. The floor is white, but a strange white, a white leeched of whiteness by the weak fluorescent light. Then you notice that the walls, the bed, the table, the chair, the television are the same, a grimy white. The only contrast is the dense grey static of the television screen. A brooding disquiet settles on your skin like a layer of dust. You stand up and walk to the television. There is no switch to turn it on or off, no control knobs or buttons. You look behind the television. There is no electrical cord.

You think it's a dream. You return to the bed, to sleep. You think to yourself that when you wake up, everything will be back to normal.

FLUORESCENT LIGHT pries your eyes open. You blink. You see the windowless walls, the table, the chair, the television, the mindless static.

Nothing has changed.

Panic curls in your stomach, and then spreads like venom to the extremities of your limbs. You hope you are still dreaming. You get out of the bed and kick the leg of the table with your bare foot. The pain tells you. You are not dreaming.

YOU SEARCH the walls for a hidden door.

You scream and the sound of your scream is swallowed up by the silence of the room.

You look under the bed, under the mattress. You toss the table and chair.

You look behind the television again, for something, anything, a hidden camera, perhaps.

You bang the walls with your fists.

You scream again.

You wonder if the amount of air in the room is finite. Your anxiety escalates and you begin to hyperventilate. Then you realise your foolishness. You lie down on the bed and calm yourself with measured breaths.

You have forgotten you are naked. After a while you realise your eyes are stinging with tears.

YOU ARE NOT DREAMING.

You are in a prison. You think it's a prison. Then you become aware that your mind is in a prison too, the prison of your head. Solitary confinement. Your tangled thoughts, the fog of your feelings, in a cell within a cell.

AFTER WAKING from a fitful sleep, it strikes you that there is no food, no water. But then you realise that you are neither hungry nor thirsty. Your body has no urge to defecate or piss.

You keep thinking it's a dream. It has to be a dream.

Your body seems alien, separate from yourself. You are conscious of your body, conscious that it is not you, yet you are conscious of inhabiting this body, you recognise it as your body.

Then you sense something. You throw the sheet off and you see it. Your penis, erect. The shock of it like an electric chair. It doesn't seem right, an erection in this room, this white room.

The television, like the single horrifying eye of a Cyclops, continues to glare at you.

TIME is rubbery, slippery. You have no sense of day or night. Impossible to tell how long you've been in the room. You have forgotten what month it is, what year. You wonder how you got here, who brought you, and for what purpose, but faced with the unyielding wall of the unimaginable your thoughts disintegrate into nothingness.

YOU ARE SITTING in the chair when you notice that the television is flickering differently from before. Something is struggling to emerge on the screen. The pained birth of an image. You get up and stare at the television, willing the formless thing to take shape. A moment later, the image resolves into a face, the face of a woman, in black and white. You have never seen her before but the vision of the woman awakens within you the ephemeral vestige of a long-forgotten memory, like an evaporating breath on a cold window. She could be twenty; she could be thirty-five. You can't tell. Her face has an indeterminate expression. She is looking directly at you. Her lips move. She is speaking but there is no sound. You try to read her lips but thick lines of roving static rupture her face. The woman and the television appear to be warring for dominance. The television wins. The woman's face breaks up, shattering into blades of grey light that shear across the screen. She vanishes into an electronic quicksand.

You kneel in front of the television and press your face against the glass. Blips of reception swarm on the screen like a colony of electronic ants.

YOU ARE RIDDLED with inertia. You sleep, wake, sleep again. You have no choice.

You wonder what you have done to deserve this punishment, this incarceration. You try to remember the awful things you've done, but they're not so awful, merely the ordinary crimes of life. You never killed anyone. You don't remember killing anyone.

YOU WAKE UP and she's there, in the room, the woman from the television. You are not dreaming. She is real. Her tangibility dumbfounds you. Words form in your mouth only to shrivel and die when you open your lips. You try to envisage how she got from the television into the room, but you can't. She is standing at the foot of the bed, looking at you. She is naked. She appears unaffected by her nudity. You think she must be a delusion but you can sense the blood pulsing beneath her skin. Her chest rises and falls with the inhalation and exhalation of air. You are conscious of breathing in the same air that she breathes out. The woman is slender, her features clear, unclouded, her body curved with supple flesh. There is an openness about her, an intelligence. You feel drawn to her, inescapably drawn. You wonder who she is and why she is here. And then you wonder if you are dead, if this is your afterlife. You ask these questions of yourself knowing that it is impossible to deduce the answers. You close your eyes and wait for her to speak but she says nothing. When you open your eyes again, she's gone.

You weep.

YOU DREAM. In your dream, the woman lies next to you, asleep. Her hand is holding your sex. You want to move, push your groin against her hand, the instinctive urge to thrust, but in the dream, you don't. In the dream, her touch is enough.

The scene changes. A dark, glistening image forms, crystallising the inchoate thoughts that seep from your memory. You see a great cavern of wet black rock and an ancient river snaking through the subterranean darkness. You realise that you have always sensed the existence of this underground river but you have never seen it until now.

Then you see the spectre of the woman's face floating in the blackness of the water.

THE DREAM DISSOLVES. You wake and your breath catches in your throat like a fishhook. The woman has returned. She is standing by the side of the bed, her gaze upon you. Again, she is naked. You cast a nervous glance at the singular eye of the television screen. The static burns with angry intensity.

You desire the woman but you are frightened. You don't know her. You don't know what she wants or what will happen. It becomes clear to you, however, that despite your fear, only one course of action is possible. You reach out and touch her. You place your hand on her hip, gently, as if touching the most fragile thing you've ever known.

Your hand remains still. Her skin, soft as cotton, exudes warmth, heat. You try to remember if you've ever felt such heat. You can't remember. She leans her hip faintly, almost imperceptibly, into your hand. The subtlety of this movement arouses you. You keep your hand there, not wanting to break contact. Then you look up at the woman and ask, "Who are you?"

She doesn't reply straight away. She looks at you intently for several moments, as if to ascertain your preparedness for her answer, and then says, "I'm the one you've always wanted."

Her voice is a balm. She bends down, touches her lips to yours. The connection, shockingly soft, transfixes you. Then she whispers, "You have never seen me, but you have always known me."

There is a truth to her words that you sense deep within but do not fully understand.

"I am the woman you have been seeking, the woman behind the faces and between the legs of all the lovers you have ever known. You have only seen fragments of me. Now you see me whole."

A realisation cracks through the layers of your mind. "You know me."

"I have always known you," says the woman, a tender smile emerging on her face. "I've been waiting."

You place your hands on her waist, draw her to you. "Where am I? Why am I here?"

"This room is you. And you are here because you finally wanted me enough."

The woman lies next to you on the bed. You tell yourself it is not a dream. You touch her body and she responds. You kiss her, she responds. You remember her words to you. You don't know her, you have always known her. And so you make love to her, knowingly and unknowingly, under the thin fluorescent light, under the omniscient gaze of the television, within the impenetrable walls of the square room. You sense that you are inside a mystery conjured from the unseen particles between yourself and the woman, a mystery that is potent because it eludes dissection. You take her breast into your mouth. You suckle on the mystery, drink it in. You cannot stop, nor do you want to. You kiss her lips, her face, her neck. You kiss the whole of her body, taste the electricity of her skin. She opens herself to you. You enter her. Flesh within flesh. You are filled with the desire to know her, to lose yourself in her, to forget, to remember. She envelops all that is you. You penetrate to her core and swim in a sea of juices, nectars, unguents.

You love her. You think it is love.

SLEEP descends upon you. You dream of heaven, or rather, a kind of heaven. You dream of the woman, with you, in a perfectly white room and in the dream you live in this room forever.

WHEN you wake up, the memory of the dream lingers in your mind, and for a few moments you allow yourself to be comforted by the artificial glow of the fluorescent light.

Then you become aware of an absence. Dread grips you like the hand of a monster. You leap up from the bed, scrutinise the room, your gaze filled with terror. The woman has gone.

You turn to the television and your stomach feels sick. The woman's face is on the screen, cruelly distorted behind an electrified fence of shifting static. She is looking at you. Her lips mutely enunciate your name, over and over. Your fingers tremble as they touch the television screen.

Then something catches your eye, something that wasn't there a moment ago that you are certain has never been there before. On the wall to the right of the television you see the rectangular outline of a door. An *exit*. You look back at the woman on the screen. The static is weakening. The image of her face is becoming clearer, more distinct. You know you can bring her back. You know. You just need time. But something tells you that the materialised presence of the door is transitory, fleeting.

You realise then that you have two options.

You choose one.

HURRICANE LOVE
ALICIA NIGHT ORCHID

"If you don't like my ocean, don't fish in my sea
Stay out of my valley and let my mountains be."

Don't Fish in My Sea — Ma Rainey (1926)

JIMMY FRUGE held a six-by-eight piece of plywood in his right hand. He spit an eight-penny nail into his left and lifted the plywood sheet to the window. He used a heavy hammer to nail it to the frame. It required twelve nails, three on each side, to complete the job. He had eight windows down.

He lowered his long, lean body off the ladder, removed his T-shirt, and used it to mop sweat off his face and chest. He sunk into a lawn chair and drew on a warm Dixie beer. His ancient transistor radio continued to beam hurricane warnings. Out in the Gulf, Katrina danced and swayed. Category 4, maybe even 5.

If the bitch hit the city head-on, she'd wash her away.

But Fruge had been weathering storms most of his life and he'd never seen one hit full-force head-on. They usually faltered or turned west after making landfall, blowing themselves out in the bayous between New Orleans and Baton Rouge.

He figured Katrina to be no different.

Anyway, it would take more than a storm to run him out of the city and away from this place on Magazine. He'd bought when the neighborhood was nothing but crack houses inhabited by drug dealers and whores. Now, two years later, things were turning around, prices were up, and Fruge had reshaped the property into an updated bed and breakfast within walking distance of the Quarter. He was fully booked through the fall and into the spring, Jazz Festival and Mardi Gras.

Except now this damn hurricane was fucking with him.

He stood, finished his beer, picked up his tools and another sheet of plywood. His right knee was painfully stiff and that left shoulder was acting up again. He'd just reached the top of the ladder, when his cell phone rang. He grimaced, made his way back down, and found the phone under the *Times Picayune,* next to his empty.

"Hey, babe." He knew who was calling.

"Jimmy, what are you doing?"

"Boarding up my windows."

"They're going to need it. This is looking bad, really bad."

"They've been saying that for two days."

"Yeah, but the mayor just announced a mandatory evacuation. Everyone's leaving the city."

"Nothing's mandatory."

"Jimmy, please. We're leaving for Jackson in an hour. You need to come with us."

Jessie Claiborne was thirty-eight, divorced, and the mother of a ten-year old boy. Descended from one of the oldest families in the city, she was attractive, smart, and respectable, the kind of woman a man like him would be lucky to settle down with. They'd met when he'd hired her out of the Yellow Pages to help him with the interior design of his B and B.

"Jessie, I can't leave."

"Honey, you can't stay. This storm's the real deal. It's the Big One."

"This place is all I got."

"What about Nathan and me? You've got us."

"I know. I just meant…"

There was a long sigh on the other end. "You are one stubborn Cajun."

"We only come in one size. You going with your folks?"

"We're taking Daddy's Hummer, so there's plenty of room for one more. We'll be staying at Cecily's house."

Jessie's daddy was the senior partner at the biggest law firm in the city. Fruge winced at the thought of spending six hours on the road in close proximity to Adam Claiborne. The old man probably liked the idea less than he did. Then there would be days, cooped up with the whole family, Cecily and her smart-ass husband Dennis, another lawyer. Plus, Nathan and his rowdy cousins would be running around like banshees.

"I don't think so, Jessie."

Another sigh. "Jimmy, please. We shouldn't be apart through something like this."

"It's all right. Go on. Be safe. Don't worry about me."

"I love you, Jimmy."

"I know. Me too."

"I'll call from the road."

"I'll be right here."

He jammed the cell phone into his pocket and remounted the ladder. A long time ago, the knee had taken shrapnel outside of a place called Thuong Duc. The shoulder had been shot through by a sniper in a Viet Namese jungle.

Four more windows to go.

LATE AFTERNOON, he caught her scent. It was Africa, the islands, and the sea. It was Gulf oil rigs and uprooted lives. The wind rattled in the Live Oaks and low clouds skittered across the sky.

He stepped out onto the sidewalk. Quiet, even for a Sunday. The coffee shop that stood where a meth lab had once operated was boarded up, the lesbian chicks that ran it gone to Panama City. The second-hand clothing store now owned by a pair of retirees from Michigan, the same. They were off to Dallas.

He walked up to St. Charles. The street car line was down, the hotels, restaurants, and stores deserted. He watched an old woman push a grocery cart down the middle of the street, one hand clutching the cart, the other her purple hat. A gang of teenage boys rounded a corner on skate boards. One of them flipped him the bird.

Fruge headed home when a police car appeared in the distance, cops with bullhorns warning folks to leave or take shelter. Last chance, they said.

The air felt heavy, balmy, like always before a storm. She'd come ashore, blow and raise hell. She'd dump rain from black skies. Then she'd move on and things would return to normal. For weeks afterward, folks would sit at Pat O'Brien's and talk about how dumb they'd been to leave the city. They'd sip Hurricanes and say they'd never leave again.

It was always the same.

He was a half block from his place when he saw her, that crazy Creole girl. She lived with the old Voodoo Maman who ran the fortune-telling business over the organic food store next to his place. She sat on his stoop, leaning back on her hands, girlish legs open, thin cotton dress barely to her knees.

"Girl, where's your granny?" Fruge asked.

She was the color of pecans, with large brown eyes and thick black hair erupting in a fountain of dreads. She spoke with a lilt, when she spoke at all. Mostly, she let those eyes do her talking. She was always hanging around, stealing sips from his beer when she thought he wasn't looking, pestering him with questions. The coffee shop lesbians said she had a crush. The Voodoo Maman gave him the evil eye.

"Gone," the girl said. "She left early dis morning. She say dis storm 'bout to wash us away."

"Gone where?"

"She got people in 'Bama."

"Why didn't you go with her?"

"My magic tell me to stay."

"And she let you stay on your own?"

"She don' tell me what to do. She know my magic stronger than her's. 'Sides, I'm not alone. I'm wit' you."

Fruge studied her face, the full lips and proud nose. Firm breasts filled the top of her dress, a *gris-gris* bag dangling between them. Her name was Simone.

"You can't stay here, girl. They're taking people got nowhere to go at the Superdome. I'll run you up there."

She grinned, broad and white. "Shit, I ain't be goin' to no damn Superdome. I'm stayin' wit' you in this big old house."

"I can't be responsible..."

She stood, tall as him and lithe as a deer. "Chile, neither of us responsible. We caught between de magic and dat big ole 'cane. De only thing save us now is de magic."

THE BREEZE picked up. Fruge had been in the city for Camille. Winds hit 75 to 100 miles per hour. Strong enough to push a car along a slick street, up-end Live Oaks, and scatter rooftops like match sticks. It reminded him of war.

You had to be very sober or very stoned to survive, and even then there were no guarantees.

He opened a beer, and when the girl took it from him without asking, he opened another for himself.

"You're too young to drink," he said. He guessed her to be anywhere from fifteen to twenty.

"I tol' you I was eighteen, if I was a day."

"Eighteen my ass."

"Eighteen," she said, "turned eighteen in the spring."

They'd moved inside after he'd made her help him pick up his yard. He was at the kitchen table. She sat cross-legged on the counter. Even in the failing light of day, he could see all the way up her dress to the white panties underneath.

"So, why don't you go to school or get a job?"

She tilted her head back and drank deeply from the bottle. "I been to school and I have a job. I schooled wit' de devil back on de island. I help my granny wit' de ju-ju and dem spells."

"The devil, huh?"

She laughed. "Don't you b'lieve in de devil? Dat ole serpent?"

He thought about it a minute. He'd seen his share of evil in the spring of '70. He'd spilled plenty of blood to mark it. As for the devil, he couldn't say. "So, what kind of spells you work up with your granny?"

Her tongue licked her lips. "Mos' people want spells 'bout lovin'. How to keep der husband or wife. How to get a man or a woman. Some want to keep de devil away. Some want to sic him on another."

Fruge didn't have much use for religion or superstition. New Orleans Voodoo or high mass with the pope, it was all the same to him. Outside, it was nearly dark.

"I better fix dinner, while we've still got power," he said.

"Oh, yeah, you better. You goin' to need your strength."

HE RUMMAGED through his refrigerator and found Andouille sausage, stewed chicken left over from earlier in the week, and half a pound of shrimp bought fresh the day before. He chopped onion, celery, and bell pepper, while she watched and opened another beer for both of them.

"You mind if I smoke?" she asked.

She produced a reefer from inside a dress pocket. It had a good, tight roll. He'd always admired a woman who rolled her own. She lit up before he could answer.

"Does it matter what I say?"

She slid off the counter and sidled next to him. While holding her toke, she brought the reefer, the pinched end wet from her lips, to his mouth. He grabbed a toke of his own and held on. He hadn't smoked in years.

She exhaled, giggling. "I knew you won't say no."

He brought half a stick of butter to a sizzle in a heavy skillet, and then added flour. He stirred and stirred, and then stirred some more. "You ever make a roux?" he asked.

"Pretty girl don' need to cook."

She stood at his shoulder while they traded hits and sipped beer. The roux turned blonde, then brown. Through the reefer, she smelled like island spices, ginger and cinnamon, cumin and chilies. Her granny had told him that Simone was from St. Lucia. How she got here, no one said and he hadn't asked.

He added the vegetables to the skillet. The roux darkened to a rich mahogany, darker than her skin. He added chicken stock, sausage, and left-over chicken. He seasoned with salt, pepper, cayenne, and a dash of filé.

"It needs to simmer for a while," he said.

"Smells good."

He cleaned the shrimp, and then chopped okra. "We'll put that in at the end."

She leaned over and kissed him just below the ear, then backed away giggling. "Shoulda' seen de look on your face."

"What the hell are you doing?"

"Messin' wit' ya."

"Well, stop that shit, or I'll throw you out in the storm."

"You ain't throw me out. Dat fat woman of yours gone, anyway."

"She's not fat."

"'Sides, she on the wrong side a forty."

"She's only thirty-eight."

"And I'm Queen Latifah. I bet she never brought you no reefer."

Simone was right about that. The Claibornes could drink single malt Scotch and fine wines with the best of them, but no one ever torched a joint. Maybe they smoked, but they never inhaled.

"You love her?"

"She's a good woman."

Simone's eyes widened. "But do you love her?"

Fruge couldn't hold her gaze. "Look, I'm not getting any younger and we've all got our faults."

"You ain't dat old.'"

"Yeah, well, I feel old."

"You still a good-lookin' man. Bet you quite de ladies' man."

Simone sat on the counter again. She had the best legs he'd ever seen, and he'd seen a few.

"How come your woman won't stay wit' ya?" she asked.

"She's got to think of her son."

"Dat little brat a her's? He needs a hickory switch on his fanny."

"He's all right."

"How come you don't stay wit' her? Get away from dis storm?"

"I've got to take care of my place."

She darted in, too quick for him, and nipped his other ear. "Nah, you stay here, 'cause I put de Voodoo on you wit' my *gris-gris*."

"The Voodoo?"

"Dat right, Jimmy Fruge. I got you under my spell."

"Girl, you better settle down."

WHILE he finished making their gumbo, cooked rice, and assembled salads, she turned his radio up as loud as it would go and danced barefoot on the table. She whirled, shook, and shimmied to a blend of hip-hop and reggae. They drank more beer and smoked another reefer. After a while, hungry as a horse, he barked her off the table, set plates, and opened a bottle of wine.

Her hair was damp with sweat. Droplets stood on her forehead. Outside, it began to rain, so dark he couldn't see his hand in front of his face. A few more hours, they'd need candles. Landfall was predicted early the next morning, but Katrina would rage all night. Between songs, the radio predicted winds to 145 miles per hour.

He wondered if either of them had the balls for it.

She ate, head down, bread in one hand, fork in the other, neither talking nor looking up. He wondered where she put it. When she finished eating, she drank her wine in two gulps and leaned back, bare feet on the table. She smoked a cigarette while he ate a second helping.

"Not bad gumbo for a white boy," she said.

"You are one cocky-ass little bitch."

The hem of her skirt was in her lap, her brown thighs smooth as his roux.

"How you learn to cook like dat?"

"I worked as a cook on the oil rigs. Then later on in the Quarter."

"You a cook?"

"I've done other things." He finished his seconds and poured more wine for both of them. "Give me one of them smokes."

"I didn't think you smoked."

"Only during hurricanes."

She shook out a cigarette and lit it for him. Then she took his hand in both of hers. She studied his palm, running her fingertips over its length and breadth.

"You been in a war."

He was feeling the beer, the reefer, and the wine. "Yeah, before you were born, I was a heartbreaker and a life taker."

Her eyes flashed. "You killed other men."

"I never said I was an angel. Mostly, I was scared."

"Nah, you won a medal."

A Silver Star, but how the hell did she know?

"Had a hard time after the war," she continued.

"I ran with a rough crowd."

"Yer white woman know 'bout dat?"

He shrugged. He hadn't seen the point of bringing up ancient history with Jessie Claiborne.

"Then," Simone said, "you went to prison."

"I've made mistakes."

"Bet yer woman don' know 'bout dat either."

"I've straightened out."

She grinned her toothy grin. "Nah, you still got a kink."

"You don't know as much as you think you do."

"I know you stole money to buy dis place."

His jaw dropped. There had been that bank job in Baton Rouge, but he'd gotten away clean. There was no way...

She released his hand. "Why you think dat woman want to be wit' you?"

He treated Jessie and Nathan well, and his ownership of the B and B wrapped him in a cloak of propriety. He liked to think of himself as charming. "I don't know. Why do you think?"

"Ass dat broad, wrinkles 'round her eyes, baggage like dat little boy? Where she goin' to find another man?"

Fruge frowned. "That's a helluva thing to say."

"She love you up good?"

He mashed out his cigarette. "You ask too many questions."

"She take you in her mouth?"

He stood and picked up their dishes. "Girl..."

"Give you her big ole ass?"

"Goddammit..."

Simone laughed, spewing smoke. "I bet she ain't no kinda' lover."

"Mind your own damn business."

HE OPENED another bottle of wine and they smoked the last of the grass. The power cut off just before midnight and he lit candles. The wind blew so hard the candlelight flickered with the gusts.

"Here she come," Simone said, "rockin' and a rollin'. You 'fraid a dis storm?"

She sat across from him, her face obscured by the red glow of a cigarette. The air was so heavy it was hard to breathe. She'd taken off her dress and wore only a bra and panties. He'd removed his shirt. Sweat poured off of him.

"Not yet. Besides, your magic's strong. It'll keep us safe, right?"

"Don't be makin' fun a my magic. You think I ain't seen de devil?"

"You're saying this hurricane's the devil?"

"Nah, mostly de devil inside. He be gnawin' at us, causin' us to doubt, causin' us to do de easy thing, 'stead of de right thing."

He wondered where she got her material. She was too young to know about self-doubt, too young to know about selling yourself short. "What're you talking about?"

"You know you ain't fancy people like dem Claibornes. You know dat old man he look down on you. And dat brother-in-law play you for de fool."

"They're decent, upstanding citizens."

"Some folks walk in de light, others in de shadow. You an'me, we walkin' in de shadow."

"What does that mean?"

"It mean you ain't never fit in wi' dem folk."

Her words made him sweat even more. "What other magic you got?"

She leaned forward and spoke in a hushed voice. "A woman wanta keep her man from another woman, she put her blood in his coffee. A woman sprinkle salt in another woman's house, dat other woman have bad luck 'til she clean up the salt and put pepper in her doorway. You want harm on another man, get a lock a his hair, burn some, and throw de rest away."

"You believe that?"

"I don't b'lieve it, I know it."

"What's that bag around your neck?"

"Dat my love potion for you. Jimson Weed, Chicken Bones, a dead man's ashes."

"Why you have a love potion for me?"

"So, you don't make a big mistake wi' dat fat woman."

He stood and crossed the room. Through a crack in the plywood, he could see outside. The rain blew sideways, the wind a steady roar. A box the size of a refrigerator tumbled down the street.

He felt her presence behind him. She placed a hand on his shoulder. "Lookie here."

In her other hand, she held a tiny figure made of cloth, stuffed with cotton. Somehow, it resembled him. One straight pin pierced the doll's knee, another its shoulder.

"What the fuck?"

"It you, Jimmy Fruge."

He took a step backwards. "Jesus Christ."

"I makin' you better," she said. "I talk to dis doll and your knee don' hurt and your shoulder get well. All dose bad memories and dreams, dey gone."

"You're fucking crazy."

She must have heard him bitch about his knee and shoulder. But the war dreams that continued to haunt his sleep, she had to be guessing.

She reached out and touched his face. "I'm not crazy, Jimmy Fruge. I jus' tellin' you what you already know."

HE FELL ASLEEP on the sofa. Once, he awoke, deep in the night, and saw the girl dancing in the candlelight. She dipped and swirled and chanted words he'd never heard.

After that, he dreamed she found a snake in his house, a Cotton Mouth or Moccasin come calling from the bayou. Quick as lightning, her hand grasped that snake behind the head. She lifted it high and whirled. Then, taking the serpent by the tail, she cracked it like a whip, ending its life.

There were other dreams. Chains dragging, people calling out. Bloated bodies floating in black water. A chicken with its head cut off.

Finally, he roused to the fury of the storm. They say a hurricane makes the sound of a freight train. This was like a train running though his house. The candles were burned down, but the gray-green light of a hurricane dawn illuminated the room.

Katrina had come ashore and stalked them like a predator.

Simone slept on the other end of the sofa. Clutched in her hand was that damn Jimmy doll.

He sat up and straightened his bad knee, expecting the pain and stiffness that usually accompanied his awakening. But there was no pain. He stood, walked over to the refrigerator, and drank half a bottle of tepid water. That knee felt better than it had felt in years. He rotated his shoulder. Damn! Good as new. He rubbed the flesh where white scar tissue marked his wound. He couldn't believe it, the scar was gone.

No fucking way.

Outside, a tree branch cracked. A moment later a thud caused the house to shudder. The Live Oak in the garden had fallen on the roof.

He turned and saw Simone rubbing her eyes.

"We need to get in the closet." He had to shout to be heard over the wind.

The house shuddered again. Debris pinged the walls like machine-gun fire and his ears popped from the low pressure. He feared losing what was left of the roof.

"C'mon, girl." He pulled her after him.

The coat closet was long and narrow. It was located in the middle of the house, under the stairs. Walls on both sides offered protection. The day before, he'd placed a mattress on the floor. Pillows and blankets were scattered around. There were water bottles and a battery-powered lantern. He switched on the lantern and hung it on a hook.

"Over here," he called to Simone.

He scrunched in a corner. She threw her arms around him and held on tight. He pulled the blankets and pillows over them.

"It's all right," he said. "We'll be all right."

"I ain't scared."

"Maybe you should be."

She buried her face in the nape of his neck. Her breasts pushed against his chest, her nipples hard as bullets.

THERE WAS a rhythm to it. The house rocked. The wind howled, and then let up a moment or two before the next onslaught.

Under their blanket, she touched the place where his scar had been. "How dat feel?"

"You can't make that go away."

"I already made it go away."

"You didn't do that. It's not possible."

She reached lower and massaged his knee. "You all better there, too."

"Sometimes it's better than others."

She shifted her body so that her pelvis pressed against his thigh. She ground against him, damp and hot. "How 'bout dat, Jimmy Fruge? How dat feel?"

"Stop it, now. I mean it, this ain't no time..."

"Nossir, dis is jus' de time."

"Time for what?"

"Dat hurricane love. "

"What..."

She giggled. "You hear what I said. Dat wild love like your woman never give you."

Then her lips were on his. He made a feeble effort to turn away, but her tongue darted in his mouth like a feral animal.

"Wait." It took all his strength to push her off of him.

She reached behind and undid her bra. Underneath the blankets and pillows, he could just make out her nakedness. Her breasts sat high and proud, large aureoles and nipples darker than the rest.

"What you waitin' for?"

"I've got to know something."

She wriggled free of her panties. Her hips flared from a hard and muscled torso and between her legs was a patch of wiry black fuzz. "What you need to know?"

"Are you...are you the..."

Her hand slid down his belly, under his waistband, and grasped him through his undershorts. "You know de answer to dat."

"Look, I've got a woman. And you're just a kid."

"Yeah, but dis ain't 'bout me. Dis 'bout you."

Fruge closed his eyes. He didn't love Jessie Claiborne, and he hated her family. He'd reached for respectability, but it had been too far a reach. The girl was right, he walked in the shadows. Always had, always would.

He touched her breast. Simone unloosed his belt and unzipped him. He hardened in her hand.

"Dat's it," she whispered. "I knew you liked me."

"Sweet Jesus."

She pushed her breasts into his face and held them to his mouth. Under the covers, her gasps were as loud as Katrina's blow.

His hands explored her body, the firm belly, the hard ass, and those long, lean thighs. His hard-on raged, but when he tried her pull her on top, she pinned him to the mattress with one hand. While licking her lips, her eyes locked on his, she reached between her legs with the other. Then she offered him her fingers and he licked them clean.

"You like dat pussy?" she teased.

Outside, another crash and the sound of timbers groaning.

"Come here, girl, I'll fuck you good."

"Not yet you don't."

She was stronger than she looked. She'd straddled him, grinning, her sweetness just inches from his face. "You goin' to eat dat pussy, 'fore you fuck it."

She leaned back, her hands on his chest for balance.

Nearly smothered, he took what she offered. He flicked and sucked, his face slick with her juices. His tongue darted and danced like the serpent's tongue until he felt her buck, clinch and release, clinch and release. When the aftershocks had quit her, she slid down his belly and kissed him. "Damn, you know how to treat a woman."

He held her face in his hands. "You're beautiful."

She sat up, grasped him in her hand and guided him to her opening. She sat back and he thrust. She squeezed him inside and rode him with the storm. He didn't last long, but neither did she.

Only after she'd rolled off and lay beside him, did he hear Katrina's roar again. He wondered if there would be anything left.

THEY STAYED in the closet the rest of the morning. He took her twice more, once in her mouth, while she knelt beside him, rubbing hard and fast. The last time in her ass. He entered from behind, Simone on her hands and knees, wailing like that bitch outside.

Afterwards, he slept again. She lay in his arms, sticky and sweet as a mango.

Late afternoon, he awoke to silence. Simone still slept, her mouth open, her body tangled in his. He slid out from under her, pulled on his jeans, and ventured out.

Things weren't as bad as he'd expected. He'd lost the Live Oak and the roof was damaged, but he'd needed to replace the roof anyway. Now, the insurance would pay for it.

He found the ladder in the street, along with other debris, a stop sign, broken glass, an overturned car that looked like it had been hit by an RPG. He set the ladder next to the house and clambered onto what was left of the roof. His knee offered no pain and that scar on his shoulder, gone, even in the light of day.

Simone was suddenly behind him, trailing along in that cotton dress. Hand in hand, they stood together, three stories up.

That's when he figured it out.

This storm had turned east, not west. The city had caught a break, missing the brunt. Clouds were breaking over Metarie, but toward Slidell and Mobile the sky remained black. The Alabama coast was taking a beating.

He sighted through his Army surplus binoculars. He could see as far as Lake Ponchartrain and across the river into the Ninth Ward. "Shit," he said.

"What?" she asked, reaching for the binoculars.

He pointed. The storm surge had broken through the levees. Chantilly and Carrollton were taking water. He guessed the Ninth Ward was already knee deep. Chances were, things would only get worse. He was glad they were on the high ground.

"De roof 'bout gone on de Superdome," she said. "I had a bad feelin' 'bout dat."

He reached for the binoculars and peered out over the city again. The water was rising fast. "What's going to happen here?"

"Things never be like they was."

Even Fruge could see that, and he didn't have the magic.

He felt a vibration in his pocket. His cell phone. He hadn't checked it since saying goodbye to Jessie the day before. There were three new messages. He figured one more wouldn't hurt, and let the call roll to voicemail.

"Dat yer woman?" Simone asked.

"Yep."

"She not comin' back."

"She's not?"

"Rich white folks don' want nothin' to do wi' dis mess. 'Sides, she got her doubts 'bout you now."

Of course she was right. His staying behind while Jessie rode out the storm with her family would put a dent in their relationship. She'd see it as a subtle betrayal. Now, with the flood, she'd have an excuse not to come home. Jessie would find a new life in Jackson with Cecily and her brother-in-law.

In a way, he was grateful for the flood. It saved him the task of breaking things off. Jessie would never have to know he'd left her, before she'd left him.

He studied the blackness over the Alabama coast. "Your granny's not coming back either, is she?" he asked.

The girl shook her head. "Nah, she gone, too. De wind and de water got her. You lookin' at de new Voodoo Maman."

"What about us?" he asked.

Simone grinned, her arms crossed at her breasts. "Dey ain't no us. Dey jus' de hurricane love. Now you find a woman who love you for who you are."

"But we did that, right? It was real, wasn't it, the hurricane love?"

"Real as anything, but who know what's real?"

He waved his hand, encompassing the flooded city. "So, what's next?" he asked. "What's going to happen?"

She turned on her heel. Over her shoulder, she said, "Shit, white boy, how you 'xpect me to know dat?"

ABOUT THE AUTHORS

VICTOR J. BANIS is the critically acclaimed author of several novels and shorter works. He lives in West Virginia's beautiful Blue Ridge.

KEVIN JAMES BREAUX is an award-winning author and artist. He is a member of the HWA and EAA. Along with having published several short stories, Kevin's first novel, *Soul Born*, an epic fantasy, will be published in 2010. He can be reached at www.Kevinbreaux.com or follow Kevin on twitter@Kevinbreaux.

ROBERT BUCKLEY is the fiction editor for the Erotica Readers and Writers Association. His stories have appeared in multiple editions of *Mammoth Book of Best New Erotica* and the *Coming Together* series. He is a blue-collar, triple-decker bred Boston Irish.

AMANDA FOX is a wife, mother, writer, teacher, and hopeful humanitarian. As one-half of a vanilla-chocolate affair that has spanned more than twenty years, she enjoys contemplating the uniqueness of interracial relationships, though savoring the complexities of more mainstream liaisons is a passion of hers as well. Online, she has written for *Clean Sheets* and *The Erotic Woman*, and her work in print is featured in *Sweet Love* and *The Mammoth Book of Best New Erotica 9*.

AKUA LEZLI HOPE creates as an award-winning poet, fiction writer, designer, and artist. She has won a Creative Writing Fellowship from the National Endowment for the Arts, two Artists Fellowships from the New York Foundation for the Arts, a Ragsdale U.S. Africa Fellowship, among other honors. Her collection, *Embouchure: Poems on Jazz and Other Musics,* won the Writer's Digest poetry book award. Her work appears in several anthologies including

Sisterfire, Erotique Noire, Confirmation, Dark Matter and numerous literary magazines.

JOLENE HUI is a writer of literary and erotic fiction and about anything else her fingers feel like typing. She's been known to write a horror column for the *The Flesh Farm* and a hockey column for *Inside Hockey*. One of Tonto Books' first authors, her literary fiction has been published in their *Tonto Short Stories, Tonto Christmas Stories,* and *More Tonto Short Stories* anthologies. Published by a variety of newspapers, magazines, and websites she has contributed stories to Cleis Press, Pretty Things Press, Logical-Lust Publications, loveyoudevine, and Alyson Books. She is a member of several organizations, including the Sapphic Planet community. She lives in Los Angeles.

HZAL is the author of *Seso The Prophet: The Cry of Beauty* and several volumes of poetry. He has written and produced two original plays: *Migration* and *They Sing Songs About This.* A native of Cleveland, Ohio, he now resides in Atlanta, Georgia with his wife. Check out his writings at www.bluzcloud.webs.com.

DEAN JEAN-PIERRE, a native of St. Croix, U.S. Virgin Island. He is a gifted writer and storyteller. His first collection, *The Pussy Whispers*, was published in 2009. His first novel is scheduled to be released shortly.

D.L. KING is a smut writing and editing New Yorker who lives somewhere between the Wonder Wheel at Coney Island and the Chrysler Building. She edited *Where The Girls Are,* a Lambda Literary Award finalist, as well as *The Sweetest Kiss* and *Spank!* Her short stories can be found in several anthologies such as *The Mammoth Book of Best New Erotica, Best Women's Erotica, Best Lesbian Erotica, Fast Girls, Sex in the City: New York, Please Ma'am, Sweet Love, The Cougar Book, Girl Crazy, Broadly Bound, Frenzy,* among others. She is the author of two novels of female domination and male submission, *The Melinoe Project* and *The Art of Melinoe.* She is also the publisher and editor of the erotica site *Erotica Revealed.* Find out more about her at www.dlkingerotica.blogspot.com and www.dlkingerotica.com.

BECKY KYLE as had both fiction and nonfiction published in various publications. In addition, she is the senior nonfiction editor for *Conclave: A Journal of Character.* She lives with her husband of twenty-eight years and four cats somewhere between the Smoky and Cumberland Mountains ranges.

MAXMILIAN LAGOS, a reformed journalist, has published many of his stories in *Literotica, MySpace* and the Erotica Readers & Writers Association. He is a polyamorous, bisexual married man, the doting father of two children. He lives in Toronto, Canada.

C. DENNIS MOORE lives and writes in St. Joseph, Missouri. He has published over sixty short stories as well as novellas and poetry. His short fiction collection, *Terrible Thrills,* which he dedicated to his three children, received critical acclaim.

DORLA MOOREHOUSE is a writer and dancer living in Austin, Texas. Though she prefers the more traditional ballroom styles, she's also willing to admit a love for the sultry sexiness of blues and swing. Dorla's fiction has most recently appeared at *The Erotic Woman, Every Night Erotica, Tinglemedia.com,* and in *Eat Me: Seven Sexy Stories of Gluttony.* Read more about her at
http://dorlamoorehouse.blogspot.com

NICK NICHOLSON has pursued a variety of creative vocations upon completing a university degree in music, working for many years as a performer, composer, teacher, and lecturer. Later, he ventured into the visual arts, completing post-graduate studies in photography and painting. In 2006, he took up another creative pursuit: writing. He lives in Australia.

ALICIA NIGHT ORCHID is a lawyer, a chef by taste, and a writer by necessity. Her mainstream fiction has appeared in several literary journals under another name. Her erotic stories have been published online in *Cleansheets, Ruthie's Club, Oysters and Chocolate, For The Girls,* and the Erotica Readers and Writers Association. Her award-winning stories have been collected in a bestselling volume, *Tight Women in Hard Places* in 2010, published by Logical-Lust Publications.

ART NIXON has publishing poetry in several anthologies, beginning with *The Muntu Poets of Cleveland* at the tender age of twenty, edited by innovative poet, literary theorist and composer Russell Atkins. Since then, his poetry has appeared in *Black American Literature Forum, The Drumming Between Us, Catch The Fire!: A Cross-Generational Anthology of Contemporary African-American Poetry,* and *Voices From Leimert Park*. He has been a featured on NPR – Pacifica Radio's Inspiration house several times. He has written articles for the Swedish-American *Vestkusten* and *The L.A. Weekly*. He has two sons, Adilifu Nama, a professor of Pan-African studies at California State University at Northridge, and Bjorn Kristoffer Nixon, a DJ in Oslo, Norway.

GARY PHILLIPS is a noted writer whose latest efforts include *The Underbelly*, a mystery novella about a semi-homeless Vietnam vet's search for a disabled friend who has disappeared from LA's Skid Row. He is an editor and contributor to the bestselling *Orange County Noir* anthology and continues to write the further adventures of pulp-era super spy Jimmy Christopher, *Operator 5*, for Moonstone Comics.

REMITTANCE GIRL lives in exile in Ho Chi Minh City, Vietnam where she writes, steals mangos, and grows orchids. For her stories, opinions, and books, go to www.remittancegirl.com.

THOMAS S. ROCHE is primarily known as a widely published author of erotic short stories but is also known as a writer of crime-noir and horror. His work has appeared several times in Susie Bright's *Best American Erotica* series, Maxim Jakubowski's *Best New Erotica* series, and in *The Mammoth Book of Pulp Fiction*. The editor of the *Noirerotica* series of erotic crime-noir anthologies and of four anthologies of horror and fantasy fiction, he is also contributed in stories in the collections, *Dark Matter* and *Parts of Heaven*, as well as the collaborations, *His and Hers* with Alison Tyler. He co-teaches a twice-yearly training on sexual health and sex education at San Francisco Sex Information (www.sfsi.org), a nonprofit educational organization. His writing has been translated into German, French, Italian, Turkish, Russian, Greek, Dutch, Norwegian, and Danish.

KALAMU YA SALAAM is a New Orleans writer, filmmaker, and educator. He is co-director of Students at the Center, a writing program in the New Orleans Public Schools (http://sacnola.com). He is also the moderator of Breath of Life, a Black music website (http://www.kalamu.com/bol). Kalamu blogs at (http://kalamu.posterous.com) and can be reached at kalamu@aol.com.

LISABET SARAI has been writing fiction and poetry ever since she learned how to hold a pencil. She has published several erotic novels and two short story collections, including *Fire In The Blood, Necessary Madness, Truce of Trust, Crossed Hearts, Serpent's Kiss, Raw Silk,* and *Chemistry,* which all proceeds of this book benefits AIDS research. She has edited several erotica anthologies and reviews erotic books and films for ERWA (www.erotica-readers.com) and *Erotica Revealed* (www.eroticarevealed.com). She has been married for more than 28 years and has two "two exceptional felines in Southeast Asia, where she pursues an alternative career that is completely unrelated to my creative writing."

SAVANNAH STEPHENS SMITH has been published fiction in print and online since 1996. A mild-mannered Canadian office worker by day, she enjoys creating erotic fiction at night. It's more fun than doing housework. She's given up on television, loves Bruce Springsteen, and drinks an astonishing amount of tea.

ALICE STURDIVANT lives and works in South Carolina where she drinks too much sweet tea, attempts to garden, is fascinated by Twitter, writes erotica when no one is looking, and occasionally battles her muse. Her articles and fiction have appeared on various blogs and websites, including *intelligentlysexy.com, oystersandchocolate.com,* and *interracialerotica.net.* Her erotica has been featured in print in the anthologies, *Oysters and Chocolate: Erotic Stories of Every Flavor* and the bestselling *Succulent: Chocolate Flava II.*

ANNE TOURNEY is a much-honored writer and photographer who explores some of the most provocative sexual fantasies. Her short fiction combines the essence of sexuality and spirituality. She has written several novels including *Head-On-Heart, Taming Jeremy, Lying In Mid Air, Unnatural Selection, Switching Hands,* and others.

ALEGRA VERDE (aka Esperanza Cintron) lives, writes, and teaches college literature in Detroit, Michigan. Her erotic fiction has been published in the Virgin Black Lace anthologies *Misbehaviour* and *The Affair,* and also in *Fairy Tale Lust* for Cleis Press. Two of her shorts will be published by Mira Spice in the spring of 2011. She has recently completed a collection of short erotic tales.

ZANDER VYNE has developed a large following of readers who enjoy intelligent, literary erotica with through his numerous publications in anthologies, magazines and on the web. Check out his website:

JAYME WHITFIELD, a native of Florida, lives in a small town with her husband and children. Coming from a background of writing for trade magazines and a local newspaper, she has "turned a spicier side of storytelling." Recently, she authored *Prisoner To Lust* for Ellora's Cave.

ABOUT THE EDITOR

COLE RILEY is the author of several street classics: *Hot Snake Nights, Rough Trade, The Devil To Pay, The Killing Kind, Dark Blood Moon,* and recently, *Harlem Confidential* and *Guilty As Sin.* His erotica and reviews have been featured on several websites and anthologies including *Intimacy* and Maxim Jakubowski's *The Mammoth Book of Best New Erotica.* In 2010, he edited an anthology, *Making The Hook-Up: Edgy Sex With Soul,* for Cleis Press. He lives in New York.

PUBLISHER' S NOTE

ACKNOWLEDGEMENTS

We know all about the warning concerning copyright restrictions. A wise legal woman, who worked with me on a previous book of this sort, reminded me that the content can only be used for study, scholarship, or research.

And that is what we have done with the tiny smattering of lyrics in the book. To fit under the protection clause, we must list what sources of research were used:

- **Vintage Sex Songs** – The Primo Collection – 2CD set **(PRMCD6077)**
- **Dirty Blues** – 2cd set- Allegro – **(CRG220113)**
- **The Best of Muddy Waters** – MCA Records – **(CHD31268)**
- **Eat To The Best: The Dirtiest Of Them Dirtiest Blues** – Bear Family Records **(LC05197)**
- **Sugar In My Bowl: Hard Driving Mamas** – **Vintage Sex Songs 1923-1952** – Buzzola Records **(BZCD002)**
- **Sex-Rated Blues For Grown Folks** – Ecko Records **(ECD1099)**
- **Raunchy Business: Hot Nuts & Lollypops** – Columbia Legacy **(CK46783)**
- **Blues Chicago Style** – **Volume One** – Pazzazz Records **(1PA220014-1)**
- **Blues Chicago Style** – **Volume Two** – Pazzazz Records **(1PAZZ014-1)**
- **The Copulating Blues** – JASS Records **(JASS J-CD-1)**
- **DirtyBlues 3** – Allegro – **(CRG120091)**

Look up the songs in these records. Listen to their power. Buy and support the magic of the blues.

OTHER TITLES BY THE PUBLISHER

The Cougar Book

Cougar women are smart. Cougar Women are sexy. Cougar women are *hot*.

Read this scintillating collection of Cougar stories edited by Jolie du Pré and featuring the best erotica writers around.

Includes an introduction by the original *Cougar* – Valerie Gibson.

$13.99 US, £9.99 UK, $4.99 eBook download

Swing! Adventures in Swinging by Today's Top Erotica Writers

Whether you are a swinger, think about swinging, or just interested in reading about it, *Swing!* has something for you!

Another acclaimed collection by Jolie du Pré and featuring the top erotica writers.
$14.99 US, £9.99 UK, $4.99 eBook download

Best S&M Erotica Vol III

Logical-Lust is the publisher for the third in M. Christian's series of "Best S&M Erotica" volumes. In these pages you'll find light stories, dark stories, powerful stories, subtle stories, fierce stories, and even romantic stories – but all of them dealing with the basic idea of consensually giving up, or taking, sexual power and control.
$11.99 US, £8.99 UK, $4.99 eBook downloads

Messalina: Devourer of Men

Eva Cavell is a woman with an embarrassing secret...

A tenure-track instructor at a private Denver college, despite desperate attempts to maintain control, Eva's world is spiralling into chaos. As emotional pressures build inside her, an explosion is imminent. Will she ever be able to live her life how she wants and without shame?

Spank!

With an introduction by well-known disciplinarian, Ms Cassandra Park, these spanking-hot stories are brought to you by one of today's bestselling editors of erotica, D. L. King. From the story of a man's hands-on tutelage in what makes spanking erotic in A.D.R. Forte's, "Anything But Ordinary" to the idea that eavesdropping can lead to a very happily ever after, in Cervo's "The Royal Montague," *Spank!* delivers.Sure to get your motor running, these stories will really warm your—heart!

Tight Women in Hard Places

Although told from a woman's point of view, don't expect mushy, romantic, happy-ever-ending stories here. Instead, meet real women making tough choices and getting on with imperfect lives. These women don't always get what they want, but they usually get what they need, both in life and in bed.
These are tight women in hard places.

ABOUT THE PUBLISHER

Logical-Lust Publications

...concentrates on quality books. We are very selective, and this successful approach has resulted in three awards and four other major finalists in just three years. We like to *"take the reader down a different path"*.

Visit the website www.logical-lust.com, or find our books on Amazon, Barnes and Noble, the iBookstore, AllRomanceebooks, Omnilit, KoboBooks, and other great online stockists, in both paperback and ebooks.